# Dictionary of Internetworking Terms and Acronyms

January 2001

**Corporate Headquarters**
Cisco Systems, Inc.
170 West Tasman Drive
San Jose, CA 95134-1706
USA

http:///www.cisco.com

Tel:  408 526-4000
      800 553-NETS (6387)
Fax: 408 526-4100

# Dictionary of Internetworking Terms and Acronyms

Cisco Systems, Inc.

Copyright © 2001 Cisco Systems, Inc.

Cisco Press logo is a trademark of Cisco Systems, Inc.

Published by:
Cisco Press
201 West 103rd Street
Indianapolis, IN 46290 USA

Printed in the United States of America 3 4 5 6 7 8 9 0

ISBN: 1-58720-045-7

Library of Congress Cataloging-in-Publication Number: 20-01086612

3rd Printing May 2001

| | |
|---|---|
| Publisher | John Wait |
| Editor-in-Chief | John Kane |
| Cisco Systems Program Manager | Bill Warren |
| Managing Editor | Patrick Kanouse |
| Compositor/Interior Design | Steve Gifford |
| Cover Designer | Louisa Klucznik |

**CISCO SYSTEMS**

**Corporate Headquarters**
Cisco Systems, Inc.
170 West Tasman Drive
San Jose, CA 95134-1706
USA
http://www.cisco.com
Tel:  408 526-4000
      800 553-NETS (6387)
Fax: 408 526-4100

**European Headquarters**
Cisco Systems Europe
11 Rue Camille Desmoulins
92782 Issy-les-Moulineaux
Cedex 9
France
http://www-
europe.cisco.com
Tel:  33 1 58 04 60 00
Fax: 33 1 58 04 61 00

**Americas Headquarters**
Cisco Systems, Inc.
170 West Tasman Drive
San Jose, CA 95134-1706
USA
http://www.cisco.com
Tel:  408 526-7660
Fax: 408 527-0883

**Asia Pacific Headquarters**
Cisco Systems Australia,
Pty., Ltd
Level 17, 99 Walker Street
North Sydney
NSW 2059 Australia
http://www.cisco.com
Tel: +61 2 8448 7100
Fax: +61 2 9957 4350

Cisco Systems has more than 200 offices in the following countries. Addresses, phone numbers, and fax numbers are listed on the Cisco Web site at www.cisco.com/go/offices

Argentina • Australia • Austria • Belgium • Brazil • Bulgaria • Canada • Chile • China • Colombia • Costa Rica • Croatia • Czech Republic • Denmark • Dubai, UAE • Finland • France • Germany • Greece • Hong Kong • Hungary • India • Indonesia • Ireland Israel • Italy • Japan • Korea • Luxembourg • Malaysia • Mexico • The Netherlands • New Zealand • Norway • Peru • Philippines Poland • Portugal • Puerto Rico • Romania • Russia • Saudi Arabia • Scotland • Singapore • Slovakia • Slovenia • South Africa • Spain Sweden • Switzerland • Taiwan • Thailand • Turkey • Ukraine • United Kingdom • United States • Venezuela • Vietnam • Zimbabwe

# Introduction

Internetworking continues to be one of the fastest developing high-technology fields today. Businesses and individuals have come to depend on the Internet for completing a wide range of their daily operations and activities.

It is no secret that Cisco Systems has capitalized on the Internet's potential, doing many of their business operations and functions across the Web, including over 85% of their annual sales transactions across the Internet.

For these reasons, the World Wide Web and the field of internetworking continue to grow at accelerated speeds. Cisco Systems, which provides the backbone for more than 60% of the world's networking systems, has created this Cisco Press internetworking reference in order to provide professionals both inside and outside the field of networking with definitions and meanings for the terms and acronyms used in the area of internetworking.

Many terms are included that relate to specific networking technology areas such as telephony, broadband, and wireless. Because comprehensive glossaries exist for these technologies elsewhere, and because including every term for all related technologies would prove unrealistic and burdensome, only those terms which are in some way related to networking are included here.

Additionally, because Cisco continues to lead the networking industry by developing and releasing new products in new areas of networking year after year, this book contains a section of Cisco-related terms for Cisco-specific and Cisco-product-specific terms.

We at Cisco Press hope you find this reference useful, whether you are a student or professional working in the field of internetworking, or someone who uses the Internet in his or her daily operations at work or at home. Because of the dynamic pace at which this field is developing, we realize that some of the information in this book may have changed by press time. For this reason, we have included a feedback card, which we hope you will use to provide us with information for future editions. Additionally, the feedback card contains online addresses so that you can contact us via the Web. Please do so—we look forward to hearing from you.

# Numerics

### 1+1

A method of protecting traffic in which a protection channel exists for each working traffic channel. For optical systems, the protection channel fibers can be routed over a path separate from the working fibers. The traffic signal is bridged to both the working and protection transmitters so the protection signal can be selected quickly if the working channel fails.

### 1:n

A method of protecting traffic in which one protection channel exists for $n$ traffic channels. Only one traffic channel can be switched to the protection channel at any given time.

### 1G mobile network

First generation mobile network. Refers to the initial category of mobile wireless networks that use analog technology only. Advanced Mobile Phone Service (AMPS) is an example of a 1G mobile network standard.

### 10Base2

10-Mbps baseband Ethernet specification using 50-ohm thin coaxial cable. 10Base2, which is part of the IEEE 802.3 specification, has a distance limit of 606.8 feet (185 meters) per segment. See also *Cheapernet, EtherChannel, IEEE 802.3,* and *Thinnet.*

### 10Base5

10-Mbps baseband Ethernet specification using standard (thick) 50-ohm baseband coaxial cable. 10Base5, which is part of the IEEE 802.3 baseband physical layer specification, has a distance limit of 1640 feet (500 meters) per segment. See also *EtherChannel* and *IEEE 802.3.*

### 10BaseF

10-Mbps baseband Ethernet specification that refers to the 10BaseFB, 10BaseFL, and 10BaseFP standards for Ethernet over fiber-optic cabling. See also *10BaseFB, 10BaseFL, 10BaseFP,* and *EtherChannel.*

### 10BaseFB

10-Mbps baseband Ethernet specification using fiber-optic cabling. 10BaseFB is part of the IEEE 10BaseF specification. It is not used to connect user stations, but instead provides a synchronous signaling backbone that allows additional segments and repeaters to be connected to the network. 10BaseFB segments can be up to 1.24 miles (2000 meters) long. See also *10BaseF* and *EtherChannel.*

### 10BaseFL

10-Mbps baseband Ethernet specification using fiber-optic cabling. 10BaseFL is part of the IEEE 10BaseF specification and, although able to interoperate with FOIRL, is designed to replace the FOIRL specification. 10BaseFL segments can be up to 3280 feet (1000 meters) long if used with FOIRL, and up to 1.24 miles (2000 meters) if 10BaseFL is used exclusively. See also *10BaseF, EtherChannel,* and *FOIRL.*

### 10BaseFP

10-Mbps fiber-passive baseband Ethernet specification using fiber-optic cabling. 10BaseFP is part of the IEEE 10BaseF specification. It organizes a number of computers into a star topology without the use of repeaters. 10BaseFP segments can be up to 1640 feet (500 meters) long. See also *10BaseF* and *EtherChannel.*

### 10BaseT

10-Mbps baseband Ethernet specification using two pairs of twisted-pair cabling (Categories 3, 4, or 5): one pair for transmitting data and the other for receiving data. 10BaseT, which is part of the IEEE 802.3 specification, has a distance limit of approximately 328 feet (100 meters) per segment. See also *EtherChannel* and *IEEE 802.3.*

### 10Broad36

10-Mbps broadband Ethernet specification using broadband coaxial cable. 10Broad36, which is part of the IEEE 802.3 specification, has a distance limit of 2.24 miles (3600 meters) per segment. See also *EtherChannel* and *IEEE 802.3.*

### 100BaseFX

A 100-Mbps baseband Fast Ethernet specification using two strands of multimode fiber-optic cable per link. To guarantee proper signal timing, a 100BaseFX link cannot exceed 1312 feet (400 meters) in length. Based on the IEEE 802.3 standard. See also *100BaseX, Fast Ethernet,* and *IEEE 802.3.*

### 100BaseT

100-Mbps baseband Fast Ethernet specification using UTP wiring. Like the 10BaseT technology on which it is based, 100BaseT sends link pulses over the network segment when no traffic is present. However, these link pulses contain more information than those used in 10BaseT. Based on the IEEE 802.3 standard. See also *10BaseT*, *Fast Ethernet*, and *IEEE 802.3*.

### 100BaseT4

100-Mbps baseband Fast Ethernet specification using four pairs of Categories 3, 4, or 5 UTP wiring. To guarantee the proper signal timing, a 100BaseT4 segment cannot exceed 328 feet (100 meters) in length. Based on the IEEE 802.3 standard. See also *Fast Ethernet* and *IEEE 802.3*.

### 100BaseTX

100-Mbps baseband Fast Ethernet specification using two pairs of either UTP or STP wiring. The first pair of wires receives data; the second transmits data. To guarantee the proper signal timing, a 100BaseTX segment cannot exceed 328 feet (100 meters) in length. Based on the IEEE 802.3 standard. See also *100BaseX*, *Fast Ethernet*, and *IEEE 802.3*.

### 100BaseX

100-Mbps baseband Fast Ethernet specification that refers to the 100BaseFX and 100BaseTX standards for Fast Ethernet over fiber-optic cabling. Based on the IEEE 802.3 standard. See also *100BaseFX*, *100BaseTX*, *Fast Ethernet*, and *IEEE 802.3*.

### 100VG-AnyLAN

100-Mbps Fast Ethernet and Token Ring media technology using four pairs of Categories 3, 4, or 5 UTP cabling. This high-speed transport technology, developed by Hewlett-Packard, can operate on existing 10BaseT Ethernet networks. Based on the IEEE 802.12 standard. See also *IEEE 802.12*.

### 1000Base-F

A 1-Gbps IEEE standard for Ethernet LANs.

### 2B1Q

2 binary 1 quaternary. An encoding scheme that provides a 2 bits per baud, 80-kbaud per second, 160-kbps transfer rate. The most common signaling method on ISDN U interfaces. The 1988 ANSI spec T1.601 defines this protocol in detail.

### 2G mobile network

second generation mobile network. Refers generically to a category of mobile wireless networks and services that implement digital technology. GSM is an example of a 2G mobile network standard.

### 2G+ mobile network

second generation plus mobile network. Refers generically to a category of mobile wireless networks that support higher data rates than 2G mobile networks. GPRS is an example of a 2G+ mobile network standard.

### 24th channel signaling

See *2G mobile network*.

### 3G mobile network

third generation mobile network. Refers generically to a category of next-generation mobile networks, such as UMTS and IMT-2000.

### 370 block mux channel

See *block multiplexer channel*.

### 4B/5B local fiber

4-byte/5-byte local fiber. Fiber channel physical media used for FDDI and ATM. Supports speeds up to 100 Mbps over multimode fiber. See also *TAXI 4B/5B*.

### 6BONE

The Internet's experimental IPv6 network.

### 8B/10B local fiber

8-byte/10-byte local fiber. Fiber channel physical media that supports speeds up to 149.76 Mbps over multimode fiber.

### 802.x

A set of IEEE standards for the definition of LAN protocols.

### 822

The short form of RFC 822. Refers to the format of Internet-style e-mail as defined in RFC 822.

### 1822

A historic term that refers to the original ARPANET host-to-IMP interface. The specifications are in BBN report 1822. See also *host* and *IMP*.

## A

amperes.

## A&B bit signaling

Procedure used in T1 transmission facilities in which each of the 24 T1 subchannels devotes 1 bit of every sixth frame to the carrying of supervisory signaling information. Also called *24th channel signaling*.

## A/D

analog to digital conversion.

## AAA

authentication, authorization, and accounting. Pronounced "triple a."

## AAL

ATM adaptation layer. Service-dependent sublayer of the data link layer. The AAL accepts data from different applications and presents it to the ATM layer in the form of 48-byte ATM payload segments. AALs consist of two sublayers: CS and SAR. AALs differ on the basis of the source-destination timing used (CBR or VBR) and whether they are used for connection-oriented or connectionless mode data transfer. At present, the four types of AAL recommended by the ITU-T are AAL1, AAL2, AAL3/4, and AAL5. See also *AAL1*, *AAL2*, *AAL3/4*, *AAL5*, *ATM*, *ATM layer*, *CS*, and *SAR*.

## AAL1

ATM adaptation layer. One of four AALs recommended by the ITU-T. AAL1 is used for connection-oriented, delay-sensitive services requiring constant bit rates, such as uncompressed video and other isochronous traffic. See also *AAL*.

## AAL2

ATM adaptation layer 2. One of four AALs recommended by the ITU-T. AAL2 is used for connection-oriented services that support a variable bit rate, such as some isochronous video and voice traffic. See also *AAL*.

## AAL3/4

ATM adaptation layer 3/4. One of four AALs (merged from two initially distinct adaptation layers) recommended by the ITU-T. AAL3/4 supports both connectionless and connection-oriented links but is used primarily for the transmission of SMDS packets over ATM networks. See also *AAL*.

## AAL5

ATM adaptation layer 5. One of four AALs recommended by the ITU-T. AAL5 supports connection-oriented VBR services and is used predominantly for the transfer of classical IP over ATM and LANE traffic. AAL5 uses SEAL and is the least complex of the current AAL recommendations. It offers low bandwidth overhead and simpler processing requirements in exchange for reduced bandwidth capacity and error-recovery capability. See also *AAL* and *SEAL*.

## AARP

AppleTalk Address Resolution Protocol. A protocol in the AppleTalk protocol stack that maps a data-link address to a network address.

## AARP probe packets

Packets transmitted by AARP that determine whether a randomly selected node ID is being used by another node in a nonextended AppleTalk network. If the node ID is not being used, the sending node uses that node ID. If the node ID is being used, the sending node chooses a different ID and sends more AARP probe packets. See also *AARP*.

## ABCD signaling

4-bit telephony line signaling coding in which each letter represents 1 of the 4 bits. This often is associated with CAS or robbed-bit signaling on a T1 or E1 telephony trunk.

## ABM

**1.** Asynchronous Balanced Mode. HDLC (and derivative protocol) communication mode supporting peer-oriented, point-to-point communications between two stations, where either station can initiate the transmission.

**2.** Accunet Bandwidth Manager.

## ABR

**1.** available bit rate. QoS class defined by the ATM Forum for ATM networks. ABR is used for connections that do not require timing relationships between source and destination. ABR provides no guarantees in terms of cell loss or delay, providing only best-effort service. Traffic sources adjust their transmission rate in response to information they receive describing the status of the network and its capability to successfully deliver data. Compare with *CBR*, *UBR*, and *VBR*.

**2.** area border router. Router located on the border of one or more OSPF areas that connects those areas to the backbone network. ABRs are considered members of both the OSPF backbone and the attached areas. They therefore maintain routing tables describing both the backbone topology and the topology of the other areas

## ABRD

automatic baud rate detection.

## ABS

application bridge server. Software module that allows the ICM to share the application bridge interface from an Aspect ACD with other applications.

## Abstract Syntax Notation One

See *ASN.1*.

## AC

alternating current.

## access device

The hardware component used in the signaling controller system: access server or mux.

## access list

A list kept by routers to control access to or from the router for a number of services (for example, to prevent packets with a certain IP address from leaving a particular interface on the router).

## access method

**1.** Generally, the way in which network devices access the network medium.

**2.** Software within an SNA processor that controls the flow of information through a network.

**access server**

Communications processor that connects asynchronous devices to a LAN or WAN through network and terminal emulation software. Performs both synchronous and asynchronous routing of supported protocols. Sometimes called a *network access server.* See also *communication server.*

**access unit**

See *AU.*

**Access-Accept**

Response packet from the RADIUS server notifying the access server that the user is authenticated. This packet contains the user profile, which defines the specific AAA functions assigned to the user.

**Access-Challenge**

Response packet from the RADIUS server requesting that the user supply additional information before being authenticated.

**Access-Request**

Request packet sent to the RADIUS server by the access server requesting authentication of the user.

**accounting management**

One of five categories of network management defined by ISO for the management of OSI networks. Accounting management subsystems are responsible for collecting network data relating to resource usage. See also *configuration management, fault management, performance management,* and *security management.*

**ACD**

**1.** automatic call distributor. Programmable device at a call center that routes incoming calls to targets within that call center. After the ICM determines the target for a call, the call is sent to the ACD associated with that target. The ACD must then complete the routing as determined by the ICM.

**2.** automatic call distribution. Device or service that automatically reroutes calls to customers in geographically distributed locations served by the same CO. See also *CO.*

**ACELP**

algebraic code excited linear prediction.

**A**

### ACF

Advanced Communications Function. A group of SNA products that provides distributed processing and resource sharing. See also *ACF*.

### ACF/NCP

Advanced Communications Function/Network Control Program. The primary SNA NCP. ACF/NCP resides in the communications controller and interfaces with the SNA access method in the host processor to control network communications. See also *ACF* and *NCP*.

### ACK

See *acknowledgment*.

### acknowledgment

Notification sent from one network device to another to acknowledge that some event occurred (for example, the receipt of a message). Sometimes abbreviated *ACK*. Compare to *NAK*.

### ACO

alarm cutoff. Feature that allows the manual silencing of the office audible alarm. (Subsequent new alarm conditions might reactivate the audible alarm.)

### ACOM

Term used in G.165, "General Characteristics of International Telephone Connections and International Telephone Circuits: Echo Cancellers." ACOM is the combined loss achieved by the echo canceller, which is the sum of the echo return loss, echo return loss enhancement, and nonlinear processing loss for the call.

### ACR

allowed cell rate. A parameter defined by the ATM Forum for ATM traffic management. ACR varies between the MCR and the PCR, and is controlled dynamically using congestion control mechanisms. See also *MCR* and *PCR*.

### ACS

asynchronous communications server.

### ACSE

association control service element. The OSI convention used to establish, maintain, or terminate a connection between two applications.

**A**

**Activation**

The process of enabling a subscriber device for network access and privileges on behalf of a registered account.

**active discovery packet**

The type of packet used by PPPoE during the discovery stage.

**active hub**

A multiported device that amplifies LAN transmission signals.

**active monitor**

The device responsible for managing a Token Ring. A network node is selected to be the active monitor if it has the highest MAC address on the ring. The active monitor is responsible for such management tasks as ensuring that tokens are not lost, or that frames do not circulate indefinitely. See also *ring monitor* and *standby monitor*.

**active nonvolatile memory**

See *ANVM*.

**ActiveX**

Microsoft's Windows-specific non-Java technique for writing applets. ActiveX applets take considerably longer to download than the equivalent Java applets; however, they more fully exploit the features of Windows 95. ActiveX sometimes is said to be a superset of Java. See also *applet* and *Java*.

**ACU**

automatic calling unit.

**ACUTA**

Association of College and University Telecomm Administrators.

**AD**

administrative domain. A group of hosts, routers, and networks operated and managed by a single organization.

**adapter**

See *NIC*.

**adaptive differential pulse code modulation**

See *ADP*.

**adaptive routing**

See *dynamic routing*.

**ADC**

analog to digital converter.

**ADCCP**

Advanced Data Communications Control Protocol. ANSI standard bit-oriented data link control protocol.

**Add Path request**

A request made by the network to add a path using the Add Path packet, which establishes a multi-hop path between two network nodes. Although the two nodes are usually the source and destination nodes of a VWP, there are cases in which other nodes might want to establish a path between them. Unlike the Restore Path request, the Add Path request is never flooded; it is instead forwarded using information carried in the path itself (source routing).

**add/drop multiplexer**

See *ADM*.

**address**

Data structure or logical convention used to identify a unique entity, such as a particular process or a network device.

**address mapping**

A technique that allows different protocols to interoperate by translating addresses from one format to another. For example, when routing IP over X.25, the IP addresses must be mapped to the X.25 addresses so that the IP packets can be transmitted by the X.25 network. See also *address resolution*.

**address mask**

A bit combination used to describe which part of an address refers to the network or the subnet and which part refers to the host. Sometimes referred to simply as *mask*. See also *subnet mask*.

**address resolution**

Generally, a method for resolving differences between computer addressing schemes. Address resolution usually specifies a method for mapping network layer (Layer 3) addresses to data link layer (Layer 2) addresses. See also *address mapping*.

**Address Resolution Protocol**

See *ARP*.

**address translation gateway**

See *ATG* in the "Cisco Systems Terms and Acronyms" section.

**addressed call mode**

A mode that permits control signals and commands to establish and terminate calls in V.25bis. See also *V.25bis*.

**ADF**

adapter description file.

**adjacency**

A relationship formed between selected neighboring routers and end nodes for the purpose of exchanging routing information. Adjacency is based upon the use of a common media segment.

**adjacent channel**

A channel or frequency that is directly above or below a specific channel or frequency.

**adjacent nodes**

**1.** In SNA, nodes that are connected to a given node with no intervening nodes.

**2.** In DECnet and OSI, nodes that share a common network segment (in Ethernet, FDDI, or Token Ring networks).

**ADM**

add/drop multiplexer. Digital multiplexing equipment that provides interfaces between different signals in a network.

**ADMD**

Administration Management Domain. X.400 Message Handling System public carrier. The ADMDs in all countries worldwide together provide the X.400 backbone. See also *PRMD*.

**administrative distance**

Rating of the trustworthiness of a routing information source. Administrative distance often is expressed as a numerical value between 0 and 255. The higher the value, the lower the trustworthiness rating.

**Administrative Domain**

See *adapter*.

**administrative weight**

See *AW* and *PTSP*.

**administrator**

The person who queries the User Registrar to analyze individual subscriber status and problems and to generate aggregate statistics.

**admission control**

See *traffic profile*.

**admissions confirmation**

An RAS message sent as an admissions confirmation.

**ADP**

automatic data processing.

**ADPCM**

adaptive differential pulse code modulation. The process by which analog voice samples are encoded into high-quality digital signals.

**ADSL**

asymmetric digital subscriber line. One of four DSL technologies. ADSL is designed to deliver more bandwidth downstream (from the central office to the customer site) than upstream. Downstream rates range from 1.5 to 9 Mbps, whereas upstream bandwidth ranges from 16 to 640 kbps. ADSL transmissions work at distances up to 18,000 feet (5,488 meters) over a single copper twisted pair. See also *HDSL*, *SDSL*, and *VDSL*.

**ADSP**

AppleTalk Data Stream Protocol.

**ADSU**

ATM DSU. Terminal adapter used to access an ATM network via an HSSI-compatible device. See also *DSU*.

**ADTS**

automated digital terminal system.

**Advanced Communications Function**

See *ACF*.

**Advanced Communications Function/Network Control Program**

See *ACF/NCP*.

**Advanced CoS Management**

advanced class of service management. Essential for delivering the required QoS to all applications. Cisco switches contain per-VC queuing, per-VC rate scheduling, multiple CoS queuing, and egress queuing. This enables network managers to refine connections to meet specific application needs. Formerly called FairShare and OptiClass.

**Advanced Data Communications Control Protocol**

See *AEP*.

**Advanced Intelligent Network**

See AIN.

**Advanced Peer-to-Peer Networking**

See *APPN*.

**Advanced Program- to-Program Communication**

See *APPC*.

**Advanced Research Projects Agency**

See *ARPA*.

**Advanced Research Projects Agency Network**

See *ARPANET*.

**advanced voice busyout**

See *AVBO*.

**advertising**

The router process in which routing or service updates are sent at specified intervals so that other routers on the network can maintain lists of usable routes.

**AE**

application entity.

**AEP**

AppleTalk Echo Protocol. Used to test the connectivity between two AppleTalk nodes. One node sends a packet to another node and receives a duplicate, or echo, of that packet.

**AERM**

SS7 MTP 2 function that provides monitoring of link alignment errors.

**AFC**

See *admissions confirmation*.

**AFCEA**

Armed Forces Communications and Electronics Association.

**affinity**

Requirements of an MPLS traffic engineering tunnel on the attributes of the links it will cross. The tunnel's affinity bits and affinity mask bits of the tunnel must match the attribute bits of the various links carrying the tunnel.

**AFI**

authority and format identifier. The part of an NSAP-format ATM address that identifies the type and the format of the IDI portion of an ATM address. See also *IDI* and *NSAP*.

**AFNOR**

Association Francaise de Normalisation.

**AFP**

AppleTalk Filing Protocol. Presentation-layer protocol that allows users to share data files and application programs that reside on a file server. AFP supports AppleShare and Mac OS File Sharing.

**AFS**

Andrew File System.

**agent**

**1.** Generally, software that processes queries and returns replies on behalf of an application.

**2.** In NMSs, a process that resides in all managed devices and reports the values of specified variables to management stations.

### aggressive mode

The connection mode that eliminates several steps during IKE authentication negotiation (phase 1) between two or more IPSec peers. Aggressive mode is faster than main mode but not as secure.

### AH

Authentication Header. A security protocol that provides data authentication and optional anti-replay services. AH is embedded in the data to be protected (a full IP datagram).

### AHT

average handle time. The average time it takes for calls to a service or a skill group to be handled. Handle time includes talk time plus after-call work time.

### AI

**1.** artificial intellegence.

**2.** access interface.

### AIM

asynchronous interface module.

### AIN

Advanced Intelligent Network. In SS7, an expanded set of network services made available to the user, and under user control, that requires improvement in network switch architecture, signaling capabilities, and peripherals. See also *SS7*.

### AIO

Asynchronous input/output.

### AIP

See *AIP* in the "Cisco Systems Terms and Acronyms" section.

### Airline Control Protocol

Data link layer polled protocol that runs in full-duplex mode over synchronous serial (V.24) lines and uses the binary-coded decimal (BCD) character set.

### Airline Product Set

See *ALPS* in the in the "Cisco Systems Terms and Acronyms" section.

algorithm    **17**

**airline protocol**

Generic term that refers to the airline reservation system data and the protocols, such as P1024B (ALC), P1024C (UTS), and MATIP, that transport the data between the mainframe and the ASCUs.

**Airline X.25**

See *AX.25*.

**AIS**

**1.** alarm indication signal. In a T1 transmission, an all-ones signal transmitted in lieu of the normal signal to maintain transmission continuity and to indicate to the receiving terminal that there is a transmission fault that is located either at, or upstream from, the transmitting terminal. See also *T1*.

**2.** automatic intercept system.

**AIX**

advanced interface executive.

**alarm**

Notification that the traffic signal has degraded or failed or equipment is malfunctioning. An SNMP message notifying an operator or an administrator of a network problem. See also *event* and *trap*.

**alarm cutoff**

See *ACO*.

**alarm indication signal**

See *AIS*.

**alarm indication signal**

See *ALS*.

**a-law**

ITU-T companding standard used in the conversion between analog and digital signals in PCM systems. A-law is used primarily in European telephone networks and is similar to the North American mu-law standard. See also *companding* and *mu-law*.

**algorithm**

Well-defined rule or process for arriving at a solution to a problem. In networking, algorithms commonly are used to determine the best route for traffic from a particular source to a particular destination.

**alias**

See *entity*.

**Alien Port Adapter**

A dual-wide port adapter for the Cisco 7200 router. The Alien Port Adapter is ABR-ready and supports traffic shaping.

**alignment error**

In IEEE 802.3 networks, an error that occurs when the total number of bits of a received frame is not divisible by eight. Alignment errors usually are caused by frame damage due to collisions.

**alignment error rate monitor**

See *AERM*.

**A-link**

SS7 access link. A dedicated SS7 signaling link not physically associated with any particular link carrying traffic.

**allowed cell rate**

See *ACOM*.

**all-rings explorer packet**

See *local explorer packet*.

**all-routes explorer packet**

An explorer packet that traverses an entire SRB network, following all possible paths to a specific destination. Sometimes called *all-rings explorer packet*. See also *explorer packet*, *local explorer packet*, and *spanning explorer packet*.

**ALO transaction**

An ATP transaction in which the request is repeated until a response is received by the requester or until a maximum retry count is reached. This recovery mechanism ensures that the transaction request is executed at least once. See also *ATP*.

**ALPS**

See *ALPS* in the "Cisco Systems Terms and Acronyms" section.

**ALPS circuit**

A communication path across a TCP connection between a host reservation system and an ASCU. When MATIP encapsulation is used on an ALPS circuit, it is equivalent to a MATIP session.

**ALPS Tunneling Protocol**

See *ATP*.

**ALS**

active line state.

**alternate mark inversion**

See *AMI*.

**AM**

amplitude modulation. A modulation technique whereby information is conveyed through the amplitude of the carrier signal. Compare with *FM* and *PAM*. See also *modulation*.

**AMA**

Automatic Messaging Accounting. In OSS, the automatic collection, recording, and processing of information relating to calls for billing purposes.

**AMADNS**

AMA Data Networking System. In OSS, the next generation (formerly Bellcore) system for the collection and the transport of AMA data from central office switches to a billing system. See also *AMA*.

**AMATPS**

AMA Teleprocessing System. In OSS, the Bellcore legacy system for collecting and transporting AMA data from central office switches to a billing system. The AMATPS consists of an AMA transmitter and a collector. See also *AMA*.

**American National Standards Institute**

See *ANP*.

**American Standard Code for Information Interchange**

See *ASCII*.

**AMI**

alternate mark inversion. Line-code type used on T1 and E1 circuits. In AMI, zeros are represented by 01 during each bit cell, and ones are represented by 11 or 00, alternately, during each bit cell. AMI requires that the sending device maintain ones density. Ones density is not maintained independently of the data stream. Sometimes called *binary coded alternate mark inversion*. Compare with *bipolar 8-zero substitution*. See also *ones density*.

**amplitude**

The maximum value of an analog waveform or a digital waveform. The magnitude or strength of a varying waveform. Typically represented as a curve along the x-axis of a graph.

**amplitude modulation**

See *AM*.

**AMRL**

adjusted main ring lenth.

**analog signal**

The representation of information with a continuously variable physical quantity, such as voltage. Because of this constant changing of the wave shape with regard to its passing a given point in time or space, an analog signal might have a virtually indefinite number of states or values. This contrasts with a digital signal that is expressed as a square wave and therefore has a very limited number of discrete states.

**analog transmission**

Signal transmission over wires or through the air in which information is conveyed through the variation of some combination of signal amplitude, frequency, and phase.

**ANI**

automatic number identification. SS7 (signaling system 7) feature in which a series of digits, either analog or digital, are included in the call, identifying the telephone number of the calling device. In other words, ANI identifies the number of the calling party. See also *CLID*.

**anonymous FTP**

Allows a user to retrieve documents, files, programs, and other archived data from anywhere on the Internet without having to establish a userid and password. By using the special userid of anonymous, the network user bypasses local security checks and can access publicly accessible files on the remote system. See also *FTP*.

**ANP**

automatic numbering plan.

**ANSI**

American National Standards Institute. A voluntary organization composed of corporate, government, and other members that coordinates standards-related activities, approves U.S. national standards, and develops positions for the United States in international standards organizations. ANSI helps develop international and U.S. standards relating to, among other things, communications and networking. ANSI is a member of the IEC and the ISO. See also *IEC* and *ISO*.

**ANSI X3T9.5**

See *X3T9.5*.

**answer supervision template**

The sequence of autonomous responses to the detection of specific signaling events for outbound calls from the Cisco VCO/4K switch. See also *inpulse rule, outpulse rule*.

**answer-mode**

Specifies that the router should not attempt to initiate a trunk connection, but should wait for an incoming call before establishing the trunk.

**antenna**

A device for transmitting or receiving a radio frequency (RF). Antennas are designed for specific and relatively tightly defined frequencies and are quite varied in design. An antenna for a 2.5 GHz (MMDS) system does not work for a 28 GHz (LMDS) design.

**antenna gain**

The measure of an antenna assembly performance relative to a theoretical antenna, called an isotropic radiator (radiator is another term for antenna). Certain antenna designs feature higher performance relative to vectors or frequencies.

**anti-replay**

Security service where the receiver can reject old or duplicate packets in order to protect itself against replay attacks. IPSec provides this optional service by use of a sequence number combined with the use of data authentication.

**ANVM**

active nonvolatile memory. Memory that contains the software currently used by the network element.

**ANW**

advanced netware.

**anycast**

In ATM, an address that can be shared by multiple end systems. An anycast address can be used to route a request to a node that provides a particular service.

**AOW**

Asia and Oceania Workshop. One of the three regional OSI Implementors Workshops. See also *EWOS*.

**AP**

**1.** application process.

**2.** application processor.

**APA**

all points addressable.

**APAD**

asynchronous packet assembler/disassembler.

**APaRT**

See *APaRT* in the "Cisco Systems Terms and Acronyms" section.

**APC**

adjacent point code. The point code of the next hop in the system for the bearer channels; usually it is the STP (signal transfer point).

**APDU**

application protocol data unit.

**API**

application program interface. The means by which an application program talks to communications software. Standardized APIs allow application programs to be developed independently of the underlying method of communication. A set of standard software interrupts, calls, and data formats that computer application programs use to initiate contact with other devices (for example, network services, mainframe communications programs, or other program-to-program communications). Typically, APIs make it easier for software developers to create the links that an application needs to communicate with the operating system or with the network.

**APN**

access point name. Identifies a PDN that is configured on and accessible from a GGSN in a GPRS network.

### APNIC

Asia Pacific Network Information Center. Nonprofit Internet registry organization for the Asia Pacific region. The other Internet registries are currently IANA, RIPE NCC, and InterNIC.

### Apollo Domain

Proprietary network protocol suite developed by Apollo Computer for communication on proprietary Apollo networks.

### APPC

Advanced Program-to-Program Communication. IBM SNA system software that allows high-speed communication between programs on different computers in a distributed computing environment. APPC establishes and tears down connections between communicating programs. It consists of two interfaces: programming and data-exchange. The programming interface replies to requests from programs requiring communication; the data-exchange interface establishes sessions between programs. APPC runs on LU 6.2 devices. See also *LU 6.2*.

### applet

A small program, often used in the context of a Java-based program, that is compiled and embedded in an HTML page. See also *ActiveX* and *Java*.

### AppleTalk

A series of communications protocols designed by Apple Computer consisting of two phases. Phase 1, the earlier version, supports a single physical network that can have only one network number and be in one zone. Phase 2 supports multiple logical networks on a single physical network and allows networks to be in more than one zone. See also *zone*.

### AppleTalk Address Resolution Protocol

See *AARP*.

### AppleTalk Echo Protocol

See *AEP*.

### AppleTalk Filing Protocol

See *AFP*.

### AppleTalk Remote Access

See *ARA*.

**AppleTalk Session Protocol**

See *ASP*.

**AppleTalk Transaction Protocol**

See *ATP*.

**AppleTalk Update-Based Routing Protocol**

See *AURP*.

**AppleTalk zone**

See *zone*.

**application**

A program that performs a function directly for a user. FTP and Telnet clients are examples of network applications.

**application layer**

Layer 7 of the *OSI reference model*. This layer provides services to application processes (such as e-mail, file transfer, and terminal emulation) that are outside the OSI model. The application layer identifies and establishes the availability of intended communication partners (and the resources required to connect with them), synchronizes cooperating applications, and establishes an agreement on the procedures for error recovery and the control of data integrity. Corresponds roughly with the *transaction services layer* in the SNA model. See also *data-link layer*, *network layer*, *physical layer*, *PQ*, *session layer*, and *transport layer*.

**application programming interface**

See *API*.

**APPN**

Advanced Peer-to-Peer Networking. Enhancement to the original IBM SNA architecture. APPN handles session establishment between peer nodes, dynamic transparent route calculation, and traffic prioritization for APPC traffic. Compare with *APPN+*. See also *APPC*.

**APPN+**

Next-generation APPN that replaces the label-swapping routing algorithm with source routing. Also called *high-performance routing*. See also *APPN*.

**APS**

automatic protection switching. A method that allows transmission equipment to recover automatically from failures, such as a cut cable.

**APSB**

automatic protection switching byte (failure-condition code).

**AR**

Access Registrar. Provides RADIUS services to DOCSIS cable modems for the deployment of high-speed data services in a one-way cable plant requiring telco-return for upstream data.

**ARA**

AppleTalk Remote Access. A protocol that provides Macintosh users direct access to information and resources at a remote AppleTalk site.

**ARC**

ATM Research Consortium.

**Archie**

A system that provides lists of anonymous FTP archives. See also *Gopher*, *WAIS*, and *World Wide Web*.

**architecture**

The overall structure of a computer or communication system. The architecture influences the capabilities and limitations of the system.

**ARCnet**

Attached Resource Computer Network. 2.5-Mbps token-bus LAN developed in the late 1970s and early 1980s by Datapoint Corporation.

**area**

A logical set of network segments (CLNS-, DECnet-, or OSPF-based) and their attached devices. Areas usually are connected to other areas via routers, making up a single autonomous system. See also *autonomous system*.

**area border router**

See *ABR*.

**ARIN**

American Registry for Internet Numbers. A nonprofit organization established for the purpose of administrating and registrating IP numbers to the geographical areas currently managed by Network Solutions (InterNIC). Those areas include, but are not limited to, North America, South America, South Africa, and the Caribbean.

**ARL**

adjusted ring length.

### ARM

asynchronous response mode. HDLC communication mode involving one primary station and at least one secondary station, where either the primary or one of the secondary stations can initiate transmissions. See also *primary station* and *secondary station*.

### ARP

Address Resolution Protocol. Internet protocol used to map an IP address to a MAC address. Defined in RFC 826. Compare with *RARP*. See also *proxy ARP*.

### ARPA

Advanced Research Projects Agency. Research and development organization that is part of DoD. ARPA is responsible for numerous technological advances in communications and networking. ARPA evolved into DARPA, and then back into ARPA again (in 1994). See also *DARPA*.

### ARPANET

Advanced Research Projects Agency Network. Landmark packet-switching network established in 1969. ARPANET was developed in the 1970s by BBN and funded by ARPA (and later DARPA). It eventually evolved into the Internet. The term ARPANET was retired officially in 1990. See also *ARPA*, *BBN*, *DARPA*, and *Internet*.

### ARQ

automatic repeat request. A communication technique in which the receiving device detects errors and requests retransmissions.

### ARU

alarm relay unit.

### AS

A collection of networks under a common administration sharing a common routing strategy. Autonomous systems are subdivided by areas. An autonomous system must be assigned a unique 16-bit number by the IANA. Sometimes abbreviated as *AS*. See also *area* and *IANA*.

### ASA

average speed of answer. Average answer wait time for calls to a service or a route.

### ASAM

ATM subscriber access multiplexer. A telephone central office multiplexer that supports SDL ports over a wide range of network interfaces. An ASAM sends and receives subscriber data (often Internet services) over existing copper telephone lines, concentrating all traffic onto a single high-speed trunk for transport to the Internet or the enterprise intranet. This device is similar to a DSLAM (different manufacturers use different terms for similar devices).

### ASBR

autonomous system boundary router. ABR located between an OSPF autonomous system and a non-OSPF network. ASBRs run both OSPF and another routing protocol, such as RIP. ASBRs must reside in a nonstub OSPF area. See also *ABR*, *nonstub area*, and *OSPF*.

### ASCII

American Standard Code for Information Interchange. 8-bit code for character representation (7 bits plus parity).

### ASCU

agent-set control unit.

### ASD

automated software distribution.

### ASE

**1.** amplified spontaneous emissions. Noise that is added to an optical signal when it is amplified. This noise (or ASE) accumulates and builds in optical spans that have multiple optical amplifiers between regenerators.

**2.** application service element.

### ASI

ATM Service Interface.

### ASIC

application-specific integrated circuit.

### ASIST

Application Software Integration Support Tools. A set of C-language application development tools designed to facilitate the creation of host-controlled applications by Cisco VCO/4K customers.

**ASN**

auxiliary signal network.

**ASN.1**

Abstract Syntax Notation One. OSI language for describing data types independent of particular computer structures and representation techniques. Described by ISO International Standard 8824. See also *BER, basic encoding rules.*

**ASP**

**1.** AppleTalk Session Protocol. A protocol that uses ATP to provide session establishment, maintenance, and teardown, as well as request sequencing. See also *ATP.*

**2.** Auxiliary signal path. In telecommunications, link between TransPaths that allows them to exchange signaling information that is incompatible with the PSTN backbone network; used to provide feature transparency.

**ASPI**

advanced ssci programming interface.

**assigned numbers**

RFC [STD2] documents the currently assigned values from several series of numbers used in network protocol implementations. This RFC is updated periodically, and current information can be obtained from the IANA. If you are developing a protocol or an application that requires the use of a link, a socket, a port, a protocol, and so on, contact the IANA to receive a number assignment. See also *IANA* and *STD.*

**association control service element**

See *ACSE.*

**associative memory**

Memory that is accessed based on its contents, not on its memory address. Sometimes called *content addressable memory (CAM).*

**AST**

automatic spanning tree. A function that supports the automatic resolution of spanning trees in SRB networks, providing a single path for spanning explorer frames to traverse from a given node in the network to another. AST is based on the IEEE 802.1 standard. See also *IEEE 802.1* and *SRB.*

### ASTA

Advanced Software Technology and Algorithms. Component of the HPCC program intended to develop software and algorithms for implementation on high-performance computer and communications systems. See also *HPCC*.

### async

Subset of tty.

### Asynchronous Balanced Mode

See *ABM*.

### asynchronous response mode

See *ARM*.

### asynchronous time-division multiplexing

See *ATDM*.

### Asynchronous Transfer Mode

See *ATM*.

### asynchronous transmission

Term describing digital signals that are transmitted without precise clocking. Such signals generally have different frequencies and phase relationships. Asynchronous transmissions usually encapsulate individual characters in control bits (called start and stop bits) that designate the beginning and the end of each character. Compare with *isochronous transmission*, *plesiochronous transmission*, and *synchronous transmission*.

### AT

advanced technology.

### ATB

all trunks busy. The state of a trunk group when all trunks are in use. The trunk group cannot accept any new inbound or outbound calls in this state. The ICM tracks the amount of time during which all trunks in a trunk group are busy.

### ATCP

AppleTalk Control Protocol. The protocol that establishes and configures AppleTalk over PPP, as defined in RFC 1378. See also *PPP*.

## ATDM

asynchronous time-division multiplexing. A method of sending information that resembles normal TDM, except that time slots are allocated as needed rather than preassigned to specific transmitters. Compare with *FDM*, *statistical multiplexing*, and *TDM*.

## ATG

See *ATG* in the "Cisco Systems Terms and Acronyms" section.

## ATH

attention hangup.

## at-least-once transaction

See *ALO transaction*.

## ATM

Asynchronous Transfer Mode. The international standard for cell relay in which multiple service types (such as voice, video, or data) are conveyed in fixed-length (53-byte) cells. Fixed-length cells allow cell processing to occur in hardware, thereby reducing transit delays. ATM is designed to take advantage of high-speed transmission media, such as E3, SONET, and T3.

## ATM adaptation layer

See *AAL*.

## ATM adaptation layer 1

See *AAL1*.

## ATM adaptation layer 2

See *AAL2*.

## ATM adaptation layer 3/4

See *AAL3/4*.

## ATM adaptation layer 5

See *AAL5*.

## ATM ARP server

A device that provides address-resolution services to LISs when running classical IP over ATM. See also *LIS*.

**ATM data service unit**

See *ADSU*.

**ATM edge LSR**

A router that is connected to the ATM-LSR cloud through LSC-ATM interfaces. The ATM edge LSR adds labels to unlabeled packets and strips labels from labeled packets.

**ATM endpoint**

The point in an ATM network where an ATM connection is initiated or terminated. ATM endpoints include ATM-attached workstations, ATM-attached servers, ATM-to-LAN switches, and ATM routers.

**ATM Forum**

International organization jointly founded in 1991 by Cisco Systems, NET/ADAPTIVE, Northern Telecom, and Sprint that develops and promotes standards-based implementation agreements for ATM technology. The ATM Forum expands on official standards developed by ANSI and ITU-T, and develops implementation agreements in advance of official standards.

**ATM network interface card**

See *ATM network interface card* in the "Cisco Systems Terms and Acronyms" section.

**ATM interface processor**

See *AIS*.

**ATM layer**

Service-independent sublayer of the data link layer in an ATM network. The ATM layer receives the 48-byte payload segments from the AAL and attaches a 5-byte header to each, producing standard 53-byte ATM cells. These cells are passed to the physical layer for transmission across the physical medium. See also *AAL*.

**ATM Lite**

Entry-level port adapter (higher performance than the AIP) for Cisco 7500 and 7200 routers. The Cisco ATM Lite port adapter does not support traffic shaping or ABR.

**ATM management**

See *ATMM*.

**ATM network**

See *ATM network* in the "Cisco Systems Terms and Acronyms" section.

### ATM NIC
See *ATM network interface card* in the "Cisco Systems Terms and Acronyms" section.

### ATM service interface
See *ASCU*.

### ATM UNI
See *UNI*.

### ATM user-user connection
A connection created by the ATM layer to provide communication between two or more ATM service users, such as ATMM processes. Such communication can be unidirectional, using one VCC, or bidirectional, using two VCCs. See also *ATM layer*, *ATMM*, and *VCC*.

### ATM-LSR
A label switch router with several LSC-ATM interfaces. The router forwards the cells among these interfaces using labels carried in the VPI/VCI field of the cells.

### ATMM
ATM management. A process that runs on an ATM switch that controls VCI translation and rate enforcement. See also *ATM* and *VCD*.

### ATP
**1.** ALPS Tunneling Protocol. A protocol used to transport ALPS data across a TCP/IP network between an ALC/UTS router and an AX.25/EMTOX router. It consists of a set of messages (or primitives) to activate and deactivate ALPS ATP circuits and to pass data.

**2.** AppleTalk Transaction Protocol. A transport-level protocol that provides a loss-free transaction service between sockets. The service allows exchanges between two socket clients in which one client requests the other to perform a particular task and to report the results. ATP binds the request and the response together to ensure the reliable exchange of request-response pairs.

### Attached Resource Computer Network
See *ARCnet*.

### attachment unit interface
See *AUI*.

**A**

### attenuation

Loss of communication signal energy.

### attribute

Form of information items provided by the X.500 Directory Service. The directory information base consists of entries, each containing one or more attributes. Each attribute consists of a type identifier together with one or more values.

### AU

access unit. A device that provides ISDN access to PSNs. See also *PSN*.

### AUI

attachment unit interface. IEEE 802.3 interface between an MAU and a NIC. The term AUI also can refer to the rear panel port to which an AUI cable might attach. Also called *transceiver cable*. See also *IEEE 802.3*, *MAU*, and *NIC*.

### AUP

acceptable use policy. Many transit networks have policies that restrict the use to which the network can be put. The enforcement of AUPs varies with the network.

### AURP

AppleTalk Update-Based Routing Protocol. A method of encapsulating AppleTalk traffic in the header of a foreign protocol, allowing the connection of two or more discontiguous AppleTalk internetworks through a foreign network (such as TCP/IP) to form an AppleTalk WAN. This connection is called an AURP tunnel. In addition to its encapsulation function, AURP maintains routing tables for the entire AppleTalk WAN by exchanging routing information between exterior routers. See also *AURP* and *exterior router*.

### AURP tunnel

A connection created in an AURP WAN that functions as a single, virtual data link between AppleTalk internetworks physically separated by a foreign network (a TCP/IP network, for example). See also *AURP*.

### AUSM

ATM user service module.

### authentication

In security, the verification of the identity of a person or a process.

**authority zone**

Associated with DNS, an authority zone is a section of the domain-name tree for which one name server is the authority. See also *DNS*.

**authorization**

The method for remote access control, including one-time authorization or authorization for each service, per-user account list and profile, user group support, and support of IP, IPX, ARA, and Telnet.

**Automated Packet Recognition**

Translation

See *APaRT* in the "Cisco Systems Terms and Acronyms" section.

**automatic call distribution**

See *ACD*.

**automatic call reconnect**

Feature permitting automatic call rerouting away from a failed trunk line.

**automatic protection switching**

See *APS*.

**automatic repeat request**

See *ARQ*.

**Automatic Routing Management**

Formerly AutoRoute. The connection-oriented mechanism used in Cisco WAN switches to provide connectivity across the network. Switches perform a connection admission control (CAC) function on all types of connections in the network. Distributed network intelligence enables the CAC function to route and reroute connections automatically over optimal paths while guaranteeing the required QoS.

**automatic spanning tree**

See *AST*.

**autonomous confederation**

A group of autonomous systems that rely on their own network reachability and routing information more than they rely on that received from other autonomous systems or confederations.

### autonomous switching

See *autonomous switching* in the "Cisco Systems Terms and Acronyms" section.

### autonomous system

See *AS*.

### autonomous system boundary router

See *ASAM*.

### autoreconfiguration

The process performed by nodes within the failure domain of a Token Ring network. Nodes automatically perform diagnostics in an attempt to reconfigure the network around the failed areas. See also *failure domain*.

### availability

The amount of time that a telephone system or other device is *operational*—that is, how long it is processing telephone calls or other transactions. Availability is represented as the ratio of the total time a device is operational during a given time interval to the length of that interval. Compare with reliability.

### available bit rate

See *ABR*.

### AVBO

advanced voice busyout. The local voice busyout feature that provides a way to busy out a voice port or a DS0 group (time slot) if a state change is detected in a monitored network interface (or interfaces). When a monitored interface changes to a specified state, to out-of-service, or to in-service, the voice port presents a seized/busyout condition to the attached PBX or other customer premises equipment (CPE). The PBX or other CPE can then attempt to select an alternate route. AVBO adds the following functionality to the local voice busyout feature:

- For Voice over IP (VoIP), monitoring of links to remote, IP-addressable interfaces by the use of a real time reporter (RTR).

- Configuration by voice class to simplify and speed up the configuration of voice busyout on multiple voice ports.

- Local voice busyout is supported on analog and digital voice ports using channel-associated signalling (CAS).

**average rate**

Average rate, in kilobits per second (kbps), at which a given virtual circuit can transmit.

**AVM**

ATM voice multiplexer.

**AW**

**1.** administrative weight. The value set by the network administrator to indicate the desirability of a network link. One of four link metrics exchanged by PTSPs to determine the available resources of an ATM network.

**2.** admin workstation. A personal computer used to monitor the handling of calls in the ICM system. The AW also can be used to modify the system configuration or scripts.

**AX.25**

X.25 implementation based on a CCITT 1984 recommendation using permanent virtual circuits (PVCs) only. There is one nonstandard aspect of this protocol: packets can be sent with the m-bit set, but the size of the packet is less than the maximum packet size for the virtual circuit.

### B channel

Bearer channel. DS0 time slot that carries analog voice or digital data over ISDN. In ISDN, a full-duplex, 64-kbps channel used to send user data. Compare with *D channel*, *E channel*, and *H channel*.

### B8ZS

binary 8-zero substitution. Line-code type, used on T1 and E1 circuits, in which a special code is substituted whenever eight consecutive zeros are sent over the link. This code then is interpreted at the remote end of the connection. This technique guarantees ones density independent of the data stream. Sometimes called *bipolar 8-zero substitution*. Compare with *AMI*. See also *ones density*.

### back end

Node or software program that provides services to a front end. See also *client*, *FRF.11*, and *server*.

### back pressure

Propagation of network congestion information upstream through an internetwork.

### backbone

Part of a network that acts as the primary path for traffic that is most often sourced from, and destined for, other networks.

### backhaul

A scheme where telephony signalling is reliably transported from a gateway to a Media Gateway Controller across a packet-switched network.

### backhauling

A scheme, also called signal tunneling, where telephony signals are passed from a gateway to a separate control for processing. The gateway need not interpret the signalling information.

### backoff

The (usually random) retransmission delay enforced by contentious MAC protocols after a network node with data to transmit determines that the physical medium is already in use.

### backplane
The physical connection between an interface processor or card and the data buses and the power distribution buses inside a chassis.

### backward explicit congestion notification
See *BECN*.

### backward indicator bit
See *BIB*.

### backward learning
Algorithmic process used for routing traffic that surmises information by assuming symmetrical network conditions. For example, if node A receives a packet from node B through intermediate node C, the backward-learning routing algorithm assumes that A can reach B through C optimally.

### backward sequence number
See *BSN*.

### BAF
Bellcore AMA Format. System of abstract syntax and semantics that supports coding of AMA data into records.

### balanced configuration
In HDLC, a point-to-point network configuration with two combined stations.

### balanced, unbalanced
See *balun*.

### balun
balanced, unbalanced. Device used for matching impedance between a balanced and an unbalanced line, usually twisted-pair and coaxial cable.

### bandwidth
The difference between the highest and lowest frequencies available for network signals. The term also is used to describe the rated throughput capacity of a given network medium or protocol. The frequency range necessary to convey a signal measured in units of hertz (Hz). For example, voice signals typically require approximately 7 kHz of bandwidth and data traffic typically requires approximately 50 kHz of bandwidth.

**bandwidth allocation**

See *bandwidth reservation*.

**bandwidth reservation**

The process of assigning bandwidth to users and applications served by a network. Involves assigning priority to different flows of traffic based on how critical and delay-sensitive they are. This makes the best use of available bandwidth, and if the network becomes congested, lower-priority traffic can be dropped. Sometimes called *bandwidth allocation*. See also *call leg*.

**Banyan VINES**

See *VINES*.

**BARRNet**

Bay Area Regional Research Network. Regional network serving the San Francisco Bay Area. The BARRNet backbone is composed of four University of California campuses (Berkeley, Davis, Santa Cruz, and San Francisco), Stanford University, Lawrence Livermore National Laboratory, and NASA Ames Research Center. BARRNet is now part of BBN Planet. See also *BBN Planet*.

**baseband**

Characteristic of a network technology where only one carrier frequency is used. Ethernet is an example of a baseband network. Also called narrowband. Contrast with *broadband*.

**baseline report**

Compares two similar time ranges in a report format. A baseline time range is protected against purge action so that baseline data is available at report time. The baseline time range can be 1 to 30 days

**bash**

Bourne-again shell. Interactive UNIX shell based on the traditional Bourne shell, but with increased functionality. See also *root account*.

**basic encoding rules**

See *BER*.

**Basic Rate Interface**

See *BRI*.

**Basic Research and Human Resources**

See *BRHR*.

**baud**

Unit of signaling speed equal to the number of discrete signal elements transmitted per second. Baud is synonymous with bits per second (bps) if each signal element represents exactly 1 bit.

**Bay Area Regional Research Network**

See *BARRNet*.

**BBN**

Bolt, Beranek, and Newman, Inc. High-technology company located in Massachusetts that developed and maintained the ARPANET (and later, the Internet) core gateway system. See also *BBN Planet*.

**BBN Planet**

Subsidiary company of BBN that operates a nationwide Internet access network composed in part by the former regional networks BARRNet, NEARNET, and SURAnet. See also *BARRNet*, *BBN*, *NEARNET*, and *SURAnet*.

**Bc**

committed burst. Negotiated tariff metric in Frame Relay internetworks. The maximum amount of data (in bits) that a Frame Relay internetwork is committed to accept and transmit at the CIR. See also *Be* and *CIR*.

**BCP**

Best Current Practices. The newest subseries of RFCs that are written to describe BCPs in the Internet. Rather than specifying a protocol, these documents specify the best ways to use the protocols and the best ways to configure options to ensure interoperability between various vendors' products.

**BDCS**

Broadband Digital Cross-Connect System. SONET DCS capable of cross-connecting DS-3, STS-1 and STS-3c signals. See also *DCS*.

**Be**

excess burst. Negotiated tariff metric in Frame Relay internetworks. The number of bits that a Frame Relay internetwork attempts to transmit after Bc is accommodated. Be data, in general, is delivered with a lower probability than Bc data because Be data can be marked as DE by the network. See also *Bc* and *DE*.

**beacon**

Frame from a Token Ring or FDDI device indicating a serious problem with the ring, such as a broken cable. A beacon frame contains the address of the station assumed to be down. See also *failure domain*.

**bearer channel**

See *B channel*.

**Because It's Time Network**

See *BITNET*.

**BECN**

backward explicit congestion notification. Bit set by a Frame Relay network in frames traveling in the opposite direction of frames encountering a congested path. DTE receiving frames with the BECN bit set can request that higher-level protocols take flow control action as appropriate. Compare with *FE*.

**Bell Communications Research**

See *Bellcore*.

**Bell operating company**

See *BOC*.

**Bellcore**

Bell Communications Research. Organization that performs research and development on behalf of the RBOCs.

**Bellman-Ford routing algorithm**

See *distance vector routing algorithm*.

**BER**

**1.** bit error rate. Ratio of received bits that contain errors.

**2.** basic encoding rules. Rules for encoding data units described in the ISO ASN.1 standard. See also *ASN.1*.

**Berkeley Internet Name Domain**

See *BIND*.

**Berkeley Standard Distribution**

See *BSD*.

### BERT
bit error rate tester. Device that determines the BER on a given communications channel. See also *BER* (*bit error rate*).

### best-effort delivery
Describes a network system that does not use a sophisticated acknowledgment system to guarantee reliable delivery of information.

### BGP
Border Gateway Protocol. Interdomain routing protocol that replaces EGP. BGP exchanges reachability information with other BGP systems. It is defined by RFC 1163. See also *BGP4* and *EGP*.

### BGP4
BGP Version 4. Version 4 of the predominant interdomain routing protocol used on the Internet. BGP4 supports CIDR and uses route aggregation mechanisms to reduce the size of routing tables. See also *BGP* and *CIDR*.

### BIA
burned-in MAC address.

### BIB
Part of an SS7 MSU that when toggled signals a negative acknowledgment by the remote signaling point.

### BIC
International Telecommunication Union Telecommunication Standardization Sector (ITU-T) standard that defines the protocols and procedures needed for establishing, maintaining, and terminating broadband switched virtual connections between public networks. Also abbreviated BICI.

### BICI
Broadband Inter-Carrier Interface. ITU-T standard that defines the protocols and procedures needed for establishing, maintaining, and terminating broadband switched virtual connections between public networks. See also *BIC*.

### bidirectional PIM
See *bidir-PIM*.

### bidir-PIM

A variant of the Protocol Independent Multicast (PIM) suite of routing protocols for
IP multicast. In PIM, packet traffic for a multicast group is routed according to the
rules of the mode configured for that multicast group.

### BIGA

See *BIGA* in the "Cisco Systems Terms and Acronyms" section.

### big-endian

Method of storing or transmitting data in which the most significant bit or byte is
presented first. Compare with *little-endian*.

### binary

Numbering system characterized by ones and zeros (1 = on, 0 = off).

### binary 8-zero substitution

See *B8ZS*.

### binary coded alternate mark inversion

See *AMI*.

### binary synchronous communication

See *BSC*.

### Binary Synchronous Communication Protocol

See *bisync*.

### BIND

Berkeley Internet Name Domain. Implementation of DNS developed and distributed
by the University of California at Berkeley (United States). Many Internet hosts run
BIND, which is the ancestor of many commercial BIND implementations.

### BinHex

Binary Hexadecimal. A method for converting binary files into ASCII for
transmission by applications, such as e-mail, that can handle only ASCII.

### BIP

bit interleaved parity. In ATM, a method used to monitor errors on a link. A check bit
or word is sent in the link overhead for the previous block or frame. Bit errors in the
payload then can be detected and reported as maintenance information.

### biphase coding

Bipolar coding scheme originally developed for use in Ethernet. Clocking information is embedded into and recovered from the synchronous data stream without the need for separate clocking leads. The biphase signal contains no direct current energy.

### bipolar

Electrical characteristic denoting a circuit with both negative and positive polarity. Contrast with *unipolar*.

### bipolar 8-zero substitution

See *B8ZS*.

### bipolar violation

See *BPV*.

### BISDN

Broadband ISDN. ITU-T communication standards designed to handle high-bandwidth applications, such as video. BISDN currently uses ATM technology over SONET-based transmission circuits to provide data rates from 155 to 622 Mbps and beyond. Contrast with *N-ISDN*. See also *BRI*, *ISDN*, and *PRI*.

### bisync

Binary Synchronous Communication Protocol. Character-oriented data-link protocol for applications. Contrast with Synchronous Data Link Control (*SDLC*).

### bit

Binary digit used in the binary numbering system. Can be 0 or 1.

### bit error rate

See *BER*.

### bit error rate tester

See *BERT*.

### bit interleaved parity

See *BIP*.

### bit rate

Speed at which bits are transmitted, usually expressed in bits per second.

## BITNET

"Because It's Time" Networking Services. Low-cost, low-speed academic network consisting primarily of IBM mainframes and 9600-bps leased lines. BITNET is now part of CREN. See also *CREN*.

## BITNET III

Dial-up service providing connectivity for members of CREN. See also *CREN*.

### bit-oriented protocol

Class of data link layer communication protocols that can transmit frames regardless of frame content. Unlike byte-oriented protocols, bit-oriented protocols provide full-duplex operation and are more efficient and reliable. Compare with *byte-oriented protocol*.

## BITS

building integrated timing supply. A clock in a central office that supplies DS1 and/or composite clock timing references to all synchronous network elements in that office.

### bits per second

Abbreviated *bps*. See also *bit rate*.

### black hole

Routing term for an area of the internetwork where packets enter, but do not emerge, due to adverse conditions or poor system configuration within a portion of the network.

### block multiplexer channel

IBM-style channel that implements the FIPS-60 channel, a U.S. channel standard. This channel also is referred to as *OEMI channel* and *370 block mux channel*.

### block serial tunnel

See *BSS*.

### blocking

In a switching system, a condition in which no paths are available to complete a circuit. The term also is used to describe a situation in which one activity cannot begin until another is completed.

### blower

An internal cooling fan used in larger router and switch chassis.

## BLSR

bidirectional line switch ring. SONET ring architecture that provides working and protection fibers between nodes. If the working fiber between nodes is cut, traffic is routed automatically onto the protection fiber. See also *SONET*.

## BNC connector

The standard connector used to connect IEEE 802.3 10Base2 coaxial cable to an MAU.

## BNI

Broadband Network Interface.

## BNM

Broadband Network Module.

## BNN

boundary network node. In SNA terminology, a subarea node that provides boundary function support for adjacent peripheral nodes. This support includes sequencing, pacing, and address translation. Also called *boundary node*.

## BOBI

See *BOBI* in the "Cisco Systems Terms and Acronyms" section.

## BOC

Bell operating company. Twenty-two local phone companies formed by the breakup of AT&T. See also *RBOC*.

## Bolt, Beranek, and Newman, Inc.

See *BBN*.

## boot helper

Minimum-function Cisco IOS image that serves only to boot the full-function, operational Cisco IOS image. Also known as rxboot.

## boot programmable read-only memory

See *boot PROM*.

## boot PROM

boot programmable read-only memory. A chip mounted on a printed circuit board used to provide executable boot instructions to a computer device.

**bootflash**

Separate Flash memory device used primarily to store the Cisco IOS boot helper image, operational Cisco IOS images, and system configuration information.

**BOOTP**

Bootstrap Protocol. The protocol used by a network node to determine the IP address of its Ethernet interfaces to affect network booting.

**Bootstrap Protocol**

See *BOOTP*.

**border gateway**

A router that communicates with routers in other autonomous systems.

**Border Gateway Protocol**

See *BGP*.

**border node**

Node in one zone that connects with one or more nodes in other zones.

**boundary function**

Capability of SNA subarea nodes to provide protocol support for attached peripheral nodes. Typically found in IBM 3745 devices.

**boundary network node**

See *BNN*.

**boundary node**

See *BNN*.

**Bpdu**

Bridge Protocol Data Unit. Spanning-Tree Protocol hello packet that is sent out at configurable intervals to exchange information among bridges in the network. See also *PDU*.

**BPI**

baseline privacy interface.

**bps**

bits per second.

### BPV

bipolar violation. A one (1) in a bipolar signal that has the same polarity as the preceding one. See also *coding violation*.

### BPX Service Node

See *BPX Service Node* in the "Cisco Systems Terms and Acronyms" section.

### BRA

basic rate access. Two 64 kbps B channels + one 16 kbps D channel (2B + D), carrying user traffic and signaling information respectively to the user via twisted pair local loop.

### break-out/break-in

See *BOBI* in the "Cisco Systems Terms and Acronyms" section.

### BRF

bridge relay function.

### BRHR

Basic Research and Human Resources. Component of the HPCC program designed to support research, training, and education in computer science, computer engineering, and computational science. See also *HPCC*.

### BRI

Basic Rate Interface. ISDN interface composed of two B channels and one D channel for circuit-switched communication of voice, video, and data. Compare with *PRI*. See also *BISDN*, *ISDN*, and *N-ISDN*.

### bridge

Device that connects and passes packets between two network segments that use the same communications protocol. Bridges operate at the data link layer (Layer 2) of the OSI reference model. In general, a bridge filters, forwards, or floods an incoming frame based on the MAC address of that frame. See also *relay*.

### bridge forwarding

A process that uses entries in a filtering database to determine whether frames with a given MAC destination address can be forwarded to a given port or ports. Described in the IEEE 802.1 standard. See also *IEEE 802.1*.

### bridge group

A bridging feature that assigns network interfaces to a particular spanning-tree group. Bridge groups can be compatible with the IEEE 802.1 or the DEC specification.

### bridge number

A number that identifies each bridge in an SRB LAN. Parallel bridges must have different bridge numbers.

### Bridge Protocol Data Unit

See *Bpdu.*

### bridge static filtering

The process in which a bridge maintains a filtering database consisting of static entries. Each static entry equates a MAC destination address with a port that can receive frames with this MAC destination address and a set of ports on which the frames can be transmitted. Defined in the IEEE 802.1 standard. See also *IEEE 802.1.*

### bridge virtual interface

See BVI.

### bridge-group

A group of interfaces bridged together to emulate a multiport bridge.

### broadband

Describes facilities or services that operate at the DS3 rate and above. For example, a Broadband DCS makes cross-connections at the DS3, STS-1, and STS-Nc levels. Similarly, Broadband ISDN provides about 150 Mb/s per channel of usable bandwidth.

### broadband

**1.** Transmission system that multiplexes multiple independent signals onto one cable.

**2.** Telecommunications terminology: Any channel having a bandwidth greater than a voice-grade channel (4 kHz).

**3.** LAN terminology: A coaxial cable on which analog signaling is used. An RF system with a constant data rate at or above 1.5 Mbps. Also called *wideband.* Contrast with *baseband.*

### broadband inter-carrier interface

See *BIC.*

### Broadband ISDN

See *BISDN.*

### Broadband Network Interface

See *BNI.*

---

**Broadband Network Module**

See *BNM*.

---

**broadband switch module**

See *BXM*.

---

**broadcast**

Data packet that are sent to all nodes on a network. Broadcasts are identified by a broadcast address. Compare with *multicast* and *unicast*. See also *broadcast*.

---

**broadcast address**

A special address reserved for sending a message to all stations. Generally, a broadcast address is a MAC destination address of all ones. Compare with *multicast address* and *unicast address*. See also *broadcast*.

---

**broadcast and unknown server**

See *BUS*.

---

**broadcast domain**

Set of all devices that receive broadcast frames originating from any device within the set. Broadcast domains typically are bounded by routers because routers do not forward broadcast frames.

---

**broadcast search**

The propagation of a search request to all network nodes if the location of a resource is unknown to the requester. See also *directed search*.

---

**broadcast storm**

An undesirable network event in which many broadcasts are sent simultaneously across all network segments. A broadcast storm uses substantial network bandwidth and, typically, causes network time-outs.

---

**brouter**

Concatenation of "bridge" and "router." Used to refer to devices that perform both bridging and routing functions.

---

**browser**

GUI-based hypertext client application, such as Internet Explorer, Mosaic, and Netscape Navigator, used to access hypertext documents and other services located on innumerable remote servers throughout the WWW and Internet. See also *hypertext*, *Internet*, *Mosaic*, and *WWW*.

B

## BSC

**1.** binary synchronous communication. Character-oriented data link layer protocol for half-duplex applications. A form of telecommunication line control that uses a standard set of transmission control characters and control character sequences, for the binary synchronous transmission of binary-coded data between stations.

**2.** base station controller. In wireless, provides the control functions and physical links between the MSC and BTS in a GSM mobile wireless network. The BSC controls the interface between the SGSN and the BTS in a GPRS network. The BSC is a high-capacity telephony switch that provides handsoff functions and cell configuration data, and controls radio frequency power levels in BTSs. The combined functions of the BSC and the BTS are referred to as the BSS.

## BSD

Berkeley Standard Distribution. A term used to describe any of a variety of UNIX-type operating systems based on the UC Berkeley BSD operating system.

## BSN

Part of an SS7 MSU that acknowledges the receipt of signal units by the remote signalling point. Contains the sequence number of the signal unit being acknowledged.

## BSS

base station subsystem. Refers to the radio-related functions provided by the BTS and BSC in a GSM mobile wireless network.

## BSTUN

Block Serial Tunnel.

Note: Do not use bisync serial tunnel or BSC tunnel as synonyms.

## BT

burst tolerance. A parameter defined by the ATM Forum for ATM traffic management. For VBR connections, BT determines the size of the maximum burst of contiguous cells that can be transmitted. See also *VBR*.

## BTA

Basic Trading Area. An area or "footprint" in which an entity is licensed to transmit their frequencies. BTAs were established by Rand McNally and are defined as county lines. Rand McNally licensed their mapping data to the FCC for ease of designation for site licenses.

**BTS**

base transceiver station. A land-based station in a GSM mobile wireless network that consists of transceivers and antennas, which handle the radio interface to a mobile station. A BSC controls one or more BTSs. The combined functions of the BTS and the BSC are referred to as the BSS.

**BTU**

British thermal units.

**BTW**

by the way. One of many short-hand phrases used in chat sessions and e-mail conversations. See also *IMHO*.

**buffer**

A storage area used for handling data in transit. Buffers are used in internetworking to compensate for differences in processing speed between network devices. Bursts of data can be stored in buffers until they can be handled by slower processing devices. Sometimes referred to as a *packet buffer*.

**build**

To create flat files that are ready for use by the signaling controller database.

**building integrated timing supply**

See *BITS*.

**burst**

In data communications, a sequence of signals counted as one unit in accordance with some specific criterion or measure.

**burst tolerance**

See *BT*.

**bursty traffic**

A data communications term referring to an uneven pattern of data transmission.

**bus**

**1.** Common physical signal path composed of wires or other media across which signals can be sent from one part of a computer to another. Sometimes called a highway.

**2.** See *bus topology*.

### BUS

broadcast and unknown server. Multicast server used in ELANs that is used to flood traffic addressed to an unknown destination and to forward multicast and broadcast traffic to the appropriate clients. See also *ELAN*.

### bus and tag channel

IBM channel, developed in the 1960s, incorporating copper multiwire technology. Replaced by the ESCON channel. See also *ESCON channel* and *parallel channel*.

### Bus Interface Gate Array

See *BIGA* in the "Cisco Systems Terms and Acronyms" section.

### bus topology

Linear LAN architecture in which transmissions from network stations propagate the length of the medium and are received by all other stations. Compare with *ring topology*, *star topology*, and *tree topology*.

### BVI

Bridge Group Virtual Interface. Logical Layer 3–only interface associated with a bridge group when IRB is configured.

### BX.25

AT&T implementation of X.25. See also *X.25*.

### BXM

Broadband Switch Module. ATM port card for the Cisco BPX switch.

### bypass mode

The operating mode on FDDI and Token Ring networks in which an interface has been removed from the ring.

### bypass relay

Allows a particular Token Ring interface to be shut down and thus effectively removed from the ring.

### byte

A term used to refer to a series of consecutive binary digits that are operated upon as a unit (for example, an 8-bit byte).

**byte reversal**

The process of storing numeric data with the least-significant byte first. Used for integers and addresses on devices with Intel microprocessors.

**byte-oriented protocol**

A class of data-link communications protocols that use a specific character from the user character set to delimit frames. These protocols largely have been replaced by bit-oriented protocols. Compare with *bit-oriented protocol*.

### C/N

Difference in amplitude between the desired radio frequency (RF) carrier and the noise in a portion of the spectrum. See *carrier-to-noise*.

### CA

**1.** certification authority. Entity that issues digital certificates (especially X.509 certificates) and vouches for the binding between the data items in a certificate.

**2.** Telecommunications: call appearance.

### CA certificate

[Digital] certificate for one CA issued by another CA.

### cable

Transmission medium of copper wire or optical fiber wrapped in a protective cover.

### cable modem

Modulator-demodulator device that is placed at subscriber locations to convey data communications on a cable television system.

### cable range

Range of network numbers that is valid for use by nodes on an extended AppleTalk network. The cable range value can be a single network number or a contiguous sequence of several network numbers. Node addresses are assigned based on the cable range values.

### cable router

Modular chassis-based router optimized for data-over-CATV hybrid fiber-coaxial (HFC) applications.

### cable television

See *CATV*.

### CAC

connection admission control. Set of actions taken by each ATM switch during connection setup to determine whether a connection's requested QoS will violate the QoS guarantees for established connections. CAC also is used when routing a connection request through an ATM network.

### caching

A form of replication in which information learned during a previous transaction is used to process later transactions.

### CAF

controllable ATM fabric.

### cage

A piece of hardware into which cards are installed.

### calculated planning impairment factor

See *ICPIF*.

### California Education and Research Federation Network

See *CERFnet*.

### call

An attempted connection between a remote system and LAC, such as a telephone call through the PSTN. An incoming or outgoing call that is established successfully between a remote system and LAC results in a corresponding L2TP session within a previously established tunnel between the LAC and the LNS.

### call admission precedence

An MPLS traffic engineering tunnel with a higher priority will, if necessary, preempt an MPLS traffic engineering tunnel with a lower priority. Tunnels that are harder to route are expected to have a higher priority and to be able to preempt tunnels that are easier to route. The assumption is that a lower-priority tunnel can find another path.

### call agent

Intelligent entity in an IP telephony network that handles call control in an MGCP model voice over IP network. Also known as a Media Gateway Controller (MGC).

### call detail record

See *CDR*.

**call leg**

Discrete segment of a call connection. A call leg is a logical connection between the router and either a telephony endpoint over a bearer channel, or another endpoint using a session protocol.

**call priority**

Priority assigned to each origination port in circuit-switched systems. This priority defines the order in which calls are reconnected. Call priority also defines which calls can or cannot be placed during a bandwidth reservation. See also *bandwidth reservation*.

**call reference value**

See *CRV*.

**call setup time**

The time required to establish a switched call between DTE devices.

**caller ID**

See *CLID*.

**calling line identification**

See *CLID*.

**CAM**

content-addressable memory. See *associative memory*. See also *CAM* in the "Cisco Systems Terms and Acronyms" section.

**Canadian Standards Association**

See *CSA*.

**CAP**

Competitive Access Provider. An independent company providing local telecommunications services mainly to business customers in competition with an area's BOC or IOC. Teleport and MFS are the two major CAPs operating in major metropolitan areas in the United States. See also *BOC* and *IOC*.

---

### CAR

**1.** committed access rate. The CAR and DCAR (distributed CAR) services limit the input or output transmission rate on an interface or subinterface based on a flexible set of criteria.

**2.** Cisco Access Registrar. Provides RADIUS services to DOCSIS modems for the deployment of high-speed data services in a one-way cable plant requiring telco-return for upstream data.

---

### carrier

An electromagnetic wave or alternating current of a single frequency, suitable for modulation by another, data-bearing signal. See also *modulation*.

---

### Carrier Detect

See *CD*.

---

### Carrier Identification Code

See *CIC*.

---

### carrier sense multiple access collision detect

See *CSI*.

---

### carrier-to-noise

See *C/N*.

---

### CAS

channel associated signaling. The transmission of signaling information within the voice channel. CAS signaling often is referred to as *robbed-bit* signaling because user bandwidth is being robbed by the network for other purposes.

---

### Category 1 cabling

One of five grades of UTP cabling described in the EIA/TIA-586 standard. Category 1 cabling is used for telephone communications and is not suitable for transmitting data. Compare with *Category 2 cabling*, *Category 3 cabling*, *Category 4 cabling*, and *Category 5 cabling*. See also *EIA/TIA-586* and *UTP*.

---

### Category 2 cabling

One of five grades of UTP cabling described in the EIA/TIA-586 standard. Category 2 cabling is capable of transmitting data at speeds up to 4 Mbps. Compare with *Category 1 cabling*, *Category 3 cabling*, *Category 4 cabling*, and *Category 5 cabling*. See also *EIA/TIA-586* and *UTP*.

### Category 3 cabling

One of five grades of UTP cabling described in the EIA/TIA-586 standard. Category 3 cabling is used in 10BaseT networks and can transmit data at speeds up to 10 Mbps. Compare with *Category 1 cabling*, *Category 2 cabling*, *Category 4 cabling*, and *Category 5 cabling*. See also *EIA/TIA-586* and *UTP*.

### Category 4 cabling

One of five grades of UTP cabling described in the EIA/TIA-586 standard. Category 4 cabling is used in Token Ring networks and can transmit data at speeds up to 16 Mbps. Compare with *Category 1 cabling*, *Category 2 cabling*, *Category 3 cabling*, and *Category 5 cabling*. See also *EIA/TIA-586* and *UTP*.

### Category 5 cabling

One of five grades of UTP cabling described in the EIA/TIA-586 standard. Category 5 cabling can transmit data at speeds up to 100 Mbps. Compare with *Category 1 cabling*, *Category 2 cabling*, *Category 3 cabling*, and *Category 4 cabling*. See also *EIA/TIA-586* and *UTP*.

### catenet

A network in which hosts are connected to diverse networks, which themselves are connected with routers. The Internet is a prominent example of a catenet.

### CATV

cable television. A communication system where multiple channels of programming material are transmitted to homes using broadband coaxial cable. Formerly called Community Antenna Television.

### cause codes

Code that indicates the reason for ISDN call failure or completion.

### CBAC

Context-based Access Control. Protocol that provides internal users with secure access control for each application and for all traffic across network perimeters. CBAC enhances security by scrutinizing both source and destination addresses and by tracking each application's connection status.

### CBC

cipher block chaining. Prevents the problems associated with Electronic Codebook (ECB), where every block of "plain text" maps to exactly one block of "cipher text" by having each encrypted block XORed with the previous block of ciphertext. In this way identical patterns in different messages are encrypted differently, depending upon the difference in the previous data.

---

**CBDS**

Connectionless Broadband Data Service. European high-speed, packet-switched, datagram-based WAN networking technology. Similar to SMDS. See also *SMDS*.

---

**CBR**

constant bit rate. QoS class defined by the ATM Forum for ATM networks. CBR is used for connections that depend on precise clocking to ensure undistorted delivery. Compare with *ABR*, *UBR*, and *VBR*.

---

**CBWFQ**

class-based weighted fair queueing extends the standard WFQ functionality to provide support for user-defined traffic classes.

---

**CC**

**1.** country code. Part of a numbering plan.

**2.** VCS–call context.

---

**CCB**

call control block.

---

**CCIE**

See *CCIE* in the "Cisco Systems Terms and Acronyms" section.

---

**CCITT**

Consultative Committee for International Telegraph and Telephone. International organization responsible for the development of communications standards. Now called the ITU-T. See also *ITU-T*.

---

**CCN unit**

continuous control node unit. Provides communication between the redundant sides of the admin shelf.

---

**CCNA**

Cisco Certified Network Associate.

---

**CCO**

See *CCO* in the "Cisco Systems Terms and Acronyms" section.

---

**CCOT**

cross office transfer time.

## CCR

commitment, concurrency, and recovery. OSI application service element used to create atomic operations across distributed systems. Used primarily to implement two-phase commit for transactions and nonstop operations.

## CCS

common channel signaling. Signaling system used in telephone networks that separates signaling information from user data. A specified channel is exclusively designated to carry signaling information for all other channels in the system. See also *SS7*.

## CCSRC

See *CCSRC* in the "Cisco Systems Terms and Acronyms" section.

## CCSS7

Common Channel Signaling System 7. Protocol used by the AT&T signaling network. The ICM's NIC receives routing requests from the CCSS7 network and returns a routing label to the CCSS7 network.

## CD

Carrier Detect. A signal that indicates whether an interface is active. Also, a signal generated by a modem indicating that a call has been connected.

## CDB

call detail block. Consists of several Call Data Elements. The CDB is generated at a Certain Point in Call (PIC). For example, a CDB is generated when the call is answered, released, and so on.

## CDDI

Copper Distributed Data Interface. The implementation of FDDI protocols over STP and UTP cabling. CDDI transmits over relatively short distances (about 90 yards [100 meters]), providing data rates of 100 Mbps using a dual-ring architecture to provide redundancy. Based on the ANSI TPPMD standard. Compare with *FDDI*.

## CDE

call detail element. A data element that includes a basic information field within a billing record. Examples of a CDE are the calling number, the called number, and so on.

## CDF

channel definition format. Technology for "push" applications on the World Wide Web. CDF is an application of XML. See also *XML*.

---

**CDMA**

code division multiple access. A method of dividing a radio spectrum to be shared by multiple users through the assignment of unique codes. CDMA implements spread spectrum transmission.

---

**CDP**

See *CDP (Cisco Discovery Protocol)* in the "Cisco Systems Terms and Acronyms" chapter.

---

**CDPD**

Cellular Digital Packet Data. Open standard for two-way wireless data communication over high-frequency cellular telephone channels. Allows data transmissions between a remote cellular link and a NAP. Operates at 19.2 kbps.

---

**CDR**

call detail record.

**1.** A record written to a database for use in postprocessing activities. CDR files consist of several CDBs. These activities include many functions, but primarily are billing and network analysis. Cisco CallManager writes CDR records to the SQL database as calls are made in a manner consistent with the configuration of each individual Cisco CallManager.

**2.** Used in the original telephony networks, and now extended to mobile wireless network calls, the CDR contains billing information for charging purposes. In a GPRS network, the charging gateway sends the billing information within a CDR to the network service provider for that subscriber.

**3.** VNS record of voice or data SVCs, which includes calling and called numbers, local and remote node names, data and time stamp, elapsed time, and Call Failure Class fields.

**4.** Wireless—Used in the original telephony networks and now extended to mobile wireless network calls. The CDR contains billing information for charging purposes. In a GPRS network, the charging gateway sends the billing information within a CDR to the network service provider for that subscriber.

---

**CD-ROM**

compact disc read-only memory.

---

**CD-RW**

compact disc read/write.

**CDV**

cell delay variation. A component of cell transfer delay, which is induced by buffering and cell scheduling. CDV is a QoS delay parameter associated with CBR and VBR service. See also *CBR* and *VBR*.

**CDVT**

cell delay variation tolerance. In ATM, a QoS parameter for managing traffic that is specified when a connection is set up. In CBR transmissions, CDVT determines the level of jitter that is tolerable for the data samples taken by the PCR. See also *CBR* and *PCR*.

**CE router**

customer edge router. A router that is part of a customer network and that interfaces to a provider edge (PE) router.

**CED**

caller-entered digits. Digits entered by a caller on a touch-tone phone in response to prompts. Either a peripheral (ACD, PBX, or VRU) or the carrier network can prompt for CEDs.

**CEF**

See *CEF* in the "Cisco Systems Terms and Acronyms" section.

**cell**

The basic data unit for ATM switching and multiplexing. Cells contain identifiers that specify the data stream to which they belong. Each cell consists of a 5-byte header and 48 bytes of payload. See also *cell relay*.

**cell delay variation**

See *CDV*.

**cell delay variation tolerance**

See *CDVT*.

**cell loss priority**

See *CLP*.

**cell loss ratio**

See *CLR*.

**cell payload scrambling**

A technique using an ATM switch to maintain framing on some medium-speed edge and trunk interfaces.

**cell relay**

Network technology based on the use of small, fixed-size packets, or cells. Because cells are fixed-length, they can be processed and switched in hardware at high speeds. Cell relay is the basis for many high-speed network protocols, including ATM, IEEE 802.6, and SMDS. See also *cell*.

**cell transfer delay**

See *CTD*.

**cells per second**

Abbreviated cps.

**Cellular Digital Packet Data**

See *CDPD*.

**cellular radio**

Technology that uses radio transmissions to access telephone-company networks. Service is provided in a particular area by a low-power transmitter.

**CELP**

code excited linear prediction compression. Compression algorithm used in low bit-rate voice encoding. Used in ITU-T Recommendations G.728, G.729, G.723.1.

**CEN**

European Committee for Standardization. CEN's mission is to promote voluntary technical harmonization in Europe in conjunction with worldwide bodies and its partners in Europe. The organization works in partnership with CENELEC and ETSI (European Telecommunications Standards Institute).

**CENELEC**

Comite Europeen de Normalisation Electrotechnique. CENELEC is the European Committee for Electrotechnical Standardization. It was set up in 1973 and was officially recognised as the European Standards Organisation in its field by the European Commission in Directive 83/189 EEC. CENELEC works with 40,000 technical experts from 19 EC and EFTA countries to publish standards for the European market.

**central office**

See *CO*.

**Centrex**

LEC service that provides local switching applications similar to those provided by an onsite PBX. With Centrex, there is no onsite switching; all customer connections go back to the CO. See also *CC* and *LEC*.

**CEP**

Certificate Enrollment Protocol. Certificate management protocol jointly developed by Cisco Systems and VeriSign, Inc. CEP is an early implementation of Certificate Request Syntax (CRS), a standard proposed to the Internet Engineering Task Force (IETF). CEP specifies how a device communicates with a CA, including how to retrieve the public key of the CA, how to enroll a device with the CA, and how to retrieve a certificate revocation list (CRL). CEP uses Public Key Cryptography Standard (PKCS) 7 and PKCS 10 as key component technologies. The public key infrastructure working group (PKIX) of the IETF is working to standardize a protocol for these functions, either CRS or an equivalent. When an IETF standard is stable, Cisco will add support for it.

**CEPT**

Conférence Européenne des Postes et des Télécommunications. Association of the 26 European PTTs that recommends communication specifications to the ITU-T.

**CER**

cell error ratio. In ATM, the ratio of transmitted cells that have errors to the total cells sent in a transmission for a specific period of time.

**CERFnet**

California Education and Research Federation Network. TCP/IP network, based in Southern California, that connects hundreds of higher-education centers internationally while also providing Internet access to subscribers. CERFnet was founded in 1988 by the San Diego Supercomputer Center and General Atomics, and is funded by the NSF.

**CERN**

European Laboratory for Particle Physics. Birthplace of the World Wide Web.

**CERT**

Computer Emergency Response Team. Chartered to work with the Internet community to facilitate its response to computer security events involving Internet hosts, to take proactive steps to raise the community's awareness of computer security issues, and to conduct research targeted at improving the security of existing systems. The U.S. CERT is based at Carnegie Mellon University in Pittsburgh. Regional CERTs are, like NICs, springing up in different parts of the world.

**certificate**

Digital representation of user or device attributes, including a public key, that is signed with an authoritative private key.

**CES**

circuit emulation service. Enables users to multiplex or to concentrate multiple circuit emulation streams for voice and video with packet data on a single high-speed ATM link without a separate ATM access multiplexer.

**CET**

See *CET* in the "Cisco Systems Terms and Acronyms" section.

**CFRAD**

See *Cisco FRAD* in the "Cisco Systems Terms and Acronyms" section.

**CGI**

Common Gateway Interface. A set of rules that describe how a Web server communicates with another application running on the same computer and how the application (called a CGI program) communicates with the Web server. Any application can be a CGI program if it handles input and output according to the CGI standard.

**chaining**

An SNA concept in which RUs are grouped together for the purpose of error recovery.

**Challenge Handshake Authentication Protocol**

See *CHAP*.

**channel**

**1.** Communication path wide enough to permit a single RF transmission. Multiple channels can be multiplexed over a single cable in certain environments.

**2.** In IBM, the specific path between large computers (such as mainframes) and attached peripheral devices.

**3.** Specific frequency allocation and bandwidth. Downstream channels are used for television in the United States are 6 MHz wide.

**channel definition format.**

See *CDF*.

**Channel Interface Processor**

See *CIP* in the "Cisco Systems Terms and Acronyms" section.

**channel service unit**

See *CSU*.

**channel-attached**

Pertaining to the attachment of devices directly by data channels (input/output channels) to a computer.

**channelized E1**

Access link operating at 2.048 Mbps that is subdivided into 30 B-channels and 1 D-channel. Supports DDR, Frame Relay, and X.25. Compare with *channelized T1*.

**channelized T1**

Access link operating at 1.544 Mbps that is subdivided into 24 channels (23 B channels and 1 D channel) of 64 kbps each. The individual channels or groups of channels connect to different destinations. Supports DDR, Frame Relay, and X.25. Also called *fractional T1*. Compare with *channelized E1*.

**CHAP**

Challenge Handshake Authentication Protocol. Security feature supported on lines using PPP encapsulation that prevents unauthorized access. CHAP does not itself prevent unauthorized access, but merely identifies the remote end. The router or access server then determines whether that user is allowed access. Compare with *PAP*.

**chargen**

Character Generation. Via TCP, a service that sends a continual stream of characters until stopped by the client. Via UDP, the server sends a random number of characters each time the client sends a datagram.

**chat script**

String of text that defines the login "conversation" that occurs between two systems. Consists of expect-send pairs that define the string that the local system expects to receive from the remote system and what the local system should send as a reply.

**Cheapernet**

Industry term used to refer to the IEEE 802.3 10Base2 standard or the cable specified in that standard. Compare with *Thinnet*. See also *10Base2*, *EtherChannel*, and *IEEE 802.3*.

## checksum

Method for checking the integrity of transmitted data. A checksum is an integer value computed from a sequence of octets taken through a series of arithmetic operations. The value is recomputed at the receiving end and is compared for verification.

## child peer group

Peer group for which another peer group is the parent peer group. See also *LGN*, *peer group*, and *parent peer group*.

## choke packet

Packet sent to a transmitter to tell it that congestion exists and that it should reduce its sending rate.

## churn

Many subscriber additions and deletions.

## CIA

classical IP over ATM. Specification for running IP over ATM in a manner that takes full advantage of the features of ATM. Defined in RFC 1577.

## CIC

Prefix to select different long distance carriers; prefixes to select tielines, trunk groups, and WATS lines; and private number plans, such as seven-digit dialing.

## CICNet

Regional network that connects academic, research, nonprofit, and commercial organizations in the Midwestern United States. Founded in 1988, CICNet was a part of the NSFNET and was funded by the NSF until the NSFNET dissolved in 1995. See also *NSFNET*.

## CICS

Customer Information Control System. IBM application subsystem allowing transactions entered at remote terminals to be processed concurrently by user applications.

## CID

**1.** craft interface device. Terminal- or PC-based interface that enables the performance of local maintenance operations.

**2.** channel ID. Designates the Frame Relay subchannel ID for Voice over Frame Relay.

### CIDR

classless interdomain routing. Technique supported by BGP4 and based on route aggregation. CIDR allows routers to group routes together to reduce the quantity of routing information carried by the core routers. With CIDR, several IP networks appear to networks outside the group as a single, larger entity. With CIDR, IP addresses and their subnet masks are written as four octets, separated by periods, followed by a forward slash and a two-digit number that represents the subnet mask. See also *BGP4*.

### CIP

See *CIP* (Channel Interface Processor) in the "Cisco Systems Terms and Acronyms" section.

### Cipher

Cryptographic algorithm for encryption and decryption.

### ciphertext

Data that has been transformed by encryption so that its semantic information content (that is, its meaning) is no longer intelligible or directly available.

### CIR

committed information rate. The rate at which a Frame Relay network agrees to transfer information under normal conditions, averaged over a minimum increment of time. CIR, measured in bits per second, is one of the key negotiated tariff metrics. See also *Bc*.

### circuit

A communications path between two or more points.

### circuit group

A grouping of associated serial lines that link two bridges. If one of the serial links in a circuit group is in the spanning tree for a network, any of the serial links in the circuit group can be used for load balancing. This load-balancing strategy avoids data ordering problems by assigning each destination address to a particular serial link.

### circuit steering

Mechanism used by some ATM switches to eavesdrop on a virtual connection and copy its cells to another port where an ATM analyzer is attached. Also known as *port snooping*.

### circuit switching

The switching system in which a dedicated physical circuit path must exist between the sender and the receiver for the duration of the "call." Used heavily in the telephone company network. Circuit switching can be contrasted with *contention* and *token passing* as a channel-access method, and with *message switching* and *packet switching* as a switching technique.

### Cisco Discovery Protocol

See *CDP* in the "Cisco Systems Terms and Acronyms" section.

### Cisco FRAD

See *Cisco FRAD* in the "Cisco Systems Terms and Acronyms" section.

### Cisco Frame Relay access device

See *Cisco FRAD* in the "Cisco Systems Terms and Acronyms" section.

### Cisco Internetwork Operating System software

See *Cisco IOS* in the "Cisco Systems Terms and Acronyms" section.

### Cisco IOS

See *Cisco IOS* in the "Cisco Systems Terms and Acronyms" section.

### Cisco Link Services

See *CLS* in the "Cisco Systems Terms and Acronyms" section.

### Cisco Link Services Interface

See *CLSI* in the "Cisco Systems Terms and Acronyms" section.

### CiscoBus controller

See *SP* in the "Cisco Systems Terms and Acronyms" section.

### CiscoFusion

See *CiscoFusion* in the "Cisco Systems Terms and Acronyms" section.

### Cisco Network Registrar

A software product that provides IP addresses, configuration parameters, and DNS names to DOCSIS cable modems and PCs, based on network and service policies. CNR also provides enhanced TFTP server capabilities, including the generation of DOCSIS cable modem configuration files.

### Cisco Optical Network Planner

See *Cisco Optical Network Planner* in the "Cisco Systems Terms and Acronyms" section.

### Cisco-trunk (private line) call

See *Cisco-trunk (private line) call* in the "Cisco Systems Terms and Acronyms" section.

### CiscoView

See *Cisco-trunk (private line) call* in the "Cisco Systems Terms and Acronyms" section.

### Cisco Wavelength Router Manager

See *Cisco Wavelength Router Manager* in the "Cisco Systems Terms and Acronyms" section.

### Cisco WRM

See *Cisco WRM* in the "Cisco Systems Terms and Acronyms" section.

### Cisco WW TAC

See *Cisco WW TAC* in the "Cisco Systems Terms and Acronyms" section.

### C-ISUP

See *C-ISUP* in the "Cisco Systems Terms and Acronyms" section. See also *ISUP*.

### CIX

Commercial Internet Exchange. A connection point between the commercial Internet service providers. Pronounced "kicks." See also *FIX* and *GIX*.

### CKTINT

Circuit Interworking software. A module in the SS7 application software that translates SS7 signals for the Cisco VCO/4K and host applications. It also performs call processing and circuit maintenance tasks.

### Class A station

See *DAS*.

### Class B station

See *SAS*.

### Class of Restrictions

See *COR*.

### class of service

See *CoS*.

### classical IP over ATM

See *CIA*.

### classless interdomain routing

See *CIDR*.

### CLAW

Common Link Access for Workstations. Data link layer protocol used by channel-attached RISC System/6000 series systems and by IBM 3172 devices running TCP/IP off-load. CLAW improves the efficiency of channel use and allows the CIP to provide the functionality of a 3172 in TCP/IP environments and to support direct channel attachment. The output from TCP/IP mainframe processing is a series of IP datagrams that the router can switch without modifications.

### clear channel

A channel that uses out-of-band signaling (as opposed to in-band signaling), so the channel's entire bit rate is available.

### Clear To Send

See *CTS*.

### ClearDDTS

Distributed Defect Tracking System. Development engineers and CSEs use ClearDDTS (Rational) to track bugs for software, hardware, and microcode products. CSEs also use ClearDDTS as a formal way to escalate an issue to developers. Customers use Release Note information derived from the ClearDDTS database to troubleshoot problems or to select a software version for an upgrade.

### CLEC

competitive local exchange carrier. A company that builds and operates communication networks in metropolitan areas and provides its customers with an alternative to the local telephone company. See also *CAF*.

### CLEI

Common Language Equipment Identifier. The standard code used by suppliers to identify equipment parts and system configurations. CLEI is a registered trademark of Bellcore (now Telcordia).

### CLI

**1.** command-line interface. An interface that allows the user to interact with the operating system by entering commands and optional arguments. The UNIX operating system and DOS provide CLIs. Compare with *GUI*.

**2.** Command Language Interpreter. The basic Cisco IOS configuration and management interface.

**CLID**

calling line ID. Information about the billing telephone number from which a call originated. The CLID value might be the entire phone number, the area code, or the area code plus the local exchange. Also known as Caller ID.

**client**

Node or software program (front-end device) that requests services from a server. See also *back end*, *FRF.11*, and *server*.

**client/server computing**

Term used to describe distributed computing (processing) network systems in which transaction responsibilities are divided into two parts: client (front end) and server (back end). Both terms (client and server) can be applied to software programs or actual computing devices. Also called distributed computing (processing). Compare with *peer-to-peer computing*. See also *RFC*.

**client/server model**

Common way to describe network services and the model user processes (programs) of those services. Examples include the nameserver/nameresolver paradigm of the DNS and fileserver/file-client relationships, such as NFS and diskless hosts.

**CLNP**

Connectionless Network Protocol. The OSI network layer protocol that does not require a circuit to be established before data is transmitted. See also *CLNS*.

**CLNS**

Connectionless Network Service. The OSI network layer service that does not require a circuit to be established before data is transmitted. CLNS routes messages to their destinations independently of any other messages. See also *CLNP*.

**cloning**

Creating and configuring a virtual access interface by applying a specific virtual template interface. The template is the source of the generic user information and the router-dependent information. The result of cloning is a virtual access interface configured with all the commands in the template.

**CLP**

cell loss priority. Field in the ATM cell header that determines the probability of a cell being dropped if the network becomes congested. Cells with CLP = 0 are insured traffic, which is unlikely to be dropped. Cells with CLP = 1 are best-effort traffic, which might be dropped in congested conditions to free up resources to handle insured traffic.

### CLR

cell loss ratio. In ATM, the ratio of discarded cells to cells that are transmitted successfully. CLR can be set as a QoS parameter when a connection is set up.

### CLTP

Connectionless Transport Protocol. Provides for end-to-end Transport data addressing (via Transport selector) and error control (via checksum), but cannot guarantee delivery or provide flow control. It is the OSI equivalent of UDP.

### cluster controller

**1.** Generally, an intelligent device that provides the connections for a cluster of terminals to a data link.

**2.** In SNA, a programmable device that controls the input/output operations of attached devices. Typically, it's an IBM 3174 or 3274 device.

### CM

cable modem. Device used to connect a PC to a local cable TV line and receive data at much higher rates than ordinary telephone modems or ISDN. A cable modem can be added to or integrated with a set-top box, thereby enabling Internet access via a television set. In most cases, cable modems are furnished as part of the cable access service and are not purchased directly and installed by the subscriber.

### CMI

**1.** coded mark inversion. ITU-T line coding technique specified for STS-3c transmissions. Also used in DS-1 systems. See also *DS-1* and *STS-3c*.

**2.** control mode idle.

### CMIP

Common Management Information Protocol. OSI network management protocol created and standardized by ISO for the monitoring and control of heterogeneous networks. See also *CMIS*.

### CMIS

Common Management Information Services. OSI network management service interface created and standardized by ISO for the monitoring and the control of heterogeneous networks. See also *CMIP*.

### CMNS

Connection-Mode Network Service. Extends local X.25 switching to a variety of media (Ethernet, FDDI, Token Ring). See also *CONP*.

### CMNM

See *CMNM* in the "Cisco Systems Terms and Acronyms" section.

### CMS

**1.** call management system. A reporting package used on ACDs and PBXs made by Lucent.

**2.** configuration management system. An application that controls and monitors the Sun Netra ft 1800 hardware

### CMT

connection management. FDDI process that handles the transition of the ring through its various states (off, active, connect, and so on), as defined by the ANSI X3T9.5 specification.

### CMTS

A cable modem termination system, such as a router or a bridge, typically located at the cable headend. Any DOCSIS-compliant headend cable router, such as the Cisco uBR7246.

### CNS/AD

Cisco Networking Services for Active Directory, which consists of a port of Active Directory to Solaris and HP/UX, and an NT and UNIX client implementation of the LDAP API and GSS-API.

### CO

central office.The local telephone company office to which all local loops in a given area connect and in which circuit switching of subscriber lines occurs.

### CO FRAD

central office frame relay access device.

### coaxial cable

Cable consisting of a hollow outer cylindrical conductor that surrounds a single inner wire conductor. Two types of coaxial cable currently are used in LANs: 50-ohm cable, which is used for digital signaling, and 75-ohm cable, which is used for analog signaling and high-speed digital signaling.

**codec**

coder-decoder.

**1.** Integrated circuit device that typically uses pulse code modulation to transform analog signals into a digital bit stream and digital signals back into analog signals.

**2.** In Voice over IP, Voice over Frame Relay, and Voice over ATM, a DSP software algorithm used to compress/decompress speech or audio signals.

**coded mark inversion**

See *CMI*.

**coder-decoder**

See *codec*.

**coding**

Electrical techniques used to convey binary signals.

**coding violation**

See *CV*.

**CO-IPX**

Connection Oriented IPX. Native ATM protocol based on IPX under development by Novell.

**collapsed backbone**

Nondistributed backbone in which all network segments are interconnected by way of an internetworking device. A collapsed backbone might be a virtual network segment existing in a device, such as a hub, a router, or a switch.

**collision**

In Ethernet, the result of two nodes transmitting simultaneously. The frames from each device impact and are damaged when they meet on the physical media. See also *collision domain*.

**collision detection**

See *CSI*.

**collision domain**

In Ethernet, the network area within which frames that have collided are propagated. Repeaters and hubs propagate collisions; LAN switches, bridges, and routers do not. See also *collision*.

**COM**
common equipment. Items used by more than one channel or equipment function.

**command-line interface**
See *CLI*.

**committed burst**
See *Bc*.

**committed information rate**
See *CIR*.

**common carrier**
Licensed, private utility company that supplies communication services to the public at regulated prices.

**common channel signaling**
See *CCS*.

**Common Gateway Interface**
See *CGI*.

**Common Language Equipment Identifier**
See *CLEI*.

**Common Link Access for Workstations**
See *CLAW*.

**Common Management Information Protocol**
See *CMIP*.

**Common Management Information Services**
See *CMIS*.

**common part convergence sublayer**
See *CPCS*.

**Common Programming Interface for Communications**
See *CPI-C*.

**common transport semantic**

See *CTS*.

**communication**

Transmission of information.

**communication controller**

In SNA, a subarea node (such as an IBM 3745 device) that contains an NCP.

**communication server**

Communications processor that connects asynchronous devices to a LAN or a WAN through network and terminal emulation software. Performs only asynchronous routing of IP and IPX. Compare with *access server*.

**communications line**

Physical link (such as wire or a telephone circuit) that connects one or more devices to one or more other devices.

**community**

In SNMP, a logical group of managed devices and NMSs in the same administrative domain.

**Community Antenna Television**

Now known as CATV. See *CATV*.

**community name**

See *community string*.

**community string**

Text string that acts as a password and is used to authenticate messages sent between a management station and a router containing an SNMP agent. The community string is sent in every packet between the manager and the agent. Also called a *community name*.

**companding**

Contraction derived from the opposite processes of compression and expansion. Part of the PCM process whereby analog signal values are rounded logically to discrete scale-step values on a nonlinear scale. The decimal step number then is coded in its binary equivalent prior to transmission. The process is reversed at the receiving terminal using the same nonlinear scale. Compare with *compression* and *expansion*. See also *a-law* and *mu-law*.

**complete sequence number PDU**

See *CSNP*.

**composite clock**

A bipolar timing signal containing 64 khz bit-clock and 8 khz byte-clock frequencies (also called composite timing).

**compound option**

A DOCSIS option that is composed of a number of suboptions. For example, options 4 and 24 are compound options.

**Compressed Serial Link Internet Protocol**

See *CSI*.

**compression**

The running of a data set through an algorithm that reduces the space required to store or the bandwidth required to transmit the data set. Compare with *companding* and *expansion*.

**Computer Science Network**

See *CSNET*.

**concentrator**

See *hub*.

**CONF**

configuration failure. Resource is OOS because its provisioning information is inconsistent.

**Conférence Européenne des Postes et des Télécommunications**

See *CEPT*.

**configuration direct VCC**

In ATM, a bi-directional point-to-point VCC set up by an LEC to an LES. One of three control connections defined by Phase 1 LANE. Compare with *control distribute VCC* and *control direct VCC*.

**configuration management**

One of five categories of network management defined by ISO for the management of OSI networks. Configuration management subsystems are responsible for detecting and determining the state of a network. See also *accounting management*, *fault management*, *performance management*, and *security management*.

**configuration register**

See *configuration register* in the "Cisco Systems Terms and Acronyms" section.

**configuration tool**

**1.** Service management tool with a GUI.

**2.** Element management service tool with a GUI.

**congestion**

Traffic in excess of network capacity.

**congestion avoidance**

Mechanism by which an ATM network controls the traffic entering the network to minimize delays. To use resources most efficiently, lower-priority traffic is discarded at the edge of the network if conditions indicate that it cannot be delivered.

**congestion collapse**

Condition in which the retransmission of frames in an ATM network results in little or no traffic successfully arriving at the destination. Congestion collapse frequently occurs in ATM networks composed of switches that do not have adequate and effective buffering mechanisms complimented by intelligent packet discard or ABR congestion feedback mechanisms.

**connection admission control**

See *CAC*.

**connection management**

See *CMT*.

**connectionless**

Term used to describe data transfer without the existence of a virtual circuit. Compare with *connection-oriented*. See also *virtual circuit*.

**Connectionless Broadband Data Service**

See *CBDS*.

**Connectionless Network Protocol**

See *CLNP*.

**Connectionless Network Service**

See *CLNS*.

**Connection-Mode Network Service**

See *CMNS*.

**connection-oriented**

Term used to describe data transfer that requires the establishment of a virtual circuit. See also *connectionless* and *virtual circuit*.

**Connection-Oriented Network Protocol**

See *CONP*.

**CONP**

Connection-Oriented Network Protocol. OSI protocol providing connection-oriented operation to upper-layer protocols. See also *CMNS*.

**CONS**

connection-oriented network service.

**console**

DTE through which commands are entered into a host.

**constant bit rate**

See *CBR*.

**constraint-based routing**

Procedures and protocols that determine a route across a backbone take into account resource requirements and resource availability instead of simply using the shortest path.

**Consultative Committee for International Telegraph and Telephone**

See *CCITT*.

**content-addressable memory**

See *associative memory*.

**contention**

Access method in which network devices compete for permission to access the physical medium. Compare with *circuit switching* and *token passing*.

**Context-based Access Control**

See *CBAC*.

### control direct VCC

In ATM, a bidirectional VCC set up by an LEC to an LES. One of three control connections defined by Phase 1 LANE. Compare with *configuration direct VCC* and *control direct VCC*.

### control distribute VCC

In ATM, a unidirectional VCC set up from an LES to an LEC. One of three control connections defined by Phase 1 LANE. Typically, the VCC is a point-to-multipoint connection. Compare with *configuration direct VCC* and *control direct VCC*.

### control messages

Signalling messages that provide the control of setup, maintenance, and teardown of L2TP sessions and tunnels.

### control point

See *CP*.

### control signal distribution box

See *CSD box*.

### convergence

Speed and ability of a group of internetworking devices running a specific routing protocol to agree on the topology of an internetwork after a change in that topology.

### convergence sublayer

See *CS*.

### conversation

In SNA, an LU 6.2 session between two transaction programs.

### cookie

A piece of information sent by a Web server to a Web browser that the browser is expected to save and send back to the Web server whenever the browser makes additional requests of the Web server.

### Cooperation for Open Systems Interconnection Networking in Europe

See *COSINE*.

### COOS

Commanded OOS. A resource is OOS because it was entered as a command. See also *OOS* in the "Cisco Systems Terms and Acronyms" section.

**Copper Distributed Data Interface**

See *CDDI*.

**COPS**

Common Open Policy Service. Quality of service (QoS) policy exchange protocol proposed as an IETF standard for communicating network QoS policy information.

**COR**

Functionality that provides the capability to deny certain call attempts based on the incoming and outgoing class of restrictions provisioned on the dial peers. This functionality provides flexibility in network design, allows users to block calls (for example, to 900 numbers), and applies different restrictions to call attempts from different originators. COR specifies which incoming dial peer can use which outgoing dial peer to make a call.

**CORBA**

Common Object Request Broker Architecture. OMG's answer to the need for interoperability among the rapidly proliferating number of hardware and software products available today. Simply stated, CORBA allows applications to communicate with one another no matter where they are located or who has designed them. See also *IIOP*.

**core gateway**

Primary routers in the Internet.

**core router**

In a packet-switched star topology, a router that is part of the backbone and that serves as the single pipe through which all traffic from peripheral networks must pass on its way to other peripheral networks.

**Corporation for Open Systems**

See *COS*.

**Corporation for Research and Educational Networking**

See *CREN*.

**CoS**

class of service. An indication of how an upper-layer protocol requires a lower-layer protocol to treat its messages. In SNA subarea routing, CoS definitions are used by subarea nodes to determine the optimal route to establish a given session. A CoS definition comprises a virtual route number and a transmission priority field. Also called *ToS*.

## COS

Corporation for Open Systems. Organization that promulgates the use of OSI protocols through conformance testing, certification, and related activities.

## COSINE

Cooperation for Open Systems Interconnection Networking in Europe. European project financed by the EC to build a communication network between scientific and industrial entities in Europe. The project ended in 1994.

## cost

An arbitrary value, typically based on hop count, media bandwidth, or other measures, that is assigned by a network administrator and used to compare various paths through an internetwork environment. Routing protocols use cost values to determine the most favorable path to a particular destination: the lower the cost, the better the path. Sometimes called *path cost*. See also *routing metric*.

## COT

Continuity Test. Requirement of the SS7 protocol specifications. It tests the bearer channels' status using either loopback or tone detection and generation. Used to test individual DS0 channels via either loopback or tone detection and generation.

## count to infinity

Problem that can occur in routing algorithms that are slow to converge, in which routers continuously increment the hop count to particular networks. Typically, some arbitrary hop-count limit is imposed to prevent this problem.

## CP

**1.** control point. In SNA networks, an element that identifies the APPN networking components of a PU 2.1 node, manages device resources, and provides services to other devices. In APPN, CPs can communicate with logically adjacent CPs by way of CP-to-CP sessions. See also *EN* and *NN*.

**2.** Telecommunications: control processor.

## CPC

calling party category.

### CPCS

**1.** common part convergence sublayer. One of the two sublayers of any AAL. The CPCS is service-independent and is divided further into the CS sublayer and the SAR sublayer. The CPCS is responsible for preparing data for transport across the ATM network, including the creation of the 48-byte payload cells that are passed to the ATM layer. See also *AAL*, *ATM layer*, *CS*, *SAR*, and *SSCS*.

**2.** Telecommunications: call processing control system.

### CPE

customer premises equipment. Terminating equipment, such as terminals, telephones, and modems, supplied by the telephone company, installed at customer sites, and connected to the telephone company network. Can also refer to any telephone equipment residing on the customer site.

### CPI-C

common programming interface for communications. Platform-independent API developed by IBM and used to provide portability in APPC applications. See also *APPC*.

### CPNIE

called party number information element.

### CPP

See *CPP* (Combinet Proprietary Protocol) in the "Cisco Systems Terms and Acronyms" section.

### cps

cells per second. Unit of measure used for ATM switch volumes.

### CQ

custom queuing.

### craft interface device

See *CID*.

### crankback

A mechanism used by ATM networks when a connection setup request is blocked because a node along a selected path cannot accept the request. In this case, the path is rolled back to an intermediate node, which attempts to discover another path to the final destination using GCAC. See also *GCAC*.

## CRC

cyclic redundancy check. Error-checking technique in which the frame recipient calculates a remainder by dividing frame contents by a prime binary divisor and compares the calculated remainder to a value stored in the frame by the sending node.

## CREN

Corporation for Research and Educational Networking. The result of a merger of BITNET and CSNET. CREN is devoted to providing Internet connectivity to its members, which include the alumni, the students, the faculty, and other affiliates of participating educational and research institutions, via BITNET III. See also *BITNET*, *BITNET III*, and *CSNET*.

## CRF

Concentrator Relay Function CRM cell rate margin. One of three link attributes exchanged using PTSPs to determine the available resources of an ATM network. CRM is a measure of the difference between the effective bandwidth allocation per traffic class as the allocation for sustainable cell rate.

## CRL

certificate revocation list. Data structure that enumerates digital certificates that have been invalidated by their issuer prior to when they were scheduled to expire.

## cross talk

Interfering energy transferred from one circuit to another.

## CRP

customer routing point. AT&T's terminology for third-party processors that accept routing requests from the CCSS7 network. Within the ICM, the Network Interface Controller (NIC) acts as a CRP.

## CRV

call reference value. Number carried in all Q.931 (I.451) messages that provides an identifier for each ISDN call.

## cryptographic algorithm

Algorithm that employs the science of cryptography, including encryption algorithms, cryptographic hash algorithms, digital signature algorithms, and key agreement algorithms.

## cryptographic key

Usually shortened to just "key." Input parameter that varies the transformation performed by a cryptographic algorithm.

## CS

convergence sublayer. One of the two sublayers of the AAL CPCS, which is responsible for padding and error checking. PDUs passed from the SSCS are appended with an 8-byte trailer (for error checking and other control information) and are padded, if necessary, so that the length of the resulting PDU is divisible by 48. These PDUs then are passed to the SAR sublayer of the CPCS for further processing. See also *AAL*, *CPCS*, *SAR*, and *SSCS*.

## CSA

Canadian Standards Association. Canadian agency that certifies products that conform to Canadian national safety standards.

## CS-ACELP

Conjugate Structure Algebraic Code Excited Linear Prediction. CELP voice compression algorithm providing 8 kbps, or 8:1 compression, standardized in ITU-T Recommendation G.729.

## CSD box

control signal distribution box. Bulkhead splitter box that distributes the clock and control system signals within a system.

## CSFS

customer support forwarding service. Facility within the ICM Logger that receives events from all parts of the ICM, filters them, and saves the appropriate messages. The Data Transfer Process (DTP) sends these messages to Cisco Customer Support.

## CSI

called subscriber identification. An identifier whose coding format contains the telephone number from a remote fax terminal.

## CSLIP

Compressed Serial Link Internet Protocol. Extension of SLIP that, when appropriate, allows just header information to be sent across a SLIP connection, reducing overhead and increasing packet throughput on SLIP lines. See also *SLIP*.

## CSM

**1.** call switching module.

**2.** See *CSM* in the "Cisco Systems Terms and Acronyms" section.

### CSMA/CD

carrier sense multiple access collision detect. Media-access mechanism wherein devices ready to transmit data first check the channel for a carrier. If no carrier is sensed for a specific period of time, a device can transmit. If two devices transmit at once, a collision occurs and is detected by all colliding devices. This collision subsequently delays retransmissions from those devices for some random length of time. Ethernet and IEEE 802.3 use CSMA/CD access.

### CSNET

Computer Science Network. Large internetwork consisting primarily of universities, research institutions, and commercial concerns. CSNET merged with BITNET to form CREN. See also *BITNET* and *CREN*.

### CSNP

complete sequence number PDU. PDU sent by the designated router in an OSPF network to maintain database synchronization.

### CSO

composite second order beat. Peak of the average level of distortion products due to second-order non-linearities in cable system equipment.

### CSU

channel service unit. Digital interface device that connects end-user equipment to the local digital telephone loop. Often referred to together with DSU, as *CSU/DSU*. See also *DSU*.

### CSV

comma separated values. Commonly used no-frills text file format used for import from and import to spreadsheets and SQL databases.

### CTB

composite triple beat. Peak of the average level of distortion components due to third-order non-linearities in cable system equipment.

### CTD

cell transfer delay. In ATM, the elapsed time between a cell exit event at the source UNI and the corresponding cell entry event at the destination UNI for a particular connection. The CTD between the two points is the sum of the total inter-ATM node transmission delay and the total ATM node processing delay.

## CTI

computer telephony integration. The name given to the merger of traditional telecommunications (PBX) equipment with computers and computer applications. The use of caller ID to retrieve customer information automatically from a database is an example of a CTI application.

## CTS

**1.** Clear To Send. Circuit in the EIA/TIA-232 specification that is activated when DCE is ready to accept data from a DTE.

**2.** common transport semantic. Cornerstone of the IBM strategy to reduce the number of protocols on networks. CTS provides a single API for developers of network software and enables applications to run over APPN, OSI, and TCP/IP.

## CU

coding unit. A type of access device. See also *access device*.

## Customer Information Control System

See *CICS*.

## customer premises equipment

See *CPE*.

## cut-through packet switching

A packet switching approach that streams data through a switch so the leading edge of a packet exits the switch at the output port before the packet finishes entering the input port. A device using cut-through packet switching reads, processes, and forwards packets as soon as the destination address is looked up and the outgoing port is determined. Also known as *on-the-fly packet switching*. Compare with *store and forward packet switching*.

## CWAF

See *CWAF* in the "Cisco Systems Terms and Acronyms" section.

## CV

coding violation. Occurrence of transmission bit error(s) in paths and lines, as detected by examining a redundancy check code embedded within the signal format. CV also refers to the performance parameter, which is the count of transmission error detections at line, path, and section levels.

**CxBus**

See *CxBus* (Cisco Extended Bus) in the "Cisco Systems Terms and Acronyms" section.

**Cyberspace**

Term coined by William Gibson in his fantasy novel Neuromancer to describe the "world" of computers and the society that gathers around them. Often used to refer to the Internet, the World Wide Web, or some combination thereof.

**cycles per second**

See *hertz*.

**cyclic redundancy check**

See *CRC*.

### D channel

**1.** data channel. Full-duplex, 16-kbps (BRI), or 64-kbps (PRI) ISDN channel. Compare with *B channel*, *E channel*, and *H channel*.

**2.** In SNA, a device that connects a processor and main storage with peripherals.

### D4 framing

See *SF*.

### DAC

**1.** dual-attached concentrator. FDDI or CDDI concentrator capable of attaching to both rings of a FDDI or CDDI network. It also can be dual-homed from the master ports of other FDDI or CDDI concentrators.

**2.** discretionary access control. An access control service that enforces a security policy based on the identity of system entities and their authorizations to access system resources.

### DACS

Digital Access and Crossconnect System. AT&T's term for a digital crossconnect system.

### DAP

Directory Access Protocol. Protocol used between a DUA and a DSA in an X.500 directory system. See also *LDAP*.

### dark fiber

Unused fiber optic cable. When it is carrying a signal, it is called lit fiber.

### DARPA

Defense Advanced Research Projects Agency. U.S. government agency that funded research for and experimentation with the Internet. Evolved from ARPA, and then, in 1994, back to ARPA. See also *ARPA*.

**DARPA Internet**

Obsolete term referring to the Internet. See *internet*.

**DAS**

**1.** dual attachment station. Device attached to both the primary and the secondary FDDI rings. Dual attachment provides redundancy for the FDDI ring: If the primary ring fails, the station can wrap the primary ring to the secondary ring, isolating the failure and retaining ring integrity. Also called a *Class A station*. Compare with *SAS*.

**2.** dynamically assigned socket. Socket that is assigned dynamically by DDP upon request by a client. In an AppleTalk network, the sockets numbered 128 to 254 are allocated as DASs.

**data bus connector**

See *DB connector*.

**data channel**

See *D channel*.

**data circuit-terminating equipment**

See *DCE*.

**data communications channel**

See *DCC*.

**data communications equipment**

See *DCE*.

**Data Country Code**

See *DCC*.

**data direct VCC**

In ATM, a bi-directional point-to-point VCC set up between two LECs. One of three data connections defined by Phase 1 LANE. Data direct VCCs do not offer any type of QOS guarantee, so they typically are used for UBR and ABR connections. Compare with *control distribute VCC* and *control direct VCC*.

**Data Encryption Standard**

See *DES*.

**Data Exchange Interface**

See *DXI*.

**data flow**

Grouping of traffic, identified by a combination of source address/mask, destination address/mask, IP next protocol field, and source and destination ports, where the protocol and port fields can have the values of any. In effect, all traffic matching a specific combination of these values is grouped logically together into a data flow. A data flow can represent a single TCP connection between two hosts, or it can represent all the traffic between two subnets. IPSec protection is applied to data flows.

**data flow control layer**

Layer 5 of the SNA architectural model. This layer determines and manages interactions between session partners, particularly data flow. Corresponds to the *session layer* of the OSI model. See also *data-link control layer*, *path control layer*, *physical control layer*, *presentation services layer*, *transaction services layer*, and *transmission control layer*.

**Data Movement Processor**

See *DMP* in the "Cisco Systems Terms and Acronyms" section.

**Data Network Identification Code**

See *DNIC*.

**data service unit**

See *DSU*.

**data set ready**

See *DSR*.

**data sink**

Network equipment that accepts data transmissions.

**data stream**

All data transmitted through a communications line in a single read or write operation.

**data terminal equipment**

See *DTE*.

**data terminal ready**

See *DTR*.

**database object**

A piece of information that is stored in a database.

**DATABASE2**

See *DB2*.

**datagram**

Logical grouping of information sent as a network layer unit over a transmission medium without prior establishment of a virtual circuit. IP datagrams are the primary information units in the Internet. The terms *cell*, *frame*, *message*, *packet*, and *segment* also are used to describe logical information groupings at various layers of the OSI reference model and in various technology circles.

**Datagram Delivery Protocol**

See *DDP*.

**Datakit**

AT&T proprietary packet switching system widely deployed by the RBOCs.

**data-link connection identifier**

See *DLCI*.

**data-link control layer**

Layer 2 in the SNA architectural model. Responsible for the transmission of data over a particular physical link. Corresponds roughly to the *data-link layer* of the OSI model. See also *data flow control layer*, *path control layer*, *physical control layer*, *presentation services layer*, *transaction services layer*, and *transmission control layer*.

**data-link layer**

Layer 2 of the OSI reference model. Provides reliable transit of data across a physical link. The data-link layer is concerned with physical addressing, network topology, line discipline, error notification, ordered delivery of frames, and flow control. The IEEE divided this layer into two sublayers: the MAC sublayer and the LLC sublayer. Sometimes simply called link layer. Roughly corresponds to the *data-link control layer* of the SNA model. See also *application layer*, *LLC*, *MAC*, *network layer*, *physical layer*, *PQ*, *session layer*, and *transport layer*.

**data-link switching**

See *DLSw*.

**data-link switching plus**

See *DLSw+* in the "Cisco Systems Terms and Acronyms" section.

**DAVIC**

Digital Audiovisual Council. DAVIC, now defunct, was established in 1994 with the aim of promoting the success of interactive digital audio-visual applications and services by promulgating specifications of open interfaces and protocols that maximize interoperability, not only across geographical boundaries but also across diverse applications, services, and industries.

**dB**

decibels. Unit for measuring relative power ratios in terms of gain or loss. Units are expressed in terms of the logarithm to base 10 of a ratio and typically are expressed in watts. dB is not an absolute value, rather it is the measure of power lost or gained between two devices. For example, a -3dB loss indicates a 50% loss in power; a +3dB reading is a doubling of power. The rule of thumb to remember is that 10 dB indicates an increase (or a loss) by a factor of 10; 20 dB indicates an increase (or a loss) of a factor of 100; 30 dB indicates an increase (or a loss) by a factor of 1000.

Because antennas and other RF devices/systems commonly have power gains or losses on the orders of magnitude or even orders of four orders of magnitude, dB is a more easily used expression.

**DB connector**

data bus connector. Type of connector used to connect serial and parallel cables to a data bus. DB connector names are in the format DB-*x*, where *x* represents the number of wires within the connector. Each line is connected to a pin on the connector, but in many cases, not all pins are assigned a function. DB connectors are defined by various EIA/TIA standards.

**DB2**

DATABASE2. IBM relational database management system.

**dBi**

dB referenced to an isotropic antenna, which theoretically is perfect in terms of symmetric patterns of radiation. Real world antennas do not perform with even nominal amounts of symmetry, but this effect generally is used to the advantage of the system designer.

**dBm**

decibels per milliwatt. 0 dBm is defined as 1 mw at 1 kHz of frequency at 600 ohms of impedance.

**dBmV**

Decibels with respect to one millivolt in a 75-ohm system. The unit of RF power used in CATV work in North America.

**dBW**

dB referencing 1 watt.

**DCA**

Defense Communications Agency. U.S. government organization responsible for DDN networks, such as MILNET. Now called DISA. See also *DISA*.

**DCC**

**1.** data communications channel. Channel that carries provisioning and maintenance data/information between network elements in the SONET overhead.

**2.** Data Country Code. One of two ATM address formats developed by the ATM Forum for use by private networks. Adapted from the subnetwork model of addressing in which the ATM layer is responsible for mapping network layer addresses to ATM addresses. Compare with *ICD*.

**DCE**

**1.** data communications equipment (EIA expansion).

**2.** data circuit-terminating equipment (ITU-T expansion). Devices and connections of a communications network that comprise the network end of the user-to-network interface. The DCE provides a physical connection to the network, forwards traffic, and provides a clocking signal used to synchronize data transmission between DCE and DTE devices. Modems and interface cards are examples of DCE. Compare with *DTE*.

**DCF**

dispersion compensating fiber. A fiber that has the opposite dispersion of the fiber being used in a transmission system. It is used to nullify the dispersion caused by that fiber.

**DCN**

data communications network. An out-of-band network that provides connectivity between network elements and their respective operations support systems (OSSs). Its primary function is enabling the surveillance and the status of a telco/PTT network but it also facilitates network operations and management, such as provisioning, billing, planning, and service assurance.

### DCOM

Distributed Component Object Model. Protocol that enables software components to communicate directly over a network. Developed by Microsoft and previously called Network OLE, DCOM is designed for use across multiple network transports, including such Internet protocols as HTTP. See also *IIOP*.

### DCS

Digital Crossconnect System. Network element providing automatic cross-connection of a digital signal or its constituent parts.

### DCT

discrete cosine transform.

### DDIC

DVB/DAVIC Interoperability Consortium. Founded in October 1998 by an international group of manufacturers, including Cisco, the Consortium promotes and supports product interoperability between member vendors employing the DVB-RCCL/DAVIC international standards. An independent verification process allows DDIC members to offer tested and documented interoperable products, thereby allowing cable network operators to choose reliable and highly intergratable, standards-based DVB solutions.

### DDM

distributed data management. Software in an IBM SNA environment that provides peer-to-peer communication and file sharing. One of three SNA transaction services. See also *DIA* and *SNADS*.

### DDN

Defense Data Network. U.S. military network composed of an unclassified network (MILNET) and various secret and top-secret networks. DDN is operated and maintained by *DISA*. See also *DISA* and *MILNET*.

### DDP

Datagram Delivery Protocol. AppleTalk network layer protocol that is responsible for the socket-to-socket delivery of datagrams over an AppleTalk internetwork.

### DDR

dial-on-demand routing. Technique whereby a router can automatically initiate and close a circuit-switched session as transmitting stations demand. The router spoofs keepalives so that end stations treat the session as active. DDR permits routing over ISDN or telephone lines using an external ISDN terminal adaptor or modem.

---

**DDSN**

Distributed Diagnostics and Service Network. Facilities that gather events within the ICM and automatically report any unexpected behavior to Cisco Customer Support. The DDSN includes the Customer Support Forwarding Service (CSFS) and the DDSN Transfer Process (DTP).

---

**DE**

discard eligible. If the network is congested, DE traffic can be dropped to ensure the delivery of higher priority traffic. See *tagged traffic*.

---

**de facto standard**

Standard that exists by nature of its widespread use. Compare with *de jure standard*. See also *standard*.

---

**de jure standard**

Standard that exists because of its approval by an official standards body. Compare with *de facto standard*. See also *standard*.

---

**DEA**

Data Encryption Algorithm. Symmetric block cipher, defined as part of the U.S. Government's Data Encryption Standard. DEA uses a 64-bit key, of which 56 bits are independently chosen and 8 are parity bits, and maps a 64-bit block into another 64-bit block.

---

**de-activation**

Process of disabling network access and privileges for a subscriber device, and reclaiming device attributes for other subscriber devices; de-activation occurs as part of subscriber account deprovisioning, or as part of activation of a replacement subscriber device; some device attributes (such as IP address leases) might not be reclaimable until the leases have expired.

---

**deadlock**

**1.** Unresolved contention for the use of a resource.

**2.** In APPN, when two elements of a process each wait for action by or a response from the other before they resume the process.

---

**decibels**

Abbreviated *dB*.

### DECnet

Group of communications products (including a protocol suite) developed and supported by Digital Equipment Corporation. DECnet/OSI (also called DECnet Phase V) is the most recent iteration and supports both OSI protocols and proprietary Digital protocols. Phase IV Prime supports inherent MAC addresses that allow DECnet nodes to coexist with systems running other protocols that have MAC address restrictions. See also *DNA*.

### DECnet routing

Proprietary routing scheme introduced by Digital Equipment Corporation in DECnet Phase III. In DECnet Phase V, DECnet completed its transition to OSI routing protocols (ES-IS and IS-IS).

### decrypt

Cryptographically restore ciphertext to the plaintext form it had before encryption.

### decryption

Reverse application of an encryption algorithm to encrypted data, thereby restoring that data to its original, unencrypted state. See also *encryption*.

### dedicated LAN

Network segment allocated to a single device. Used in LAN switched network topologies.

### dedicated line

Communications line that is indefinitely reserved for transmissions, rather than switched as transmission is required. See also *leased line*.

### default route

Routing table entry that is used to direct frames for which a next hop is not explicitly listed in the routing table.

### Defense Advanced Research Projects Agency

See *DARPA*.

### Defense Communications Agency

See *DCA*.

### Defense Data Network

See *DDN*.

### Defense Information Systems Agency

See *DISA*.

**Defense Intelligence Agency**

See *DIA*.

**DEK**

data encryption key. Used for the encryption of message text and for the computation of message integrity checks (signatures).

**delay**

The time between the initiation of a transaction by a sender and the first response received by the sender. Also, the time required to move a packet from source to destination over a given path.

**demand priority**

Media access method used in 100VG-AnyLAN that uses a hub that can handle multiple transmission requests and can process traffic according to priority, making it useful for servicing time-sensitive traffic, such as multimedia and video. Demand priority eliminates the overhead of packet collisions, collision recovery, and broadcast traffic typical in Ethernet networks. See also *100VG-AnyLAN*.

**demarc**

Demarcation point between carrier equipment and CPE.

**demodulation**

Process of returning a modulated signal to its original form. Modems perform demodulation by taking an analog signal and returning it to its original (digital) form. See also *modulation*.

**demodulator**

Device for assembling signals after they have been received by an antenna. A demodulator is typically the first major device downstream from an antenna receiving system and exists on the block diagram prior to various Cisco devices. The corresponding device on the transmission side of a system is a modulator.

**demultiplexer**

See *demux*.

**demultiplexing**

Separating of multiple input streams that were multiplexed into a common physical signal back into multiple output streams. See also *multiplexing*.

**demux**

demultiplexer. Device used to separate two or more signals that previously were combined by a compatible multiplexer and are transmitted over a single channel.

**dense mode PIM**

See *PIM dense mode*.

**dense wavelength division multiplexing**

See *DWDM*.

**Department of Defense**

See *DoD*.

**Dependent LU**

See *DLU*.

**Dependent LU Requester**

See *DLUR*.

**Dependent LU Server**

See *DLUS*.

**deprovisioning**

Elimination of an existing subscriber account; deprovisioning of a subscriber account includes subscriber account deregistration and device de-activation.

**DER**

Distinguished Encoding Rules. Subset of the Basic Encoding Rules, which gives exactly one way to represent any ASN.1 value as an octet string [X690].

**DES**

**1.** Data Encryption Standard. Standard cryptographic algorithm developed by the U.S. National Bureau of Standards.

**2.** destination end station.

**designated bridge**

Bridge that incurs the lowest path cost when forwarding a frame from a segment to the root bridge.

**designated router**

OSPF router that generates LSAs for a multiaccess network and has other special responsibilities in running OSPF. Each multiaccess OSPF network that has at least two attached routers has a designated router that is elected by the OSPF Hello protocol. The designated router enables a reduction in the number of adjacencies required on a multiaccess network, which in turn reduces the amount of routing protocol traffic and the size of the topological database.

**destination address**

Address of a network device that is receiving data. See also *source address*.

**destination MAC**

See *DMAC*.

**destination node**

Termination of an end-to-end channel or virtual wavelength path (VWP).

**destination service access point**

See *DSAP*.

**deterministic load distribution**

Technique for distributing traffic between two bridges across a circuit group. Guarantees packet ordering between source-destination pairs and always forwards traffic for a source-destination pair on the same segment in a circuit group for a given circuit-group configuration.

**Deutsche Industrie Norm**

See *DIN*.

**Deutsche Industrie Norm connector**

See *DIN connector*.

**device**

See *node*.

### D-H

Diffie-Hellman. The Diffie-Hellman algorithm, introduced by Whitfield Diffie and Martin Hellman in 1976, was the first system to utilize "public-key" or "asymmetric" cryptographic keys. Today Diffie-Hellman is part of the IPSec standard. A protocol known as OAKLEY uses Diffie-Hellman, as described in RFC 2412. OAKLEY is used by the Internet Key Exchange (IKE) protocol (see *RFC 2401*), which is part of the overall framework called Internet Security Association and Key Management Protocol (ISAKMP; see *RFC 2408*).

### DHCP

Dynamic Host Configuration Protocol. Provides a mechanism for allocating IP addresses dynamically so that addresses can be reused when hosts no longer need them.

### DIA

Document Interchange Architecture. Defines the protocols and the data formats needed for the transparent interchange of documents in an SNA network. One of three SNA transaction services. See also *DDM* and *SNADS*.

### dial backup

Feature that provides protection against WAN downtime by allowing the network administrator to configure a backup serial line through a circuit-switched connection.

### dial peer

Addressable call endpoint. In Voice over IP, there are two kinds of dial peers: POTS and VoIP.

### dial-on-demand routing

See *DDR*.

### dial-up line

Communications circuit that is established by a switched-circuit connection using the telephone company network.

### DID

direct inward dial. Allows a user outside a company to dial an internal extension number without needing to pass through an operator or an attendant. The dialed digits are passed to the PBX, which then completes the call.

### DID/DNIS

Direct Inward Dialing/Dialed Number Identification Service. When a call arrives at an ACD or PBX, the carrier sends a digital code on the trunk line. The switch can read this code to determine how it should dispatch the call. Typically, this value is the specific number dialed by the user. By mapping each possible code with an internal extension, the switch can provide direct inward dialing (DID).

The ICM uses the DID/DNIS value to specify the service, the skill group, or the specific agent to whom the switch should route the call. The switch reads the value from the trunk line when the call arrives and dispatches the call appropriately.

### differential encoding

Digital encoding technique whereby a binary value is denoted by a signal change rather than a particular signal level.

### differential Manchester encoding

Digital coding scheme where a mid–bit-time transition is used for clocking, and a transition at the beginning of each bit time denotes a zero. This coding scheme is used by IEEE 802.5 and Token Ring networks.

### differentiated service

A paradigm for providing QoS on the Internet by employing a small, well-defined set of building blocks from which a variety of services can be built.

### Diffie-Hellman key exchange

A public key cryptography protocol that allows two parties to establish a shared secret over insecure communications channels. Diffie-Hellman is used within Internet Key Exchange (IKE) to establish session keys. Diffie-Hellman is a component of Oakley key exchange. Cisco IOS software supports 768-bit and 1024-bit Diffie-Hellman groups.

### Diffusing Update Algorithm

See *DUAL* in the "Cisco Systems Terms and Acronyms" section.

### digital certificate

Certificate document in the form of a digital data object (a data object used by a computer) to which is appended a computed digital signature value that depends on the data object.

**digital envelope**

Digital envelope for a recipient is a combination of (a) encrypted content data (of any kind) and (b) the content encryption key in an encrypted form that has been prepared for the use of the recipient.

**digital information signal**

T.30 Digital Information Signal that provides the capabilities of a receiving fax machine.

**Digital Network Architecture**

See *DNA*.

**digital signal level 0**

See *DS-0*.

**digital signal level 1**

See *DS-1*.

**digital signal level 3**

See *DS-3*.

**digital signature**

Value computed with a cryptographic algorithm and appended to a data object in such a way that any recipient of the data can use the signature to verify the data's origin and integrity.

**Dijkstra's algorithm**

See *SPF*.

**DIN**

Deutsche Industrie Norm. German national standards organization.

**DIN connector**

Deutsche Industrie Norm connector. Multipin connector used in some Macintosh and IBM PC-compatible computers, and on some network processor panels.

**direct memory access**

See *DMA*.

### directed search

Search request sent to a specific node known to contain a resource. A directed search is used to determine the continued existence of the resource and to obtain routing information specific to the node. See also *broadcast search*.

### directed tree

Logical construct used to define data streams or flows. The origin of a data stream is the root. Data streams are unidirectional branches directed away from the root and toward targets, and targets are the leaves of the directed tree.

### direct-inward-dial

Calls in which the gateway uses the number initially dialed (DNIS) to make the call, as opposed to a prompt to dial additional digits.

### directory enabled networking

An LDAP-based information model for networked devices.

### directory services

Services that help network devices locate service providers.

### DISA

Defense Information Systems Agency. Formerly DCA. U.S. military organization responsible for implementing and operating military information systems, including the DDN. See also *DDN* and *dBm*.

### discard eligible

See *DE*.

### discovery architecture

APPN software that enables a machine configured as an APPN EN to find primary and backup NNs automatically when the machine is brought onto an APPN network.

### discovery mode

Method by which an AppleTalk interface acquires information about an attached network from an operational node, and then uses this information to configure itself. Also called dynamic configuration.

### Disengage Request

Message with the Billing Information Token (which contains the duration of the call) sent by the gateway to the gatekeeper when a call ends.

### Distance Vector Multicast Routing Protocol

See *DXI*.

### distance vector routing algorithm

Class of routing algorithms that iterate on the number of hops in a route to find a shortest-path spanning tree. Distance vector routing algorithms call for each router to send its entire routing table in each update, but only to its neighbors. Distance vector routing algorithms can be prone to routing loops, but are computationally simpler than link state routing algorithms. Also called Bellman-Ford routing algorithm. See also *link-state routing algorithm* and *SPF*.

### distortion delay

Problem with a communication signal resulting from nonuniform transmission speeds of the components of a signal through a transmission medium. Also called group delay.

### distributed CEF

One of two modes of CEF operation that enables line cards to perform the express forwarding between port adapters.

### distributed computing (processing)

See *client/server computing*.

### Distributed Data Management

See *DDM*.

### Distributed Queue Dual Bus

See *DQDB*.

### Distributed Relational Database Architecture

See *DRDA*.

### distribution point

X.500 Directory entry or other information source that is named in a v3 X.509 public-key certificate extension as a location from which to obtain a CRL that might list the certificate.

### DIT

Directory Information Tree. Global tree of entries corresponding to information objects in the OSI X.500 Directory.

### DLCI

data-link connection identifier. Value that specifies a PVC or an SVC in a Frame Relay network. In the basic Frame Relay specification, DLCIs are locally significant (connected devices might use different values to specify the same connection). In the LMI extended specification, DLCIs are globally significant (DLCIs specify individual end devices). See also *LMDS*.

### DLL

dynamic link library.

### DLSw

data-link switching. Interoperability standard, described in RFC 1434, that provides a method for forwarding SNA and NetBIOS traffic over TCP/IP networks using data-link layer switching and encapsulation. DLSw uses SSP instead of SRB, eliminating the major limitations of SRB, including hop-count limits, broadcast and unnecessary traffic, timeouts, lack of flow control, and lack of prioritization schemes. See also *SRB* and *SSP* (Switch-to-Switch Protocol).

### DLSw+

See *DLSw+* (*data-link switching plus*) in the "Cisco Systems Terms and Acronyms" section.

### DLU

Dependent LU. LU that depends on the SSCP to provide services for establishing sessions with other LUs. See also *LU* and *SSCP*.

### DLUR

Dependent LU Requester. Client half of the Dependent LU Requestor/Server enhancement to APPN. The DLUR component resides in APPN ENs and NNs that support adjacent DLUs by securing services from the DLUS. See also *APPN*, *DLU*, and *DLUS*.

### DLUR node

In APPN networks, an EN or an NN that implements the DLUR component. See also *DLUR*.

### DLUS

Dependent LU Server. Server half of the Dependent LU Requestor/Server enhancement to APPN. The DLUS component provides SSCP services to DLUR nodes over an APPN network. See also *APPN*, *DLU*, and *DLUR*.

**DLUS node**

In APPN networks, an NN that implements the DLUS component. See also *DLUS*.

**DMA**

direct memory access. Transfer of data from a peripheral device, such as a hard disk drive, into memory without that data passing through the microprocessor. DMA transfers data into memory at high speeds with no processor overhead.

**DMAC**

destination MAC. The MAC address specified in the Destination Address field of a packet. Compare with *SMAC*. See also *MAC address*.

**DMDP**

DNSIX Message Deliver Protocol. DMDP provides a basic message-delivery mechanism for all DNSIX elements.

**DMM**

**1.** dual MICA module. Contains 12 discrete modems.

**2.** DuoDecimal Modem Module. MICA technologies hardware packaging with 12 modems on a daughter card unit.

**DMP**

**1.** device management protocol. The session-layer communications protocol used within the ICM. Different application-level protocols might be running beneath DMP.

**2.** See *DMP (Data movement processor)* in the "Cisco Systems Terms and Acronyms" section.

**DN**

**1.** dialed number. Number that a caller dialed to initiate a call; for example, 800-555-1212.

**2.** Distinguished Name. Global, authoritative name of an entry in the OSI Directory (X.500).

**DNA**

**1.** DoNotAge. Most significant bit of the LS Age field. LSAs having the DoNotAge bit set are not aged as they are in the link-state database of the OSPF router, which means that these LSAs need not be refreshed every 30 minutes.

**2.** Digital Network Architecture. Network architecture developed by Digital Equipment Corporation. The products that embody DNA (including communications protocols) are referred to collectively as DECnet. See also *DECnet*.

## DNIC

Data Network Identification Code. Part of an X.121 address. DNICs are divided into two parts: the first specifying the country in which the addressed PSN is located and the second specifying the PSN itself. See also *X.121*.

## DNIS

dialed number identification service (the called number). Feature of trunk lines where the called number is identified; this called number information is used to route the call to the appropriate service. DNIS is a service used with toll-free dedicated services whereby calls placed to specific toll-free numbers are routed to the appropriate area within a company to be answered.

## DNS

Domain Name System. System used on the Internet for translating names of network nodes into addresses. See also *authority zone*.

## DNS zone

domain name server zone. Point of delegation in the DNS tree. It contains all names from a certain point downward except those for which other zones are authoritative. Authoritative name servers can be asked by other DNSs for name-to-address translation. Many name servers can exist within an organization, but only those known by the root name servers can be queried by the clients across the Internet. The other name servers answer only internal queries.

## DNSIX

Department of Defense Intelligence Information System Network Security for Information Exchange. Collection of security requirements for networking defined by the U.S. Defense Intelligence Agency.

## DOCSIS

Data-over-Cable Service Interface Specifications. Defines technical specifications for equipment at both subscriber locations and cable operators' headends. Adoption of DOCSIS will accelerate the deployment of data-over-cable services and will ensure interoperability of equipment throughout system operators' infrastructures.

## DOCSIS CM

DOCSIS cable modem. DOCSIS CMs obtain boot configuration using DHCP, Time, and TFTP client implementations.

**D**

### DOCSIS CMTS

DOCSIS cable modem termination system. The Cisco 7246 or 7223 router is a leading router implementation of a DOCSIS CMTS.

### DOCSIS configuration file

File containing configuration parameters for a DOCSIS cable modem. The cable modem obtains this file at boot time using the TFTP protocol.

### Document Interchange Architecture

See *DIA*.

### DoD

Department of Defense. U.S. government organization that is responsible for national defense. The DoD frequently has funded communication protocol development.

### DoD Intelligence Information System Network Security for Information

See *DNSIX*.

### DOI

domain of interpretation. In IPSec, an ISAKMP/IKE DOI defines payload formats, exchange types, and conventions for naming security-relevant information such as security policies or cryptographic algorithms and modes.

### domain

**1.** On the Internet, a portion of the naming hierarchy tree that refers to general groupings of networks based on organization type or geography.

**2.** In SNA, an SSCP and the resources it controls.

**3.** In IS-IS, a logical set of networks.

**4.** In security, an environment or context that is defined by a security policy, a security model, or a security architecture to include a set of system resources and the set of system entities that have the right to access the resources.

### Domain

Networking system developed by Apollo Computer (now part of Hewlett-Packard) for use in its engineering workstations.

### domain name

The style of identifier—a sequence of case-insensitive ASCII labels separated by dots ("bbn.com.")—defined for subtrees in the Internet Domain Name System [R1034] and used in other Internet identifiers, such as host names, mailbox names, and URLs.

**Domain Name System**

See *DNS*.

**domain specific part**

See *DSP*.

**dot address**

Refers to the common notation for IP addresses in the form *n.n.n.n* where each number *n* represents, in decimal, 1 byte of the 4-byte IP address. Also called dotted notation and four-part dotted notation.

**dotted decimal notation**

Syntactic representation for a 32-bit integer that consists of four 8-bit numbers written in base 10 with periods (dots) separating them. Used to represent IP addresses on the Internet, as in 192.67.67.20. Also called dotted quad notation.

**dotted notation**

See *dot address*.

**downlink station**

See *ground station*.

**downstream**

Frequency multiplexed band in a CATV channel that distributes signals from a headend facility to subscribers.

**downstream physical unit**

See *DSPU*.

**DPM**

call defect per million. Lost stable (connected call) or non-stable (call being setup) call due to any hardware or software failure, procedural error, or other causes. Note that a Call Defect does not include misrouted calls or loss of call features.

**DQDB**

Distributed Queue Dual Bus. Data-link layer communication protocol, specified in the IEEE 802.6 standard, designed for use in MANs. DQDB, which permits multiple systems to interconnect using two unidirectional logical buses, is an open standard that is designed for compatibility with carrier transmission standards, and is aligned with emerging standards for BISDN. SIP is based on DQDB. See also *MAN*.

**D**

## DRAM

dynamic random-access memory. RAM that stores information in capacitors that must be refreshed periodically. Delays can occur because DRAMs are inaccessible to the processor when refreshing their contents. However, DRAMs are less complex and have greater capacity than SRAMs. See also *SRAM*.

## DRDA

Distributed Relational Database Architecture. IBM proprietary architecture.

## drop

Point on a multipoint channel where a connection to a networked device is made.

## drop and insert

Allows DSO channels from one T1 or E1 facility to be cross-connected digitally to DS0 channels on another T1 or E1. By using this method, channel traffic is sent between a PBX and a CO PSTN switch or other telephony device, so that some PBX channels are directed for long-distance service through the PSTN while the router compresses others for interoffice VoIP calls. In addition, Drop and Insert can cross-connect a telephony switch (from the CO or PSTN) to a channel bank for external analog connectivity. Also called *TDM Cross-Connect*.

## drop cable

Cable that connects a network device (such as a computer) to a physical medium. A type of AUI. See also *AU*.

## DRP

See *DRP* (Director Response Protocol) in the "Cisco Systems Terms and Acronyms" section.

## DS0

digital service zero (0). Single timeslot on a DS1 (also known as T1) digital interface—that is, a 64-kbps, synchronous, full-duplex data channel, typically used for a single voice connection on a PBX. See also *DS1* and *PBX*.

## DS-0

digital signal level 0. Framing specification used in transmitting digital signals over a single channel at 64-kbps on a T1 facility. Compare with *DS-1* and *DS-3*.

### DS1

digital service 1. Interface with a 1.544-Mbps data rate that often carries voice interface connections on a PBX. Each DS1 (also known as T1) has 24 DS0 channels framed together so that each DS0 timeslot can be assigned to a different type of trunk group, if desired.

### DS-1

digital signal level 1. Framing specification used in transmitting digital signals at 1.544-Mbps on a T1 facility (in the United States) or at 2.108-Mbps on an E1 facility (in Europe). Compare with *DS-0* and *DS-3*. See also *E1* and *T1*.

### DS-1 domestic trunk interface

See *DS-1/DTI*.

### DS-1/DTI

DS-1 domestic trunk interface. Interface circuit used for DS-1 applications with 24 trunks.

### DS-3

digital signal level 3. Framing specification used for transmitting digital signals at 44.736 Mbps on a T3 facility. Compare with *DS-0* and *DS-1*. See also *E3* and *T.120*.

### DSA

Directory System Agent. Software that provides the X.500 Directory Service for a portion of the directory information base. Generally, each DSA is responsible for the directory information for a single organization or organizational unit.

### DSAP

destination service access point. SAP of the network node designated in the Destination field of a packet. Compare with *SSAP*. See also *SAP (service access point)*.

### DSF

dispersion-shifted fiber. A type of single-mode fiber designed to have zero dispersion near 1550 nm.

### DSL

digital subscriber line. Public network technology that delivers high bandwidth over conventional copper wiring at limited distances. There are four types of DSL: ADSL, HDSL, SDSL, and VDSL. All are provisioned via modem pairs, with one modem located at a central office and the other at the customer site. Because most DSL technologies do not use the whole bandwidth of the twisted pair, there is room remaining for a voice channel. See also *ADSL*, *HDSL*, and *VDSL*.

**D**

## DSLAM

digital subscriber line access multiplexer. A device that connects many digital subscriber lines to a network by multiplexing the DSL traffic onto one or more network trunk lines.

## DSn

digital signal level n. A classification of digital circuits. The DS technically refers to the rate and the format of the signal, whereas the T designation refers to the equipment providing the signals. In practice, DS and T are used synonymously; for example, DS1 and T1, DS3 and T3.

## DSN

delivery status notification. Message returned to the originator indicating the delivery status of an e-mail message. A sender can request three types of delivery status notifications: delay, success, and failure. RFC 1891, RFC 1892, RFC 1893, and RFC 1894 describe specifications for DSN.

## DSP

**1.** domain specific part. Part of an NSAP-format ATM address that contains an area identifier, a station identifier, and a selector byte. See also *NSAP*.

**2.** digital signal processor. A DSP segments the voice signal into frames and stores them in voice packets.

## DSPU

downstream physical unit. In SNA, a PU that is located downstream from the host. See also *DSPU concentration* in the "Cisco Systems Terms and Acronyms" section.

## DSPU concentration

See *DSPU concentration* in the "Cisco Systems Terms and Acronyms" section.

## DSPWare

Firmware running on the DSP coprocessor.

## DSR

data set ready. EIA/TIA-232 interface circuit that is activated when DCE is powered up and ready for use.

## DSU

data service unit. Device used in digital transmission that adapts the physical interface on a DTE device to a transmission facility, such as T1 or E1. The DSU also is responsible for such functions as signal timing. Often referred to together with CSU, as *CSU/DSU*.

## DSX-1

Crossconnection point for DS-1 signals.

## DTE

data terminal equipment. Device at the user end of a user-network interface that serves as a data source, destination, or both. DTE connects to a data network through a DCE device (for example, a modem) and typically uses clocking signals generated by the DCE. DTE includes such devices as computers, protocol translators, and multiplexers. Compare with *DCE*.

## DTL

designated transit list. List of nodes and optional link IDs that completely specify a path across a single PNNI peer group.

## DTMF

dual tone multifrequency. Tones generated when a button is pressed on a telephone, primarily used in the U.S. and Canada.

## DTMF relay

dual-tone multifrequency relay. Mechanism whereby a local Voice over IP gateway listens for DTMF digits (during a call), and then sends them uncompressed as either RTP or H.245 packets to the remote Voice over IP gateway, which regenerates DTMF digits and prevents digit loss due to compression.

## DTP

DDSN Transfer Protocol. Process on the ICM Logger that connects to Cisco Customer Support and delivers any messages saved by the Customer Support Forwarding Service (CSFS). The DTP is part of the Distributed Diagnostics and Service Network (DDSN), which ensures that Cisco Customer Support is informed promptly of any unexpected behavior within the ICM.

## DTR

data terminal ready. EIA/TIA-232 circuit that is activated to let the DCE know when the DTE is ready to send and receive data.

## DUA

Directory User Agent. Software that accesses the X.500 Directory Service on behalf of the directory user. The directory user can be a person or another software element.

## DUAL

See *DUAL (Diffusing update algorithm)* in the "Cisco Systems Terms and Acronyms" section.

**D**

**dual attachment station**

See *DAS*.

**dual counter-rotating rings**

Network topology in which two signal paths, whose directions are opposite each other, exist in a token-passing network. FDDI and CDDI are based on this concept.

**dual homing**

Network topology in which a device is connected to the network by way of two independent access points (points of attachment). One access point is the primary connection, and the other is a standby connection that is activated in the event of a failure of the primary connection.

**Dual IS-IS**

See *Integrated IS-IS*.

**dual tone multifrequency**

See *DTMF*.

**dual-attached concentrator**

See *DAC*.

**dual-homed station**

Device attached to multiple FDDI rings to provide redundancy.

**DVB**

Digital Video Broadcasting. Consortium of around 300 companies in the fields of broadcasting, manufacturing, network operation, and regulatory matters working to establish common international standards for the move from analog to digital broadcasting. The DVB Project Office and its 3.5 staff are based in Geneva, Switzerland.

**DVB-C**

DVB digital cable delivery system. Digital cable system that is compatible with DVB-S.

**DVMRP**

Distance Vector Multicast Routing Protocol. Internetwork gateway protocol, largely based on RIP, that implements a typical dense mode IP multicast scheme. DVMRP uses IGMP to exchange routing datagrams with its neighbors. See also *IGMP*.

**DVVI**

data, voice, video integration.

## DWDM

dense wavelength division multiplexing. Optical transmission of multiple signals over closely spaced wavelengths in the 1550 nm region. (Wavelength spacings are usually 100 GHz or 200 GHz, which corresponds to 0.8 nm or 1.6 nm.)

## DXI

Data Exchange Interface. ATM Forum specification, described in RFC 1483, that defines how a network device, such as a bridge, a router, or a hub, effectively can act as an FEP to an ATM network by interfacing with a special DSU that performs packet segmentation and reassembly.

### dynamic adaptive routing

Automatic rerouting of traffic based on a sensing and analysis of current actual network conditions, not including cases of routing decisions taken on predefined information.

### dynamic address resolution

Use of an address resolution protocol to determine and store address information on demand.

### Dynamic Buffer Management

Frame Relay and ATM service modules are equipped with large buffers and the patented Dynamic Buffer Management scheme for allocating and scaling traffic entering or leaving a node on a per-VC basis. The WAN switch dynamically assigns buffers to individual virtual circuits based upon the amount of traffic present and service-level agreements. This deep pool of available buffers readily accommodates large bursts of traffic into the node.

### dynamic configuration

See *discovery mode*.

### Dynamic IISP

Dynamic Interim-Interswitch Signaling Protocol. Basic call routing protocol that automatically reroutes ATM connections in the event of link failures. Dynamic IISP is an interim solution until PNNI Phase 1 is completed. Contrast with *IISP*.

### dynamic random-access memory

See *DRAM*.

### dynamic routing

Routing that adjusts automatically to network topology or traffic changes. Also called adaptive routing.

**dynamic switched call**

Telephone call dynamically established across a packet data network based on a dialed telephone number. In the case of VoFR, a Cisco proprietary session protocol similar to Q.931 is used to achieve call switching and negotiation between calling endpoints. The proprietary session protocol runs over FRF.11-compliant subchannels.

### E channel

echo channel. 64-kbps ISDN circuit-switching control channel. The E channel was defined in the 1984 ITU-T ISDN specification but was dropped in the 1988 specification. Compare with *B channel*, *D channel*, and *H channel*.

### E&M

recEive and transMit (or ear and mouth).

**1.** Trunking arrangement generally used for two-way switch-to-switch or switch-to-network connections. Cisco's analog E&M interface is an RJ-48 connector that allows connections to PBX trunk lines (tie lines). E&M also is available on E1 and T1 digital interfaces.

**2.** A type of signaling traditionally used in the telecommunications industry. Indicates the use of a handset that corresponds to the ear (receiving) and mouth (transmitting) component of a telephone.

### E&M signaling

Method of signaling on a DS0 timeslot such that the signaling bits are used to indicate call states, such as on-hook, off-hook, alerting, and dial pulsing. See also *E&M*.

### E.164

**1.** ITU-T recommendation for international telecommunication numbering, especially in ISDN, BISDN, and SMDS. An evolution of standard telephone numbers.

**2.** Name of the field in an ATM address that contains numbers in E.164 format.

### E1

Wide-area digital transmission scheme used predominantly in Europe that carries data at a rate of 2.048 Mbps. E1 lines can be leased for private use from common carriers. Compare with *T1*. See also *DS-1*.

### E2A

Legacy protocols for providing OAM&P functions between a network element and an operations support system. See also *OAM&P*.

### E3

Wide-area digital transmission scheme used predominantly in Europe that carries data at a rate of 34.368 Mbps. E3 lines can be leased for private use from common carriers. Compare with *T.120*. See also *DS-3*.

### EAP

Extensible Authentication Protocol. Framework that supports multiple, optional authentication mechanisms for PPP, including cleartext passwords, challenge-response, and arbitrary dialog sequences.

### early packet discard

See *EPD*.

### early token release

Technique used in Token Ring networks that allows a station to release a new token onto the ring immediately after transmitting instead of waiting for the first frame to return. This feature can increase the total bandwidth on the ring. See also *Token Ring*.

### EARN

European Academic Research Network. European network connecting universities and research institutes. EARN merged with RARE to form TERENA. See also *RARE* and *TERENA*.

### EAS

expert agent selection. Mode for the Lucent Definity ECS ACD. In this mode, agents are added automatically to pre-assigned skill groups at login. Calls can be routed either to the agent's physical extension or to the agent's login ID. In non-EAS mode, agents must add themselves manually to hunt groups and calls can be routed only to physical extensions.

### EBCDIC

extended binary coded decimal interchange code. Any of a number of coded character sets developed by IBM consisting of 8-bit coded characters. Older IBM systems and telex machines use this character code. Compare with *ASCII*.

### EBONE

European Backbone. Pan-European network backbone service.

### EBU

European Broadcasting Union. Founded in 1950 and headquartered in Geneva, the European Broadcasting Union (EBU) is an association of national broadcasters that negotiates broadcasting rights for major sports events, operates the Eurovision and Euroradio networks, organizes program exchanges, stimulates and coordinates co-productions, and provides operational, commercial, technical, legal, and strategic services.

### EC

European Community.

### ECDSA

Elliptic Curve Digital Signature Algorithm. Standard [A9062] that is the elliptic curve cryptography analog of the Digital Signature Algorithm.

### echo

Telephony—Audible and unwanted leak-through of one's own voice into one's own receive (return) path. Hence signal from the transmission path is returning to one's ear through the receive path.

### echo cancellation

Method for removing unwanted signals from the main transmitted voice telephony signal.

### echo channel

See *E channel*.

### echoplex

Mode in which keyboard characters are echoed on a terminal screen upon return of a signal from the other end of the line indicating that the characters were received correctly.

### ECM

Error Correction Mode. An option defined in T.30 and available in many fax machines that allows a fax page to be broken into HDLC-like frames that allow transmission errors to be detected.

### ECM disable

Feature that disables ECM capability advertised in a fax DIS signal.

### ECMA

European Computer Manufacturers Association. Group of European computer vendors who have done substantial OSI standardization work.

### EDFA

erbium-doped fiber amplifier. Optical fibers doped with the rare earth element erbium, which can amplify light in the 1550 nm region when pumped by an external light source.

### edge device

**1.** Physical device that is capable of forwarding packets between legacy interfaces (such as Ethernet and Token Ring) and ATM interfaces based on data-link and network layer information. An edge device does not participate in the running of any network layer routing protocol but it obtains forwarding descriptions using the route distribution protocol.

**2.** Any device that is not an ATM switch that can connect to an ATM switch.

### Edge LSR

Edge Label Switch Router. The role of an Edge LSR is to turn unlabeled packets into labeled packets, and vice versa. Formerly known as Tag Edge Router (TER).

### EDI

electronic data interchange. Electronic communication of operational data, such as orders and invoices, between organizations.

### EDIFACT

Electronic Data Interchange for Administration, Commerce, and Transport. Data exchange standard administered by the United Nations to be a multi-industry EDI standard.

### EECM

end-to-end call manager.

### EEPROM

electrically erasable programmable read-only memory. EPROM that can be erased using electrical signals applied to specific pins. See also *EPROM*.

### EFCI

Explicit Forward Congestion Indication. In ATM, one of the congestion feedback modes allowed by ABR service. A network element in an impending congestion state or in a congested state can set the EFCI. The destination end-system can implement a protocol that adaptively lowers the cell rate of the connection based on the value of the EFCI. See also *ABR*.

### EFF

Electronic Frontier Foundation. Foundation established to address social and legal issues arising from the impact on society of the increasingly pervasive use of computers as the means of communication and information distribution.

### EGP

exterior gateway protocol. Internet protocol for exchanging routing information between autonomous systems. Documented in RFC 904. Not to be confused with the general term *exterior gateway protocol*. EGP is an obsolete protocol that was replaced by BGP. See also *BGP*.

### egress

Traffic leaving the network.

### EHSA

enhanced high system availability. Processor redundancy scheme that reduces switchover time by requiring that the redundant processor be running in hot standby mode.

### EIA

Electronic Industries Alliance. Group that specifies electrical transmission standards. The EIA and the TIA have developed numerous well-known communications standards, including EIA/TIA-232 and EIA/TIA-449. See also *TIA*.

### EIA/TIA-232

Common physical layer interface standard, developed by EIA and TIA, that supports unbalanced circuits at signal speeds of up to 64 kbps. Closely resembles the V.24 specification. Formerly called RS-232.

### EIA/TIA-449

Popular physical layer interface developed by EIA and TIA. Essentially, a faster (up to 2 Mbps) version of EIA/TIA-232 capable of longer cable runs. Formerly called RS-449. See also *EIA-530*.

**EIA/TIA-586**

Standard that describes the characteristics and applications for various grades of UTP cabling. See also *Category 1 cabling*, *Category 2 cabling*, *Category 3 cabling*, *Category 4 cabling*, *Category 5 cabling*, and *UTC*.

**EIA-530**

Refers to two electrical implementations of EIA/TIA-449: RS-422 (for balanced transmission) and RS-423 (for unbalanced transmission). See also *RS-422*, *RS-423*, and *EIA/TIA-449*.

**EIGRP**

See *EIGRP* in the "Cisco Systems Terms and Acronyms" section.

**EIP**

See *EIP* in the "Cisco Systems Terms and Acronyms" section.

**EIRP**

Effective Isotropic Radiated Power. Term for the expression of the performance of an antenna in a given direction relative to the performance of a theoretical (isotropic) antenna and is expressed in watts or dBW. EIRP is the sum of the power sent to the antenna plus antenna gain.

**EISA**

Extended Industry-Standard Architecture. 32-bit bus interface used in PCs, PC-based servers, and some UNIX workstations and servers. See also *ISA*.

**E-ISUP**

Extended-ISUP. Originally a subset of Q.761 ISUP. It is expanding in to a superset of ITU and ANSI ISUP. In addition, it supports the delivery of SDP parameters via generic digits. E-ISUP runs over IP and therefore uses IP addresses instead of point codes.

**ELAN**

emulated LAN. ATM network in which an Ethernet or Token Ring LAN is emulated using a client-server model. ELANs are composed of an LEC, an LES, a BUS, and an LECS. Multiple ELANs can exist simultaneously on a single ATM network. ELANs are defined by the LANE specification. See also *BUS*, *LANE*, *LEC*, *LECS*, and *LES*.

**ELAP**

EtherTalk Link Access Protocol. Link-access protocol used in an EtherTalk network. ELAP is built on top of the standard Ethernet data link layer.

**electrically erasable programmable read-only memory**
See *EECM*.

**electromagnetic interference**
See *EMI*.

**electromagnetic pulse**
See *EMP*.

**electromagnetic spectrum**
Full range of a electromagnetic (same as magnetic) frequencies, the subset of which is used in commercial RF systems. Commercial RF systems typically are classified in ranges that include MF, HF, VHF, SHF, and EHF. Military systems typically include frequencies outside these types.

**electronic data interchange**
See *EDI*.

**Electronic Data Interchange for Administration, Commerce, and Transport**
See *EDIFACT*.

**Electronic Frontier Foundation**
See *EFF*.

**Electronic Industries Association**
See *EIA*.

**electronic mail**
See *e-mail*.

**Electronic Messaging Association**
See *EMA*.

**electrostatic discharge**
See *ESD*.

**ELMI**
Enhanced Local Management Interface.

## EMA

**1.** Enterprise Management Architecture. Digital Equipment Corporation network management architecture, based on the OSI network management model.

**2.** Electronic Messaging Association. Forum devoted to standards and policy work, education, and development of electronic messaging systems, such as e-mail, voice mail, and facsimile.

## e-mail

electronic mail. Widely used network application in which text messages are transmitted electronically between end users over various types of networks using various network protocols.

## EMI

electromagnetic interference. Interference by electromagnetic signals that can cause reduced data integrity and increased error rates on transmission channels.

## EMIF

ESCON Multiple Image Facility. Mainframe I/O software function that allows one ESCON channel to be shared among multiple logical partitions on the same mainframe. See also *ESCON*.

## EMP

electromagnetic pulse. Caused by lightning and other high-energy phenomena. Capable of coupling enough energy into unshielded conductors to destroy electronic devices. See also *Tempest*.

## EMS

**1.** Event Management Service. A software module within the ICM that processes use to report events to other processes within the system.

**2.** Element Management System.

## EMTOX

Exchange of Mixed Traffic over X.25. Specification for transmitting airline protocol data over standard X.25 switched virtual circuits (SVCs).

## emulated LAN

See *EMA*.

## emulation mode

Function of an NCP that enables it to perform activities equivalent to those performed by a transmission control unit.

### EN

end node. APPN end system that implements the PU 2.1, provides end-user services, and supports sessions between local and remote CPs. ENs are not capable of routing traffic and rely on an adjacent NN for APPN services. Compare with *NN*. See also *CP*.

### encapsulation

Wrapping of data in a particular protocol header. For example, Ethernet data is wrapped in a specific Ethernet header before network transit. Also, when bridging dissimilar networks, the entire frame from one network is simply placed in the header used by the data link layer protocol of the other network. See also *tunneling*.

### encapsulation bridging

Carries Ethernet frames from one router to another across disparate media, such as serial and FDDI lines. Contrast with *translational bridging*.

### encoder

Device that modifies information into the required transmission format.

### encryption

Application of a specific algorithm to data so as to alter the appearance of the data making it incomprehensible to those who are not authorized to see the information. See also *decryption*.

### encryption certificate

Public-key certificate that contains a public key that is intended to be used for encrypting data, rather than for verifying digital signatures or performing other cryptographic functions.

### end node

See *EN*.

### end of transmission

See *EOT*.

### end point

Device at which a virtual circuit or virtual path begins or ends.

### end system

See *ES*.

### End System-to-Intermediate System

See *ES-IS*.

**endpoint**

H.323 terminal or gateway. An endpoint can call and be called. It generates and terminates the information stream.

**end-to-end encryption**

Continuous protection of data that flows between two points in a network, provided by encrypting data when it leaves its source, leaving it encrypted while it passes through any intermediate computers (such as routers), and decrypting only when the data arrives at the intended destination.

**Energy Sciences Network**

See *ESnet*.

**Enhanced IGRP**

See *EIGRP* in the "Cisco Systems Terms and Acronyms" section.

**Enhanced Interior Gateway Routing Protocol**

See *EIGRP* in the "Cisco Systems Terms and Acronyms" section.

**Enhanced Monitoring Services**

See *Enhanced Monitoring Services* in the "Cisco Systems Terms and Acronyms" section.

**Enterprise Management Architecture**

See *EMA*.

**enterprise network**

Large and diverse network connecting most major points in a company or other organization. Differs from a WAN in that it is privately owned and maintained.

**Enterprise System Connection**

See *ESCON*.

**Enterprise System Connection channel**

See *ESCON channel*.

**entity**

Generally, an individual, manageable network device. Sometimes called an alias.

**entity identifier**

The unique address of an NVE socket in a node on an AppleTalk network. The specific format of an entity identifier is network-dependent. See also *NVE*.

**entity name**

Name that an NVE can assign to itself. Although not all NVEs have names, NVEs can possess several names (or aliases). An entity name is made up of three character strings: object, entity type, and zone. For example: Bldg 2 LaserJet 5:LaserWriter@Bldg 2 Zone. See also *NVE*.

**entity type**

Part of an entity name that describes the entity's class. For example, LaserWriter or AFPServer. See also *entity name*.

**EOM**

end of message. Indicator that identifies the last ATM cell containing information from a data packet that was segmented.

**EOT**

end of transmission. Generally, a character that signifies the end of a logical group of characters or bits.

**EPD**

early packet discard. Mechanism used by some ATM switches for discarding a complete AAL5 frame when a threshold condition, such as imminent congestion, is met. EPD prevents congestion that would otherwise jeopardize the switch's capability to properly support existing connections with a guaranteed service. Compare with *TPD*.

**ephemeral key**

A public key or a private key that is relatively short-lived.

**EPROM**

erasable programmable read-only memory. Nonvolatile memory chips that are programmed after they are manufactured, and, if necessary, can be erased by some means and reprogrammed. Compare with *EECM* and *PROM*.

**equalization**

Technique used to compensate for communications channel distortions.

**ER**

explicit rate. In ATM, an RM cell used to limit the ACR for a transmission to a specific value. Usually the source sets the ER initially to a requested rate, such as the PCR. Later, any network element in the path can reduce the ER to a value that the element can sustain. See also *ACOM*, *PCR*, and *RLM*.

**erasable programmable read-only memory**

See *EPROM*.

**ERC**

Easily Recognizable Code. Part of a North American number (in the NPA position) of the pattern NXX, where N=2...9 and XX = 00, 22, 33, ... 88.

**error control**

Technique for detecting and correcting errors in data transmissions.

**error-correcting code**

Code having sufficient intelligence and incorporating sufficient signaling information to enable the detection and the correction of many errors at the receiver.

**error-detecting code**

Code that can detect transmission errors through analysis of received data based on the adherence of the data to appropriate structural guidelines.

**errored second**

See *ES*.

**ES**

**1.** end system. Nonrouting host or node in an OSI network.

**2.** errored second. A one-second interval during which one or more errors are detected; a PM parameter, measured on a per-channel basis.

**ESCON**

Enterprise System Connection. IBM channel architecture that specifies a pair of fiber-optic cables, with either LEDs or lasers as transmitters, and a signaling rate of 200 Mbps.

**ESCON channel**

IBM channel for attaching mainframes to peripherals, such as storage devices, backup units, and network interfaces. This channel incorporates fiber channel technology. The ESCON channel replaces the bus and tag channel. Compare with *parallel channel*. See also *bus and tag channel*.

**ESCON Multiple Image Facility**

See *EMIF*.

**ESD**

electrostatic discharge. Discharge of stored static electricity that can damage electronic equipment and impair electrical circuitry, resulting in complete or intermittent failures.

**ESF**

Extended Superframe. Framing type used on T1 circuits that consists of 24 frames of 192 bits each, with the 193rd bit providing timing and other functions. ESF is an enhanced version of SF. See also *SF*.

**ESI**

end system identifier. Identifier that distinguishes multiple nodes at the same level when the lower level peer group is partitioned (usually an IEEE 802 address).

**ES-IS**

End System-to-Intermediate System. OSI protocol that defines how end systems (hosts) announce themselves to intermediate systems (routers). See also *IS-IS*.

**ESMTP**

Extended Simple Mail Transfer Protocol. Extended version of the Simple Mail Transfer Protocol (SMTP), which includes additional functionality, such as delivery notification and session delivery. ESMTP is described in RFC 1869, *SMTP Service Extensions*.

**ESnet**

Energy Sciences Network. Data communications network managed and funded by the U.S. Department of Energy Office of Energy Research (DOE/OER). Interconnects the DOE to educational institutions and other research facilities.

**ESP**

**1.** Extended Services Processor.

**2.** Encapsulating Security Payload. Security protocol that provides data privacy services, optional data authentication, and anti-replay services. ESP encapsulates the data to be protected.

**ESS**

Electronic Switching System. AT&T's term for an electronic central office switch. A 5ESS is AT&T's digital central office for end office applications. A 4ESS is its digital central office for toll center application.

### ETH unit

ethernet unit. Unit that provides interfaces to the Management Bus Concentrator and the network management system (NMS).

### EtherChannel

Developed and copyrighted by Cisco Systems. Logical aggregation of multiple Ethernet interfaces used to form a single higher bandwidth routing or bridging endpoint.

### Ethernet

Baseband LAN specification invented by Xerox Corporation and developed jointly by Xerox, Intel, and Digital Equipment Corporation. Ethernet networks use CSMA/CD and run over a variety of cable types at 10 Mbps. Ethernet is similar to the IEEE 802.3 series of standards. See also *10Base2*, *10Base5*, *10BaseF*, *10BaseT*, *10Broad36*, *Fast Ethernet*, and *IEEE 802.3*.

### Ethernet Interface Processor

See *EIP* in the "Cisco Systems Terms and Acronyms" section.

### ethernet meltdown

Event that causes saturation, or near saturation, on an Ethernet. It usually results from illegal or misrouted packets and typically lasts only a short time.

### EtherTalk

Apple Computer's data-link product that allows an AppleTalk network to be connected by Ethernet cable.

### EtherTalk Link Access Protocol

See *ELAP*.

### ETSI

European Telecommunications Standards Institute. ETSI is a non-profit organization producing voluntary telecommunications standards used throughout Europe, some of which have been adopted by the EC as the technical base for Directives or Regulations.

### EUnet

European Internet. European commercial Internet service provider. EUnet is designed to provide e-mail, news, and other Internet services to European markets.

**European Academic Research Network**

See *EARN*.

**European Computer Manufacturers Association**

See *ECMA*.

**European Internet**

See *EUnet*.

**European Telecommunication Standards Institute**

See *ETSI*.

**event**

Network message indicating operational irregularities in physical elements of a network or a response to the occurrence of a significant task, typically the completion of a request for information. See also *alarm* and *trap*.

**Event Detection Point**

Intelligent Network terminology.

**EWOS**

European Workshop for Open Systems. The OSI Implementors Workshop for Europe.

**excess burst**

See *Be*.

**excess rate**

In ATM, traffic in excess of the insured rate for a given connection. Specifically, the excess rate equals the maximum rate minus the insured rate. Excess traffic is delivered only if network resources are available and can be discarded during periods of congestion. Compare with *insured rate* and *maximum rate*.

**exchange identification**

See *XID*.

**EXEC**

See *EXEC* in the "Cisco Systems Terms and Acronyms" section.

**expansion**

The process of running a compressed data set through an algorithm that restores the data set to its original size. Compare with *companding* and *compression*.

**expedited delivery**

Option set by a specific protocol layer telling other protocol layers (or the same protocol layer in another network device) to handle specific data more rapidly.

**explicit forward congestion indication**

See *EFCI*.

**explicit rate**

See *ER*.

**explicit route**

In SNA, a route from a source subarea to a destination subarea, as specified by a list of subarea nodes and transmission groups that connect the two.

**explorer frame**

Frame sent out by a networked device in an SRB environment to determine the optimal route to another networked device.

**explorer packet**

Generated by an end station trying to find its way through an SRB network. Gathers a hop-by-hop description of a path through the network by being marked (updated) by each bridge that it traverses, thereby creating a complete topological map. See also *all-routes explorer packet*, *local explorer packet*, and *spanning explorer packet*.

**Extended Binary Coded Decimal Interchange Code**

See *EBCDIC*.

**Extended Industry-Standard Architecture**

See *EISA*.

**extended label ATM interface**

Type of interface supported by the remote ATM switch driver and a particular switch-specific driver that supports MPLS over an ATM interface on a remotely controlled switch.

**Extended Services Processor**

See *ESP* in the "Cisco Systems Terms and Acronyms" section.

**Extended Superframe Format**

See *ESF*.

**exterior gateway protocol**

See *EGP*.

**exterior router**

Router connected to an AURP tunnel, responsible for the encapsulation and the deencapsulation of AppleTalk packets in a foreign protocol header (for example, IP). See also *AURP* and *AURP tunnel*.

**external ATM interface**

One of the interfaces on the controlled ATM switch other than the switch control port. Also known as an exposed ATM interface because it is available for connections outside the label controlled switch.

**EXZ**

excessive zeros.

**facility loopback**

Signal looped back toward the incoming facility.

**failure domain**

Area in which a failure occurred in a Token Ring, defined by the information contained in a beacon. When a station detects a serious problem with the network (such as a cable break), it sends a beacon frame that includes the station reporting the failure, its NAUN, and everything in between. Beaconing in turn initiates a process called autoreconfiguration. See also *autoreconfiguration*, *beacon*, and *NAUN*.

**fallback**

Mechanism used by ATM networks when rigorous path selection does not generate an acceptable path. The fallback mechanism attempts to determine a path by selectively relaxing certain attributes, such as delay, in order to find a path that meets some minimal set of desired attributes.

**fan-out unit**

Device that allows multiple devices on a network to communicate using a single network attachment.

**fantail**

Panel of I/O connectors that attaches to an equipment rack, providing easy access for data connections to a network.

**FAQ**

frequently asked questions. Usually appears in the form of a "read-me" file in a variety of Internet forums. New users are expected to read the FAQ before participating in newsgroups, bulletin boards, video conferences, and so on.

**FARNET**

Federation of American Research NETworks.

### Fast Ethernet

Any of a number of 100-Mbps Ethernet specifications. Fast Ethernet offers a speed increase 10 times that of the 10BaseT Ethernet specification while preserving such qualities as frame format, MAC mechanisms, and MTU. Such similarities allow the use of existing 10BaseT applications and network management tools on Fast Ethernet networks. Based on an extension to the IEEE 802.3 specification. Compare with *EtherChannel*. See also *100BaseFX*, *100BaseT*, *100BaseT4*, *100BaseTX*, *100BaseX*, and *IEEE 802.3*.

### Fast Ethernet Interface Processor

See *FEIP* in the "Cisco Systems Terms and Acronyms" section.

### Fast Sequenced Transport

See *FST* in the "Cisco Systems Terms and Acronyms" section.

### Fast Serial Interface Processor

See *FSIP* in the "Cisco Systems Terms and Acronyms" section.

### fast switching

See *fast switching* in the "Cisco Systems Terms and Acronyms" section.

### fault management

One of five categories of network management defined by ISO for management of OSI networks. Fault management attempts to ensure that network faults are detected and controlled. See also *accounting management*, *configuration management*, *performance management*, and *security management*.

### FCC

Federal Communications Commission. U.S. government agency that supervises, licenses, and controls electronic and electromagnetic transmission standards.

### FCFS

first come first served.

### FCS

frame check sequence. Extra characters added to a frame for error control purposes. Used in HDLC, Frame Relay, and other data link layer protocols.

**FDDI**

Fiber Distributed Data Interface. LAN standard, defined by ANSI X3T9.5, specifying a 100-Mbps token-passing network using fiber-optic cable, with transmission distances of up to 2 km. FDDI uses a dual-ring architecture to provide redundancy. Compare with *CDDI* and *FDDI II*.

**FDDI II**

ANSI standard that enhances FDDI. FDDI II provides isochronous transmission for connectionless data circuits and connection-oriented voice and video circuits. Compare with *FDDI*.

**FDDI Interface Processor**

See *FIP* in the "Cisco Systems Terms and Acronyms" section.

**FDDITalk**

Apple Computer's data-link product that allows an AppleTalk network to be connected by FDDI cable.

**FDL**

Facility Data Link. A 4-kbps channel provided by the Extended Superframe (ESF) T1 framing format. The FDL performs outside the payload capacity and allows a service provider to check error statistics on terminating equipment without intrusion.

**FDM**

frequency-division multiplexing. Technique whereby information from multiple channels can be allocated bandwidth on a single wire based on frequency. Compare with *ATDM*, *statistical multiplexing*, and *TDM*.

**FE**

Fast Ethernet.

**feature boards**

Modular system cards that perform specific functionality (DSC cards or modem cards, for example).

**FEC**

forward error correction. FEC is a class of methods for controlling errors in a one-way communication system. FEC sends extra information along with the data, which can be used by the receiver to check and correct the data.

## FECN

forward explicit congestion notification. Bit set by a Frame Relay network to inform DTE receiving the frame that congestion was experienced in the path from source to destination. DTE receiving frames with the FECN bit set can request that higher-level protocols take flow-control action as appropriate. Compare with *BECN*.

## Federal Communications Commission

See *FCC*.

## Federal Networking Council

See *FNC*.

## FEIP

See *FEIP* in the "Cisco Systems Terms and Acronyms" section.

## FEP

front-end processor. Device or board that provides network interface capabilities for a networked device. In SNA, typically an IBM 3745 device.

## FGD

Feature Group-D (FGD). Identifies a standardized service available to carriers delivered on a channelized T1 line.

## FGD-EANA

Feature Group-D (FGD) signalling protocol of type Exchange Access North American (EANA). This provides certain call services, such as emergency (USA-911) calls. The command calling number outbound is used only for FGD-EANA signalling to generate ANI digits for outgoing calls.

## Fiber Distributed Data Interface

See *FDDI*.

## fiber optics

A method for the transmission of information (audio, video, data). Light is modulated and transmitted over high purity, hair-thin fibers of glass. The bandwidth capacity of fiber optic cable is much greater than that of conventional cable or copper wire.

## fiber plant

Aerial or buried fiber optic cable that established connectivity between fiber optic transmission equipment locations.

### fiber-optic cable

Physical medium capable of conducting modulated light transmission. Compared with other transmission media, fiber-optic cable is more expensive but is not susceptible to electromagnetic interference, and is capable of higher data rates. Sometimes called *optical fiber*.

### fiber-optic interrepeater link

See *FOIRL*.

## FICON

fiber connectivity. FICON channels provide 100-Mbps bi-directional link rates at unrepeated distances of up to 20 km over fiber optic cables (compared with ESCON channels that support 17-MBps link rates at maximum unrepeated distances of up to 3 km).

## FID0

format indicator 0. One of several formats that an SNA TH can use. An FID0 TH is used for communication between an SNA node and a non-SNA node. See also *TH*.

## FID1

format indicator 1. One of several formats that an SNA TH can use. An FID1 TH encapsulates messages between two subarea nodes that do not support virtual and explicit routes. See also *TH*.

## FID2

format indicator 2. One of several formats that an SNA TH can use. An FID2 TH is used for transferring messages between a subarea node and a PU 2, using local addresses. See also *TH*.

## FID3

format indicator 3. One of several formats that an SNA TH can use. An FID3 TH is used for transferring messages between a subarea node and a PU 1, using local addresses. See also *TH*.

## FID4

format indicator 4. One of several formats that an SNA TH can use. An FID4 TH encapsulates messages between two subarea nodes that are capable of supporting virtual and explicit routes. See also *TH*.

### field replaceable unit

Hardware component that can be removed and replaced on-site. Typical field-replaceable units include cards, power supplies, and chassis components.

### FIFO

first-in, first-out. Refers to a buffering scheme where the first byte of data entering the buffer is the first byte retrieved by the CPU. In telephony, FIFO refers to a queueing scheme where the first calls received are the first calls processed.

### FIFO queueing

first-in, first-out queueing. Involves buffering and forwarding of packets in the order of arrival. FIFO embodies no concept of priority or classes of traffic. There is only one queue, and all packets are treated equally. Packets are sent out an interface in the order in which they arrive.

### file transfer

Category of popular network applications that allow files to be moved from one network device to another.

### File Transfer Protocol

See *FTP*.

### File Transfer, Access, and Management

See *FTAM*.

### filter

Generally, a process or a device that screens network traffic for certain characteristics, such as source address, destination address, or protocol, and determines whether to forward or discard that traffic based on the established criteria.

### filtering router

Internetwork router that selectively prevents the passage of data packets according to a security policy.

### finger

Software tool for determining whether a person has an account at a particular Internet site. Many sites do not allow incoming finger requests.

### FIP

See *FIP (FDDI Interface Processor)* in the "Cisco Systems Terms and Acronyms" section.

### firewall

Router or access server, or several routers or access servers, designated as a buffer between any connected public networks and a private network. A firewall router uses access lists and other methods to ensure the security of the private network.

### firmware

Software instructions set permanently or semipermanently in ROM.

### FISU

Fill-In Signal Unit. SS7 message that is sent in both directions whenever other signal units are not present. Provides a CRC checksum for use by both signalling endpoints.

### FIX

Federal Internet Exchange. Connection point between the North American governmental internets and the Internet. The FIXs are named after their geographic region, as in FIX West (Mountain View, California) and FIX East (College Park, Maryland). See also *CIX*, *GIX*, and *MAE*.

### flapping

Routing problem where an advertised route between two nodes alternates (flaps) back and forth between two paths due to a network problem that causes intermittent interface failures.

### flash memory

A special type of EEPROM that can be erased and reprogrammed in blocks instead of one byte at a time. Many modern PCs have their BIOS stored on a flash memory chip so that it can be updated easily if necessary. Such a BIOS is sometimes called a flash BIOS. Flash memory is also popular in modems because it enables the modem manufacturer to support new protocols as they become standardized.

### flash update

Routing update sent asynchronously in response to a change in the network topology. Compare with *routing update*.

### flat addressing

Scheme of addressing that does not use a logical hierarchy to determine location. For example, MAC addresses are flat, so bridging protocols must flood packets throughout the network to deliver the packet to the appropriate location. Compare with *hierarchical addressing*.

### F-link

SS7 fully associated link. An SS7 signaling link directly associated with a link carrying traffic (although not necessarily imbedded within the same physical span.

### flooding

Traffic passing technique used by switches and bridges in which traffic received on an interface is sent out all the interfaces of that device except the interface on which the information was receivedoriginally.

### flow

Stream of data traveling between two endpoints across a network (for example, from one LAN station to another). Multiple flows can be transmitted on a single circuit.

### flow control

Technique for ensuring that a transmitting entity, such as a modem, does not overwhelm a receiving entity with data. When the buffers on the receiving device are full, a message is sent to the sending device to suspend the transmission until the data in the buffers has been processed. In IBM networks, this technique is called *pacing*.

### flowspec

In IPv6, the traffic parameters of a stream of IP packets between two applications. See also *IPv6*.

### FLT

Full Line Terminal. Multiplexer that terminates a SONET span. See also *SONET*.

### FM

frequency modulation. Modulation technique in which signals of different frequencies represent different data values. Compare with *AM* and *PAM*. See also *modulation*.

### FNC

Federal Networking Council. Group responsible for assessing and coordinating U.S. federal agency networking policies and needs.

### FOIRL

fiber-optic interrepeater link. Fiber-optic signaling methodology based on the IEEE 802.3 fiber-optic specification. FOIRL is a precursor of the 10BaseFL specification, which is designed to replace it. See also *10BaseFL*.

### footprint

Geographical area in which an entity is licensed to broadcast its signal.

### foreign exchange

See *FX*.

### format indicator 0

See *FID0*.

### format indicator 1

See *FID1*.

### format indicator 2

See *FID2*.

### format indicator 3

See *FID3*.

### format indicator 4

See *FID4*.

### forward channel

Communications path carrying information from the call initiator to the called party.

### forward delay interval

Amount of time an interface spends listening for topology change information after that interface is activated for bridging and before forwarding actually begins.

### forward explicit congestion notification

See *FE*.

### forwarding

Process of sending a frame toward its ultimate destination by way of an internetworking device.

### FOTS

Fiber Optics Transmission Systems. Vendor-proprietary fiber-optic transmission equipment.

### Fourier transform

Technique used to evaluate the importance of various frequency cycles in a time series pattern.

### four-part dotted notation

See *dot address*.

### FQDN

fully qualified domain name. FQDN is the full name of a system, rather than just its host name. For example, aldebaran is a host name, and aldebaran.interop.com is an FQDN.

### fractional T1

See *channelized T1*.

### FRAD

Frame Relay access device. Any network device that provides a connection between a LAN and a Frame Relay WAN. See also *Cisco FRAD* (Cisco Frame Relay access device) and *FRAS* (*Frame Relay access suppor*t) in the "Cisco Systems Terms and Acronyms" section.

### fragment

Piece of a larger packet that has been broken down to smaller units.

### fragmentation

Process of breaking a packet into smaller units when transmitting over a network medium that cannot support the original size of the packet. See also *reassembly*.

### frame

Logical grouping of information sent as a data link layer unit over a transmission medium. Often refers to the header and the trailer, used for synchronization and error control, that surround the user data contained in the unit. The terms *cell*, *datagram*, *message*, *packet*, and *segment* also are used to describe logical information groupings at various layers of the OSI reference model and in various technology circles.

**frame check sequence**

See *FCS*.

**frame forwarding**

Mechanism by which frame-based traffic, such as *HDLC* and *SDLC*, traverses an ATM network.

**Frame Relay**

Industry-standard, switched data link layer protocol that handles multiple virtual circuits using HDLC encapsulation between connected devices. Frame Relay is more efficient than X.25, the protocol for which it generally is considered a replacement. See also *X.25*.

**Frame Relay access device**

See *FRAD*.

**Frame Relay access support**

See *FRAS* in the "Cisco Systems Terms and Acronyms" section.

**Frame Relay bridging**

Bridging technique, described in RFC 1490, that uses the same spanning-tree algorithm as other bridging functions but allows packets to be encapsulated for transmission across a Frame Relay network.

**frame switch**

See *LAN switch*.

**frames types**

- information frame (I-frame)
- supervisory frame (S-frame)
- unnumbered frame (U-frame)
- unnumbered information frame (UI-frame)

**FRAS**

See *FRAS* (*Frame Relay access support*) in the "Cisco Systems Terms and Acronyms" section.

**FRASM**

Frame Relay access service module.

### freenet

Community-based bulletin board system with e-mail, information services, interactive communications, and conferencing.

### free-trade zone

Part of an AppleTalk internetwork that is accessible by two other parts of the internetwork that cannot directly access one another.

### frequency

Number of cycles per second, measured in hertz, of an alternating current.

### frequency modulation

See *FM*.

### frequency re-use

One of the fundamental concepts on which commercial wireless systems are based that involves the partitioning of an RF radiating area (cell) into segments of a cell, which for Cisco purposes means the cell is broken into three equal segments. One segment of the cell uses a frequency that is far enough away from the frequency in the bordering segment that it does not provide interference problems.

Frequency re-use in mobile cellular systems means that each cell has a frequency that is far enough away from the frequency in the bordering cell that it does not provide interference problems. The same frequency is used at least two cells apart from each other. This practice enables cellular providers to have many times more customers for a given site license.

### frequency-division multiplexing

See *FDM*.

### FRF

Frame Relay Forum. An association of corporate members consisting of vendors, carriers, users, and consultants committed to the implementation of Frame Relay in accordance with national and international standards. See www.frforum.com.

### FRF.11

Frame Relay Forum implementation agreement for Voice over Frame Relay (v1.0 May 1997). This specification defines multiplexed data, voice, fax, DTMF digit-relay, and CAS/Robbed-bit signaling frame formats but does not include call setup, routing, or administration facilities. See www.frforum.com.

**FRF.11 Annex C**

See *FRF.12*.

**FRF.12**

The FRF.12 Implementation Agreement (also known as FRF.11 Annex C) was developed to allow long data frames to be fragmented into smaller pieces and interleaved with real-time frames. In this way, real-time voice and non real-time data frames can be carried together on lower speed links without causing excessive delay to the real-time traffic. See www.frforum.com.

**FRF.8**

Frame Relay-to-ATM Service Interworking. To communicate over WANs, end-user stations and the network cloud typically must use the same type of transmission protocol. This limitation has prevented differing networks, such as Frame Relay and ATM, from being linked. However, the Frame Relay-to-ATM Service Interworking (FRF.8) feature allows Frame Relay and ATM networks to exchange data despite differing network protocols. The Frame Relay/ATM PVC Service Interworking Implementation Agreement specified in Frame Relay Forum (FRF) document number FRF.8 provide the functional requirements for linking Frame Relay and ATM networks.

**FRF11-trunk**

Point to point permanent voice connection (private line) conforming to the FRF.11 specification.

**FRMR**

Frame REJECT.

**front end**

Node or software program that requests services of a back end. See also *back end*, *client*, and *server*.

**front-end processor**

See *FEP*.

**FRTS**

Frame Relay traffic shaping. Queueing method that uses queues on a Frame Relay network to limit surges that can cause congestion. Data is buffered and sent into the network in regulated amounts to ensure that the traffic can fit within the promised traffic envelope for the particular connection.

## FSIP

See *FSIP* in the "Cisco Systems Terms and Acronyms" section.

## FSN

Forward Sequence Number. Part of an SS7 MSU that contains the sequence number of the signal unit.

## FSSRP

Fast Simple Server Redundancy Protocol. The LANE simple server redundancy feature creates fault-tolerance using standard LANE protocols and mechanisms. FSSRP differs from LANE SSRP in that all configured LANE servers of an Emulated LAN (ELANE) are always active. See also *SSRP*.

## FST

See *FST* in the "Cisco Systems Terms and Acronyms" section.

## FTAM

File Transfer, Access, and Management. In OSI, an application layer protocol developed for network file exchange and management between diverse types of computers.

## FTP

File Transfer Protocol. Application protocol, part of the TCP/IP protocol stack, used for transferring files between network nodes. FTP is defined in RFC 959.

## full duplex

Capability for simultaneous data transmission between a sending station and a receiving station. Compare with *half duplex* and *simplex*.

## full mesh

Term describing a network in which devices are organized in a mesh topology, with each network node having either a physical circuit or a virtual circuit connecting it to every other network node. A full mesh provides a great deal of redundancy but because it can be prohibitively expensive to implement, it usually is reserved for network backbones. See also *mesh* and *partial mesh*.

## fully qualified domain name

See *FQDN*.

## FUNI

frame user network interface.

### Fuzzball

Digital Equipment Corporation LSI-11 computer system running IP gateway software. The NSFnet used these systems as backbone packet switches.

### FX

foreign exchange.

**1.** A circuit that connects a subscriber in one exchange with a central office (CO) in another exchange.

**2.** A trunk type that connects a call center with a central office in a remote exchange. This allows callers in that remote exchange. See also *CO*, *FXO*, *FXS*, and *PBX*.

### FXO

Foreign Exchange Office. An FXO interface connects to the Public Switched Telephone Network (PSTN) central office and is the interface offered on a standard telephone. Cisco's FXO interface is an RJ-11 connector that allows an analog connection at the PSTN's central office or to a station interface on a PBX.

### FXS

Foreign Exchange Station. An FXS interface connects directly to a standard telephone and supplies ring, voltage, and dial tone. Cisco's FXS interface is an RJ-11 connector that allows connections to basic telephone service equipment, keysets, and PBXs.

### G.703/G.704

ITU-T electrical and mechanical specifications for connections between telephone company equipment and DTE using BNC connectors and operating at E1 data rates.

### G.711

Describes the 64-kbps PCM voice coding technique. In G.711, encoded voice is already in the correct format for digital voice delivery in the PSTN or through PBXs. Described in the ITU-T standard in its G-series recommendations.

### G.723.1

Describes a compression technique that can be used for compressing speech or audio signal components at a very low bit rate as part of the H.324 family of standards. This CODEC has two bit rates associated with it: 5.3 and 6.3 kbps. The higher bit rate is based on ML-MLQ technology and provides a somewhat higher quality of sound. The lower bit rate is based on CELP and provides system designers with additional flexibility. Described in the ITU-T standard in its G-series recommendations.

### G.726

Describes ADPCM coding at 40, 32, 24, and 16 kbps. ADPCM-encoded voice can be interchanged between packet voice, PSTN, and PBX networks if the PBX networks are configured to support ADPCM. Described in the ITU-T standard in its G-series recommendations.

### G.728

Describes a 16-kbps low-delay variation of CELP voice compression. CELP voice coding must be translated into a public telephony format for delivery to or through the PSTN. Described in the ITU-T standard in its G-series recommendations.

### G.729

Describes CELP compression where voice is coded into 8-kbps streams. There are two variations of this standard (G.729 and G.729 Annex A) that differ mainly in computational complexity; both provide speech quality similar to 32-kbps ADPCM. Described in the ITU-T standard in its G-series recommendations.

### G.804

The ITU-T framing standard that defines the mapping of ATM cells into the physical medium.

### gain

The ratio of the output amplitude of a signal to the input amplitude of a signal. This ratio typically is expressed in dBs. The higher the gain, the better the antenna receives or transmits but also the more noise it includes.

### gatekeeper

**1.** The component of an H.323 conferencing system that performs call address resolution, admission control, and subnet bandwidth management.

**2.** Telecommunications: H.323 entity on a LAN that provides address translation and control access to the LAN for H.323 terminals and gateways. The gatekeeper can provide other services to the H.323 terminals and gateways, such as bandwidth management and locating gateways. A gatekeeper maintains a registry of devices in the multimedia network. The devices register with the gatekeeper at startup and request admission to a call from the gatekeeper.

### gateway

In the IP community, an older term referring to a routing device. Today, the term *router* is used to describe nodes that perform this function, and *gateway* refers to a special-purpose device that performs an application-layer conversion of information from one protocol stack to another. Compare with *router*.

### Gateway Discovery Protocol

See *GDP* in the "Cisco Systems Terms and Acronyms" section.

### gateway host

In SNA, a host node that contains a gateway SSCP.

### gateway NCP

NCP that connects two or more SNA networks and performs address translation to allow cross-network session traffic.

**Gateway-to-Gateway Protocol**

See *GGP*.

**Gb**

gigabit. Approximately 1,000,000,000 bits.

**GB**

gigabyte. Approximately 1,000,000,000 bytes.

**Gbps**

gigabits per second.

**GBps**

gigabytes per second.

**GCAC**

generic connection admission control. In ATM, a PNNI algorithm designed for CBR and VBR connections. Any node can use GCAC to calculate the expected CAC behavior of another node given that node's advertised link metrics and the QoS of a connection setup request. See also *CAC*.

**GCRA**

generic cell rate algorithm. In ATM, an algorithm that defines conformance with respect to the traffic contract of the connection. For each cell arrival, the GCRA determines whether the cell conforms to the traffic contract.

**GDP**

See *GDP* in the "Cisco Systems Terms and Acronyms" section.

**generic connection admission control**

See *GCAC*.

**generic routing encapsulation**

See *GRE* in the "Cisco Systems Terms and Acronyms" section.

**Get Nearest Server**

See *Gn interface*.

**GGP**

Gateway-to-Gateway Protocol. MILNET protocol specifying how core routers (gateways) should exchange reachability and routing information. GGP uses a distributed shortest-path algorithm.

---

**GGSN**

gateway GPRS support node. A wireless gateway that allows mobile cell phone users to access the public data network (PDN) or specified private IP networks.

---

**GHz**

gigahertz.

---

**Gi interface**

Reference point between a GPRS network and an external packet data network.

---

**gigabit**

Abbreviated Gb.

---

**Gigabit Ethernet**

Standard for a high-speed Ethernet, approved by the IEEE (Institute of Electrical and Electronics Engineers) 802.3z standards committee in 1996.

---

**gigabits per second**

Abbreviated Gbps.

---

**gigabyte**

Abbreviated GB.

---

**gigabytes per second**

Abbreviated GBps.

---

**gigahertz**

Abbreviated GHz.

---

**GIX**

Global Internet eXchange. Common routing exchange point that allows pairs of networks to implement agreed-upon routing policies. The GIX is intended to allow maximum connectivity to the Internet for networks all over the world. See also *CIX*, *FIX*, and *MAE*.

---

**gleaning**

The process by which a router automatically derives AARP table entries from incoming packets. Gleaning speeds up the process of populating the AARP table. See also *AARP*.

### Gn interface

An interface between GSNs within the same PLMN in a GPRS network. GTP is a protocol defined on both the Gn and Gp interfaces between GSNs in a GPRS network.

### GNS

Get Nearest Server. A request packet sent by a client on an IPX network to locate the nearest active server of a particular type. An IPX network client issues a GNS request to solicit either a direct response from a connected server or a response from a router that tells it where on the internetwork the service can be located. GNS is part of the IPX SAP. See also *IPX* and *Service Advertisement Protocol (SAP)*.

### goodput

Generally refers to the measurement of actual data successfully transmitted from the sender(s) to the receiver(s). This is often a more useful measurement than the number of ATM cells per second throughput of an ATM switch if that switch is experiencing cell loss that results in many incomplete, and therefore unusable, frames arriving at the recipient.

### Gopher

The Internet Gopher allows a neophyte user to access various types of data residing on multiple hosts in a seamless fashion.

### GOSIP

Government OSI Profile. U.S. government procurement specification for OSI protocols. Through GOSIP, the government mandates that all federal agencies standardize on OSI and implement OSI-based systems as they become commercially available.

### Government OSI Profile

See *GOSIP*.

### Gp interface

Interface between GSNs within different PLMNs in a GPRS network. GTP is a protocol defined on both the Gp and Gn interfaces between GSNs in a GPRS network.

### GPRS

general packet radio service. A service defined and standardized by the European Telecommunication Standards Institute (ETSI). GPRS is an IP packet-based data service for Global System for Mobile Communications (GSM) networks.

### grade of service

A measure of telephone service quality based on the probability that a call will encounter a busy signal during the busiest hours of the day.

### graphical user interface

See *GUI*.

### GRE

See *GRE* in the "Cisco Systems Terms and Acronyms" section.

### GRJ

A RAS message sent as a gatekeeper rejection.

### Ground Start

A method of signaling used primarily on CO trunk lines to PBXs. A ground is placed on one side of the two-wire line to indicate that it is in use so the other side of the two-wire interface does not attempt to use the line.

### ground station

The collection of communications equipment designed to receive signals from (and usually transmit signals to) satellites. Also called a *downlink station*.

### ground-start trunk

A phone line that uses a ground instead of a short (loop-start trunks use a short between tip and ring) to signal the central office for a dial tone.

### Group 3

The standard created by the ITU-T relating to fax devices. A Group 3 fax device is a digital machine containing a 14400 baud modem that can transmit an 8 1/2 by 11 inch page in approximately 20 seconds with a resolution of either 203 by 98 dots per inch (dpi) or 203 by 196 dpi (fine), using Huffman code to compress fax data. Group 3 faxes use a standard dial-up telephone line for transmission.

### group address

See *multicast address*.

**group delay**

See *distortion delay*.

**Group Matrix Card unit**

This unit, located in the Line bay, selects one of the two optical signals and routes the signal to the Matrix Card (MC) units in the Matrix bay.

**GRQ**

A RAS message sent as a gatekeeper request.

**GSM**

global system for mobile communication. A second generation (2G) mobile wireless networking standard defined by ETSI, GSM is deployed widely throughout the world. GSM uses TDMA technology and operates in the 900-MHz radio band.

**GSN**

GPRS support node. GSN (or GSNs) refers to the general functions of a group of both GGSNs and SGSNs in a GPRS network.

**GSS**

generic service state.

**GTP**

GPRS tunneling protocol. GTP handles the flow of user packet data and signaling information between the SGSN and GGSN in a GPRS network. GTP is defined on both the Gn and Gp interfaces of a GPRS network.

**GTP tunnel**

Used to communicate between an external packet data network and a mobile station in a GPRS network. A GTP tunnel is referenced by an identifier called a *TID* and is defined by two associated PDP contexts residing in different GSNs. A tunnel is created whenever an SGSN sends a Create PDP Context Request in a GPRS network.

**GTT**

Global Title Translation. A function usually performed in an STP, GTT is the procedure by which the destination signaling point and the subsystem number (SSN) is determined from digits (that is, the global title) present in the signaling message.

**guard band**

An unused frequency band between two communications channels that provides separation of the channels to prevent mutual interference.

**GUI**

graphical user interface. A user environment that uses pictorial as well as textual representations of the input and the output of applications and the hierarchical or other data structure in which information is stored. Such conventions as buttons, icons, and windows are typical, and many actions are performed using a pointing device (such as a mouse). Microsoft Windows and the Apple Macintosh are prominent examples of platforms using a GUI.

### H channel

high-speed channel. Full-duplex ISDN primary rate channel operating at 384 kbps. Compare with *B channel*, *D channel*, and *E channel*.

### H.225.0

An ITU standard that governs H.225.0 session establishment and packetization. H.225.0 actually describes several different protocols: RAS, use of Q.931, and use of RTP.

### H.245

An ITU standard that governs H.245 endpoint control.

### H.320

Suite of ITU-T standard specifications for videoconferencing over circuit-switched media, such as ISDN, fractional T-1, and switched-56 lines. Extension of ITU-T standard H.320 that enables videoconferencing over LANs and other packet-switched networks, as well as video over the Internet.

### H.323

H.323 allows dissimilar communication devices to communicate with each other by using a standardized communication protocol. H.323 defines a common set of CODECs, call setup and negotiating procedures, and basic data transport methods.

### H.323 RAS

registration, admission, and status. The RAS signaling protocol performs registration, admissions, bandwidth changes, and status and disengage procedures between the VoIP gateway and the gatekeeper.

### H.450.2

Call transfer supplementary service for H.323.

### H.450.3

Call diversion supplementary service for H.323.

## hairpin

Telephony term that means to send a call back in the direction that it came from. For example, if a call cannot be routed over IP to a gateway that is closer to the target telephone, the call typically is sent back out the local zone, back the way from which it came.

## hairpinning

An incoming PSTN call is looped back out onto the PSTN. This is done if the call cannot be delivered using IP. It also can be used by a trunking gateway to deliver a modem call to a NAS.

## half duplex

Capability for data transmission in only one direction at a time between a sending station and a receiving station. BSC is an example of a half-duplex protocol. See also *BSC*. Compare with *full duplex* and *simplex*.

## handshake

Sequence of messages exchanged between two or more network devices to ensure transmission synchronization.

## hardware address

See *MAC address*.

## HCMs

high-performance voice compression modules. Modules that provide voice compression according to the voice compression coding algorithm (codec) specified when the Cisco MC3810 multiservice concentrator is configured.

## HDB3

high density binary 3.

**1.** Zero suppression line coding used on E1 links.

**2.** Line code type used on E1 circuits.

## HDD unit

Hard Disk Drive unit. This contains two hard drives for storing the database and the software.

## HDLC

high-level data link control. Bit-oriented synchronous data link layer protocol developed by ISO. Derived from SDLC, HDLC specifies a data encapsulation method on synchronous serial links using frame characters and checksums. See also *SDLC*.

## HDS

Historical Data Server. An Admin Workstation with a special database that holds ICM historical data. In a normal configuration, historical data is stored only in the central database. When you use the HDS option, the historical data also is stored on the HDS machine, which must be a real-time distributor. Other Admin Workstations at the site can read historical data from the HDS rather than accessing the central database.

## HDSL

high-data-rate digital subscriber line. One of four DSL technologies. HDSL delivers 1.544 Mbps of bandwidth each way over two copper twisted pairs. Because HDSL provides T1 speed, telephone companies have been using HDSL to provision local access to T1 services whenever possible. The operating range of HDSL is limited to 12,000 feet (3658.5 meters), so signal repeaters are installed to extend the service. HDSL requires two twisted pairs, so it is deployed primarily for PBX network connections, digital loop carrier systems, interexchange POPs, Internet servers, and private data networks. Compare with *ADSL*, *SDSL*, and *VDSL*.

## headend

End point of a broadband network. All stations transmit toward the headend; the headend then transmits toward the destination stations.

## head-end

The upstream, transmit end of a tunnel.

## header

Control information placed before data when encapsulating that data for network transmission. Compare with *trailer*. See also *PCI*.

## heartbeat

See *SQE*.

## HEC

header error control. Algorithm for checking and correcting an error in an ATM cell. Using the fifth octet in the ATM cell header, ATM equipment checks for an error and corrects the contents of the header. The check character is calculated using a CRC algorithm allowing a single bit error in the header to be corrected or multiple errors to be detected.

### HELLO

Interior routing protocol used principally by NSFnet nodes. HELLO allows particular packet switches to discover minimal delay routes. Not to be confused with the *Hello protocol*.

### hello packet

Multicast packet that is used by routers for neighbor discovery and recovery. Hello packets also indicate that a client is still operating and network-ready.

### Hello protocol

Protocol used by OSPF systems for establishing and maintaining neighbor relationships. Not to be confused with HELLO.

### HEPnet

High-Energy Physics Network. Research network that originated in the United States but that has spread to most places involved in high-energy physics. Well-known sites include Argonne National Laboratory, Brookhaven National Laboratory, Lawrence Berkeley Laboratory, and the SLAC.

### hertz

Measure of frequency. Abbreviated Hz. Synonymous with cycles per second.

### heterogeneous network

Network consisting of dissimilar devices that run dissimilar protocols and in many cases support dissimilar functions or applications.

### HFC

hybrid fiber-coaxial. Technology being developed by the cable TV industry to provide two-way, high-speed data access to the home using a combination of fiber optics and traditional coaxial cable.

### HFE

hardware forwarding engine.

### hierarchical addressing

Scheme of addressing that uses a logical hierarchy to determine location. For example, IP addresses consist of network numbers, subnet numbers, and host numbers, which IP routing algorithms use to route the packet to the appropriate location. Compare with *flat addressing*.

**hierarchical routing**

The complex problem of routing on large networks can be simplified by reducing the size of the networks. This is accomplished by breaking a network into a hierarchy of networks, where each level is responsible for its own routing.

**High Performance Computing and Communications**

See *HPCC*.

**High Performance Computing Systems**

See *HPCS*.

**High Performance Routing**

See *HPR*.

**High Water Mark**

A counter that reports the highest number of DS0s that were in use at one time.

**High-Energy Physics Network**

See *HEPnet*.

**High-Level Data Link Control**

See *HDLC*.

**High-Performance Parallel Interface**

See *HIPPI*.

**High-Speed Communications Interface**

See *HSCI* in the "Cisco Systems Terms and Acronyms" section.

**High-Speed Serial Interface**

See *HSSI*.

**highway**

See *bus*.

**hijack attack**

Form of active wire tapping in which the attacker seizes control of a previously established communication association.

**HIP**

See *HIP* in the "Cisco Systems Terms and Acronyms" section.

## HIPPI

High-Performance Parallel Interface. High-performance interface standard defined by ANSI. HIPPI typically is used to connect supercomputers to peripherals and other devices.

## HLD

high-level designator. Designator that logically identifies the peer session endpoints used if the multiplex in the circuit is set to group.

## HLR

home location register. A database that contains information about subscribers to a mobile network. The HLR registers subscribers for a particular service provider. The HLR stores "permanent" subscriber information (rather than temporary subscriber data, which a VLR manages), including the service profile, the location information, and the activity status of the mobile user.

## HMAC

Hash-based Message Authentication Code. HMAC is a mechanism for message authentication using cryptographic hash functions. HMAC can be used with any iterative cryptographic hash function, for example, MD5, SHA-1, in combination with a secret shared key. The cryptographic strength of HMAC depends on the properties of the underlying hash function.

## HMAC-MD5

Hashed Message Authentication Codes with MD5 (RFC 2104). A keyed version of MD5 that enables two parties to validate transmitted information using a shared secret.

## HMM

Hex MICA Module. Contains six discrete modems.

### holddown

State into which a route is placed so that routers neither advertise the route nor accept advertisements about the route for a specific length of time (the holddown period). Holddown is used to flush bad information about a route from all routers in the network. A route typically is placed in holddown when a link in that route fails.

### home gateway

A router or access server that terminates VPDN tunnels and PPP sessions.

**homologation**

Conformity of a product or a specification to international standards, such as ITU-T, CSA, TUV, UL, or VCCI. Enables portability across company and international boundaries.

**hookflash**

Short on-hook period usually generated by a telephone-like device during a call to indicate that the telephone is attempting to perform a dial-tone recall from a PBX. Hookflash often is used to perform call transfer.

**Hoot and Holler**

A broadcast audio network used extensively by the brokerage industry for market updates and trading. Similar networks are used in publishing, transportation, power plants, and manufacturing.

**hop**

Passage of a data packet between two network nodes (for example, between two routers). See also *hop count*.

**hop count**

Routing metric used to measure the distance between a source and a destination. RIP uses hop count as its sole metric. See also *hookflash* and *RIP*.

**hop off**

Point at which a call transitions from H.323 to non-H.323, typically at a gateway.

**host**

Computer system on a network. Similar to node, except that host usually implies a computer system, whereas node generally applies to any networked system, including access servers and routers. See also *node*.

**host address**

See *host number*.

**host name**

Name given to a machine. See also *FQDN*.

**host node**

SNA subarea node that contains an SSCP. See also *SSCP*.

## host number

Part of an IP address that designates which node on the subnetwork is being addressed. Also called a *host address*.

## Hot Standby Router Protocol

See *HSRP* in the "Cisco Systems Terms and Acronyms" section.

## hot swapping

See *OIR* and *power-on servicing*.

## HPCC

High-Performance Computing and Communications. U.S. government–funded program advocating advances in computing, communications, and related fields. The HPCC is designed to ensure U.S. leadership in these fields through education, research and development, industry collaboration, and implementation of high-performance technology. See also the five components of the HPCC: *ASTA*, *BRHR*, *HPCS*, *IITA*, and *NREN*.

## HPCS

High-Performance Computing Systems. Component of the HPCC program designed to ensure U.S. technological leadership in high-performance computing through research and development of computing systems and related software. See also *HPCC*.

## HPR

High-Performance Routing. Second-generation routing algorithm for APPN. HPR provides a connectionless layer with nondisruptive routing of sessions around link failures, and a connection-oriented layer with end-to-end flow control, error control, and sequencing. Compare with *ISR*. See also *APPN*.

## HSCI

See *HSCI* in the "Cisco Systems Terms and Acronyms" section.

## HSRP

See *HSRP* in the "Cisco Systems Terms and Acronyms" section.

## HSSI

High-Speed Serial Interface. Network standard for high-speed (up to 52 Mbps) serial connections over WAN links.

## HSSI Interface Processor

See *HIP* in the "Cisco Systems Terms and Acronyms" section.

**HTML**

Hypertext Markup Language. Simple hypertext document formatting language that uses tags to indicate how a given part of a document should be interpreted by a viewing application, such as a Web browser. See also *hypertext* and *Web browser*.

**HTTP**

Hypertext Transfer Protocol. The protocol used by Web browsers and Web servers to transfer files, such as text and graphic files.

**hub**

**1.** Generally, a term used to describe a device that serves as the center of a star-topology network.

**2.** Hardware or software device that contains multiple independent but connected modules of network and internetwork equipment. Hubs can be active (where they repeat signals sent through them) or passive (where they do not repeat, but merely split, signals sent through them).

**3.** In Ethernet and IEEE 802.3, an Ethernet multiport repeater, sometimes called a concentrator.

**hybrid encryption**

Application of cryptography that combines two or more encryption algorithms, particularly a combination of symmetric and asymmetric encryption.

**hybrid network**

Internetwork made up of more than one type of network technology, including LANs and WANs.

**hyperlink**

Pointer within a hypertext document that points (links) to another document, which might or might not also be a hypertext document.

**hypertext**

Electronically stored text that allows direct access to other texts by way of encoded links. Hypertext documents can be created using HTML, and often integrate images, sound, and other media that are commonly viewed using a browser. See also *HTML* and *browser*.

**Hypertext Markup Language**

See *HTML*.

## Hypertext Transfer Protocol

See *HTTP*.

## Hz

See *hertz*.

## I/O

input/output.

## IAB

Internet Architecture Board. Board of internetwork researchers who discuss issues pertinent to Internet architecture. Responsible for appointing a variety of Internet-related groups,such as the IANA, IESG, and IRSG. The IAB is appointed by the trustees of the ISOC. See also *IANA, IESG, IRSG,* and *ISOC*.

## IAC

initial alignment control. SS7 MTP 2 function that provides the link alignment processing.

## IAHC

Internet International Ad Hoc Committee. A coalition of participants from the broad Internet community that works to satisfy the requirement for enhancements to the Internet's global DNS. Organizations naming members to the committee include Internet Society (ISOC), Internet Assigned Numbers Authority (IANA), Internet Architecture Board (IAB), Federal Networking Council (FNC), International Telecommunication Union (ITU), International Trademark Association (INTA), and World Intellectual Property Organization (WIPO).

## IANA

Internet Assigned Numbers Authority. Organization operated under the auspices of the ISOC as a part of the IAB. IANA delegates authority for IP address–space allocation and domain-name assignment to the InterNIC and other organizations. IANA also maintains a database of assigned protocol identifiers used in the TCP/IP stack, including autonomous system numbers. See also *ICP cell, ISOC,* and *InterNIC*.

## IBC

In-band control. Refers to issuing MICA technologies commands on the data channel, versus OBC, on the out-of-band control channel. In-band commands are passed by setting an in-band-command bit in the data buffer.

**ICANN**

Internet Corporation for Assigned Names and Numbers. Non-profit, private corporation that assumed responsibility for IP address space allocation, protocol parameter assignment, domain name system management, and root server system management functions that formerly were performed under U.S. Government contract by IANA and other entities.

**ICC**

Interface Controller Card. A high-capacity network interface card used in the Cisco VCO/4K product. The ICC is inserted into the VCO/4K midplane, connecting with a series of I/O modules specific to different network interface requirements.

**ICD**

International Code Designator. One of two ATM address formats developed by the ATM Forum for use by private networks. Adapted from the subnetwork model of addressing in which the ATM layer is responsible for mapping network layer addresses to ATM addresses. Compare with *DCC*.

**ICM**

Intelligent Call Management. The Cisco system that implements enterprise-wide call distribution across call centers. The ICM provides pre-routing, post-routing, and performance monitoring capabilities.

**ICMP**

Internet Control Message Protocol. Network layer Internet protocol that reports errors and provides other information relevant to IP packet processing. Documented in RFC 792.

**ICMP flood**

Denial of service attack that sends a host more ICMP echo request ("ping") packets than the protocol implementation can handle.

**ICMP Router Discovery Protocol**

See *IRDP*.

**ICP**

Intelligent Call Processing. AT&T's name for the facility that allows third-party products, such as the ICM, to pre-route calls.

**ICP cell**

IMA control protocol cell used for aligning the cells in multiple links.

## ICPIF

Calculated Planning Impairment Factor loss/delay busyout threshold. The ICPIF numbers represent predefined combinations of loss and delay. Packet loss and delay determine the threshold for initiating the busyout state.

## ICR

initial cell rate.

## ICRL

indirect certificate revocation list. In X.509, a CRL that may contain certificate revocation notifications for certificates issued by CAs other than the issuer of the ICRL.

## I-D

Internet-Draft. Working documents of the IETF, from its Areas and Working Groups. They are valid for a maximum of six months and might be updated, replaced, or made obsolete by other documents at any time. Very often, I-Ds are precursors to RFCs.

## IDB

interface description block. An IDB sub-block is an area of memory that is private to an application. This area stores private information and states variables that an application wants to associate with an IDB or an interface. The application uses the IDB to register a pointer to its sub-block, not to the contents of the sub-block itself.

## IDEA

International Data Encryption Algorithm. Patented, symmetric block cipher that uses a 128-bit key and operates on 64-bit blocks.

## IDI

initial domain identifier. Portion of an NSAP or NSAP-format ATM address that specifies the address allocation and the administration authority. See also *NSAP*.

## IDN

International Data Number. See *X.121*.

## IDP

initial domain part. Part of a CLNS address that contains an authority and format identifier and a domain identifier.

## IDPR

Interdomain Policy Routing. Interdomain routing protocol that dynamically exchanges policies between autonomous systems. IDPR encapsulates interautonomous system traffic and routes it according to the policies of each autonomous system along the path. IDPR is currently an IETF proposal. See also *policy-based routing*.

## IDRP

IS-IS Interdomain Routing Protocol. OSI protocol that specifies how routers communicate with routers in different domains.

## IE

information element.

## IEC

International Electrotechnical Commission. Industry group that writes and distributes standards for electrical products and components.

## IEEE

Institute of Electrical and Electronics Engineers. Professional organization whose activities include the development of communications and network standards. IEEE LAN standards are the predominant LAN standards today.

## IEEE 802.1

IEEE specification that describes an algorithm that prevents bridging loops by creating a spanning tree. The algorithm was invented by Digital Equipment Corporation. The Digital algorithm and the IEEE 802.1 algorithm are not exactly the same, nor are they compatible. See also *spanning tree*, *spanning-tree algorithm*, and *Spanning-Tree Protocol*.

## IEEE 802.12

IEEE LAN standard that specifies the physical layer and the MAC sublayer of the data link layer. IEEE 802.12 uses the demand priority media-access scheme at 100 Mbps over a variety of physical media. See also *100VG-AnyLAN*.

## IEEE 802.2

IEEE LAN protocol that specifies an implementation of the LLC sublayer of the data link layer. IEEE 802.2 handles errors, framing, flow control, and the network layer (Layer 3) service interface. Used in IEEE 802.3 and IEEE 802.5 LANs. See also *IEEE 802.3* and *IEEE 802.5*.

## IEEE 802.3

IEEE LAN protocol that specifies an implementation of the physical layer and the MAC sublayer of the data link layer. IEEE 802.3 uses CSMA/CD access at a variety of speeds over a variety of physical media. Extensions to the IEEE 802.3 standard specify implementations for Fast Ethernet. Physical variations of the original IEEE 802.3 specification include *10Base2*, *10Base5*, *10BaseF*, *10BaseT*, and *10Broad36*. Physical variations for *Fast Ethernet* include *100BaseT*, *100BaseT4*, and *100BaseX*.

## IEEE 802.4

IEEE LAN protocol that specifies an implementation of the physical layer and the MAC sublayer of the data link layer. IEEE 802.4 uses token-passing access over a bus topology and is based on the token bus LAN architecture. See also *token bus*.

## IEEE 802.5

IEEE LAN protocol that specifies an implementation of the physical layer and MAC sublayer of the data link layer. IEEE 802.5 uses token passing access at 4 or 16 Mbps over STP cabling and is similar to IBM Token Ring. See also *Token Ring*.

## IEEE 802.6

IEEE MAN specification based on DQDB technology. IEEE 802.6 supports data rates of 1.5 to 155 Mbps. See also *DQDB*.

## IEPG

Internet Engineering Planning Group. A group primarily composed of Internet service operators. Its goal is to promote a globally coordinated Internet operating environment. Membership is open to all.

## IESG

Internet Engineering Steering Group. An organization appointed by the IAB that manages the operation of the IETF. See also *ICP cell* and *IETF*.

## IETF

Internet Engineering Task Force. Task force consisting of over 80 working groups responsible for developing Internet standards. The IETF operates under the auspices of ISOC. See also *ISOC*.

## IF

intermediate frequency. Intermediate electromagnetic frequencies generated by a superheterodyne radio receiver.

### IFIP

International Federation for Information Processing. Research organization that performs OSI prestandardization work. Among other accomplishments, IFIP formalized the original MHS model. See also *MHS*.

### IF-MIB

Interfaces Group MIB. The current specification for the IF-MIB is found in RFC 2233. The MIB module to describe generic objects for network interface sublayers. This MIB is an updated version of the MIB-II if Table, and incorporates the extensions defined in RFC 1229.

### I-frame

Information frame. One of three SDLC frame formats. See also *S-frame* and *U-frame*.

### IGMP

Internet Group Management Protocol. Used by IP hosts to report their multicast group memberships to an adjacent multicast router. See also *multicast router*.

### IGP

Interior Gateway Protocol. Internet protocol used to exchange routing information within an autonomous system. Examples of common Internet IGPs include IGRP, OSPF, and RIP. See also *OSPF* and *RIP*. See also *IGRP* in the "Cisco Systems Terms and Acronyms" section.

### IGRP

See *IGRP* in the "Cisco Systems Terms and Acronyms" section.

### IIH

IS-IS Hello. Message sent by all IS-IS systems to maintain adjacencies. See also *IS-IS*.

### IINREN

Interagency Interim National Research and Education Network. Evolving operating network system. Near term research and development activities will provide for the smooth evolution of this networking infrastructure into the future gigabit NREN.

### IIOP

Internet Inter-ORB Protocol. Protocol used in the CORBA framework for accessing objects across the Internet. See also *CORBA*.

## IISP

Interim-Interswitch Signaling Protocol. ATM signaling protocol for inter-switch communication using manually configured prefix tables. When a signaling request is received by a switch, the switch checks the destination ATM address against the prefix table and notes the port with the longest prefix match. It then forwards the signaling request across that port using UNI procedures. IISP is an interim solution until PNNI Phase 1 is completed. Formerly known as PNNI Phase 0. Contrast with *Dynamic IISP*.

## IITA

Information Infrastructure Technology and Applications. Component of the HPCC program intended to ensure U.S. leadership in the development of advanced information technologies. See also *HPCC*.

## IKE

Internet Key Exchange. IKE establishes a shared security policy and authenticates keys for services (such as IPSec) that require keys. Before any IPSec traffic can be passed, each router/firewall/host must verify the identity of its peer. This can be done by manually entering pre-shared keys into both hosts or by a CA service.

## ILEC

incumbent local exchange carrier. Traditional telephone company. In the U.S., the Regional Bell Operation Companies (RBOCs) that were formed after the divestiture of AT&T and the Independent Operating Companies (IOCs) that usually are located in more rural areas or single cities are ILECs. In other areas of the world, ILECs are the Post, Telephone, and Telegraphs (PTTs), government-managed monopolies.

## ILMI

Interim Local Management Interface. Specification developed by the ATM Forum for incorporating network-management capabilities into the ATM UNI.

## IMA

inverse multiplexing over ATM. Standard protocol defined by the ATM Forum in 1997.

## IMA group

Physical links grouped to form a higher-bandwidth logical link the rate of which is approximately the sum of the individual link rates.

### IMAP

Internet Message Access Protocol. Method of accessing e-mail or bulletin board messages kept on a mail server that can be shared. IMAP permits client e-mail applications to access remote message stores as if they were local without actually transferring the message.

### IMAP4

Internet Message Access Protocol, version 4. Internet protocol by which a client workstation can access a mailbox dynamically on a server host to manipulate and retrieve mail messages that the server has received and is holding for the client.

### IMHO

"In My Humble Opinion." One of many short-form phrases seen in e-mail messages, newsgroups, and so on.

### Immediate Start

A method of E&M signaling. When the signaling leads indicate a change to an off-hook state, the interface is immediately ready to send signaling information.

### IMP

interface message processor. Old name for ARPANET packet switches. See also *ARPANET* and *packet switch*.

### IMSI

international mobile system identifier. A unique identifier stored in the SIM of a mobile station. The MS sends the IMSI to a BTS for identification of the MS in the GSM network. The BTS looks for the IMSI in the HLR.

### IMT

Inter-Machine Trunk.

### IN/AIN

Intelligent Network/Advanced Intelligent Network.

### INA

**1.** interactive network adapter. Central point or hub in broadband networks that receives signals on one set frequency band and retransmits them to another. Every transmission in a broadband network has to go through the INA or head-end. In CATV technology, the head-end is the control center for a cable system where video, audio, and data signals are processed and distributed along the coaxial cable network.

**2.** Information Networking Architecture. Bellcore object-oriented architecture for the management of ATM and SONET equipment and services in an operating company environment.

### INAP
Intelligent Network Application Part. SS7 architectural protocol layer.

### INASoft
Bellcore implementation of INA. See also *INA*.

### INB
Install Busy. Entity has just been created but has not been commanded In-Service or Out-of-Service yet.

### in-band signaling
Transmission within a frequency range normally used for information transmission. Compare with *out-of-band signaling*.

### INCRP
Intelligent Network Call Routing Protocol. The communication protocol used by ICM gateways to pass a routing request and response between two ICMs. The ICM sending the request must be set up for remote network routing and the ICM receiving the request must be running an INCRP Network Interface Controller (NIC).

### incumbent local exchange carrier
See *ILEC*.

### Industry-Standard Architecture
See *ISA*.

### INE
Intelligent Network Element. Network element that can be provisioned from a remote OSS.

### information element
In ATM, the portion of a signaling packet that carries information, such as addresses, used in the UNI specification. See also *UNI*.

### Information Infrastructure Technology and Applications
See *IITA*.

**infrared**

Electromagnetic waves whose frequency range is above that of microwaves, but below that of the visible spectrum. LAN systems based on this technology represent an emerging technology.

**ingress noise**

Over-the-air signals that are coupled inadvertently into the nominally closed coaxial cable distribution system. Ingress noise is difficult to track down and intermittent in nature.

**initial domain identifier**

See *IDI*.

**initial domain part**

See *IDP*.

**INOC**

Internet Network Operations Center. BBN group that in the early days of the Internet monitored and controlled the Internet core gateways (routers). INOC no longer exists in this form.

**inpulse rule**

A sequence of instructions that define autonomous call processing actions to be completed on incoming ports in the Cisco VCO/4K switch. See also *answer supervision template* and *outpulse rule*.

**input/output**

See *IN/AIN*.

**Institute of Electrical and Electronics Engineers**

See *IEEE*.

**insured burst**

In an ATM network, the largest burst of data above the insured rate that temporarily is allowed on a PVC and not tagged by the traffic policing function for dropping in the case of network congestion. The insured burst is specified in bytes or cells. Compare with *maximum burst*. See also *insured rate*.

**insured rate**

Long-term data throughput, in bits or cells per second, that an ATM network commits to support under normal network conditions. The insured rate is 100 percent allocated; the entire amount is deducted from the total trunk bandwidth along the path of the circuit. Compare with *excess rate* and *maximum rate*. See also *insured burst*.

**insured traffic**

Traffic within the insured rate specified for an ATM PVC. This traffic should not be dropped by the network under normal network conditions. See also *CLP* and *insured rate*.

**INTAP**

Interoperability Technology Association for Information Processing. Technical organization that has the official charter to develop Japanese OSI profiles and conformance tests.

**Integrated IS-IS**

Routing protocol based on the OSI routing protocol IS-IS but with support for IP and other protocols. Integrated IS-IS implementations send only one set of routing updates, making it more efficient than two separate implementations. Formerly called Dual IS-IS. Compare with *IS-IS*.

**Integrated Services Digital Network**

See *ISDN*.

**Integrated Services Internet**

IETF proposal for enhancing IP to allow it to support integrated or multimedia services, including traffic management mechanisms that closely match the traffic management mechanisms of ATM. An example is RSVP.

**Intelligent QoS Management Suite**

Composed of Automatic Routing Management, Advanced CoS Management, Optimized Bandwidth Management, and Dynamic Buffer Management. Formerly called Advanced Networking Features.

**interarea routing**

Term used to describe routing between two or more logical areas. Compare with *intra-area routing*.

**Interdomain Policy Routing**

See *IDPR*.

### interface

**1.** Connection between two systems or devices.

**2.** In routing terminology, a network connection.

**3.** In telephony, a shared boundary defined by common physical interconnection characteristics, signal characteristics, and meanings of interchanged signals.

**4.** Boundary between adjacent layers of the OSI model.

### interface message processor

See *IMP*.

### interface processor

See *interface processor* in the "Cisco Systems Terms and Acronyms" section.

### interference

Unwanted communication channel noise.

### Interim Local Management Interface

See *ILMI*.

### Interior Gateway Protocol

See *IGP*.

### Interior Gateway Routing Protocol

See *IGRP* in the "Cisco Systems Terms and Acronyms" section.

### intermediate routing node

See *IRN*.

### Intermediate Session Routing

See *ISR*.

### intermediate system

See *IS*.

### Intermediate System-to-Intermediate System

See *IS-IS*.

### International Code Designator

See *ICD*.

**International Data Number**

See *X.121*.

**International Electrotechnical Commission**

See *IEC*.

**International Federation for Information Processing**

See *IFIP*.

**International Organization for Standardization**

See *ISO*.

**International Standards Organization**

Erroneous expansion of the acronym ISO. See *ISO*.

**International Telecommunication Union Telecommunication Standardization Sector**

See *ITU-T*.

**internet**

Short for internetwork. Not to be confused with the Internet. See *internetwork*.

**Internet**

Largest global internetwork, connecting tens of thousands of networks worldwide and having a "culture" that focuses on research and standardization based on real-life use. Many leading-edge network technologies come from the Internet community. The Internet evolved in part from ARPANET. At one time, called the DARPA Internet. Not to be confused with the general term internet. See also *ARPANET*.

**Internet address**

See *IP address*.

**Internet Architecture Board**

See *ICP cell*.

**Internet Assigned Numbers Authority**

See *IANA*.

**Internet Control Message Protocol**

See *ICMP*.

**Internet Engineering Planning Group**

See *IEPG*.

**Internet Engineering Steering Group**

See *IESG*.

**Internet Engineering Task Force**

See *IETF*.

**Internet Group Management Protocol**

See *IGMP*.

**Internet Message Access Protocol**

See *IMAP*.

**Internet Network Operations Center**

See *INOC*.

**Internet protocol**

See also *IP*. See also *TCP/IP*.

**Internet Protocol (IP, IPv4)**

Network layer for the TCP/IP protocol suite. Internet Protocol (version 4) is a connectionless, best-effort packet switching protocol. Defined in RFC 791.

**Internet Protocol (IPng, IPv6)**

See *IPv6*.

**Internet Registry**

See *IR*.

**Internet Relay Chat**

See *IRC*.

**Internet Research Steering Group**

See *IRSG*.

**Internet Research Task Force**

See *IRTF*.

**Internet service provider**

See *ISP*.

**Internet Society**

See *ISOC*.

**Internet telephony**

Generic term used to describe various approaches to running voice telephony over IP.

**Internet-Draft**

See *I-D*.

**internetwork**

Collection of networks interconnected by routers and other devices that functions (generally) as a single network. Sometimes called an internet, which is not to be confused with the Internet.

**Internetwork Packet Exchange**

See *IPX*.

**internetworking**

General term used to refer to the industry devoted to connecting networks together. The term can refer to products, procedures, and technologies.

**InterNIC**

Organization that serves the Internet community by supplying user assistance, documentation, training, registration service for Internet domain names, and other services. Formerly called NIC.

**interoperability**

Capability of computing equipment manufactured by different vendors to communicate with one another successfully over a network.

**Inter-Switch Link**

See *ISL* in the "Cisco Systems Terms and Acronyms" section.

**Inter-Switching System Interface**

See *ISSI*.

**intra-area routing**

Term used to describe routing within a logical area. Compare with *interarea routing*.

### intrusion detection

Security service that monitors and analyzes system events for the purpose of finding (and providing real-time or near real-time warning of) attempts to access system resources in an unauthorized manner.

### Inverse Address Resolution Protocol

See *Inverse ARP*.

### Inverse ARP

Inverse Address Resolution Protocol. Method of building dynamic routes in a network. Allows an access server to discover the network address of a device associated with a virtual circuit.

### inverse multiplexing

Process whereby physical links are grouped to form a higher-bandwidth logical link whose rate is approximately the sum of the individual link rates.

### IOC

independent operating company. Independently owned company providing local telephone services to residential and business customers in a geographic area not served by an RBOC.

### IOCC

I/O channel controller.

### IONL

Internal Organization of the Network Layer. OSI standard for the detailed architecture of the network layer. Basically, it partitions the network layer into subnetworks interconnected by convergence protocols (equivalent to internet working protocols), creating what the Internet community calls a catenet or an internet.

### IOS

See *Cisco IOS* in the "Cisco Systems Terms and Acronyms" section.

### IP

Internet Protocol. Network layer protocol in the TCP/IP stack offering a connectionless internetwork service. IP provides features for addressing, type-of-service specification, fragmentation and reassembly, and security. Defined in RFC 791.

### IP address

32-bit address assigned to hosts using TCP/IP. An IP address belongs to one of five classes (A, B, C, D, or E) and is written as 4 octets separated by periods (dotted decimal format). Each address consists of a network number, an optional subnetwork number, and a host number. The network and subnetwork numbers together are used for routing, and the host number is used to address an individual host within the network or subnetwork. A subnet mask is used to extract network and subnetwork information from the IP address. CIDR provides a new way of representing IP addresses and subnet masks. Also called an Internet address. See also *CIDR*, *IP*, and *subnet mask*.

### IP datagram

Fundamental unit of information passed across the Internet. Contains source and destination addresses along with data and a number of fields that define such things as the length of the datagram, the header checksum, and flags to indicate whether the datagram can be (or was) fragmented.

### IP explicit path

A list of IP addresses, each representing a node or a link in the explicit path.

### IP multicast

Routing technique that allows IP traffic to be propagated from one source to a number of destinations or from many sources to many destinations. Rather than sending one packet to each destination, one packet is sent to a multicast group identified by a single IP destination group address.

### IP Multicast Heartbeat

Users of the multicast routing feature need a way to monitor the health of multicast delivery and be alerted when the delivery fails to meet certain parameters.

### IP multicast Multilayer Switching (MLS)

Feature that provides high-performance, hardware-based, Layer 3 switching of IP multicast traffic for routers connected to Catalyst 5000 series LAN switches. An IP multicast flow is a unidirectional sequence of packets between a multicast source and the members of a destination multicast group. Flows are based on the IP address of the source device and the destination IP multicast group address. IP multicast MLS switches IP multicast data packet flows between IP subnets using advanced, application-specific integrated circuit (ASIC) switching hardware, thereby off-loading processor-intensive, multicast packet routing from network routers. The packet forwarding function is moved onto the connected Layer 3 switch whenever a supported path exists between a source and members of a multicast group. Packets that do not have a supported path to reach their destinations still are forwarded in software by routers. Protocol Independent Multicast (PIM) is used for route determination.

### IP over ATM

Suite used to send IP datagram packets between nodes on the Internet.

### IP Precedence

A 3-bit value in the type of service (TOS) byte used for assigning precedence to IP packets.

### IP Security Option

See *IPSO*.

### IP spoofing

IP spoofing attack occurs when an attacker outside your network pretends to be a trusted user either by using an IP address that is within the range of IP addresses for your network or by using an authorized external IP address that you trust and to which you want to provide access to specified resources on your network. Should an attacker get access to your IPSec security parameters, that attacker can masquerade as the remote user authorized to connect to the corporate network.

### IP telephony

The transmission of voice and fax *phone calls* over data networks that uses the Internet Protocol (IP). IP telephony is the result of the transformation of the *circuit-switched* telephone network to a packet-based network that deploys voice-compression algorithms and flexible and sophisticated transmission techniques, and delivers richer services using only a fraction of traditional digital telephony's usual bandwidth. Compare with *VoIP*.

With Layer 2 switching, frames are switched based on Media Access Control (MAC) address information. Layer 2 switching does not look inside a packet for network-layer information as does Layer 3 switching. Layer 2 switching is performed by looking at a destination MAC address within a frame. It looks at the frame destination address and sends it to the appropriate interface if it knows the destination address location. Layer 2 switching builds and maintains a switching table that keeps track of the MAC addresses that belong to each port or interface. Compare with *Layer 3 switching*.

### IPC

interprocess communications. This mechanism makes it possible to create large systems that are complex in function, yet simple and streamlined in design.

### IPCP

IP Control Protocol. Protocol that establishes and configures IP over PPP. See also *IP* and *PPP*.

## IPng

See *IPv6*.

## IPSec

IP Security. A framework of open standards that provides data confidentiality, data integrity, and data authentication between participating peers. IPSec provides these security services at the IP layer. IPSec uses IKE to handle the negotiation of protocols and algorithms based on local policy and to generate the encryption and authentication keys to be used by IPSec. IPSec can protect one or more data flows between a pair of hosts, between a pair of security gateways, or between a security gateway and a host.

## IPSO

IP Security Option. U.S. government specification that defines an optional field in the IP packet header that defines hierarchical packet security levels on a per interface basis.

## IPv6

IP version 6. Replacement for the current version of IP (version 4). IPv6 includes support for flow ID in the packet header, which can be used to identify flows. Formerly called IPng (next generation).

## IPX

Internetwork Packet Exchange. NetWare network layer (Layer 3) protocol used for transferring data from servers to workstations. IPX is similar to IP and XNS.

## IPXCP

IPX Control Protocol. Protocol that establishes and configures IPX over PPP. See also *IPX* and *PPP*.

## IPXWAN

IPX wide-area network. Protocol that negotiates end-to-end options for new links. When a link comes up, the first IPX packets sent across are IPXWAN packets negotiating the options for the link. When the IPXWAN options are determined successfully, normal IPX transmission begins. Defined by RFC 1362.

## IR

**1.** intermediate reach. The distance specification for optical systems that operate effectively from 3 to 20 km (1.8 to 12.5 mi).

**2.** Internet Registry. IR was delegated the responsibility of network address and autonomuous system identifiers from the IANA, which has the discretionary authority to delegate portions of its responsibility.

**IRB**

integrated routing and bridging. Integrated Services Digital Network (ISDN) User Part. An upper-layer application supported by SS7 for connection set up and tear down.

**IRC**

Internet Relay Chat. World-wide "party line" protocol that allows one to converse with others in real time. IRC is structured as a network of servers, each of which accepts connections from client programs, one per user.

**IRDP**

ICMP Router Discovery Protocol. Protocol that enables a host to determine the address of a router that it can use as a default gateway. Similar to ES-IS but used with IP. See also *ES-IS*.

**IRN**

intermediate routing node. In SNA, a subarea node with intermediate routing capability.

**IRR**

A RAS message sent as an information request.

**IRSG**

Internet Research Steering Group. Group that is part of the IAB and oversees the activities of the IRTF. See also *ICP cell* and *IRTF*.

**IRTF**

Internet Research Task Force. Community of network experts that considers Internet-related research topics. The IRTF is governed by the IRSG and is considered a subsidiary of the IAB. See also *ICP cell* and *IRSG*.

**IS**

**1.** intermediate system. Routing node in an OSI network.

**2.** Telecommunications: In-Service. Entity is fully operational and capable of providing service to a requesting entity.

**ISA**

Industry-Standard Architecture. 16-bit bus used for Intel-based personal computers. See also *EISA*.

### ISAKMP

Internet Security Association and Key Management Protocol. Internet IPSec protocol [RFC 2408] that negotiates, establishes, modifies, and deletes security associations. It also exchanges key generation and authentication data (independent of the details of any specific key generation technique), key establishment protocol, encryption algorithm, or authentication mechanism.

### isarithmic flow control

Flow control technique that permits travel through the network. Isarithmic flow control is not commonly implemented.

### ISDN

Integrated Services Digital Network. Communication protocol offered by telephone companies that permits telephone networks to carry data, voice, and other source traffic. See also *BISDN*, *BRI*, *N-ISDN*, and *PRI*.

### IS-IS

Intermediate System-to-Intermediate System. OSI link-state hierarchical routing protocol based on DECnet Phase V routing, whereby ISs (routers) exchange routing information based on a single metric to determine network topology. Compare with *Integrated IS-IS*. See also *ES-IS* and *OSPF*.

### IS-IS Hello

See *IIH*.

### IS-IS Interdomain Routing Protocol

See *IDRP*.

### ISL

See *ISL* in the "Cisco Systems Terms and Acronyms" section.

### ISM

internetwork status monitor.

### ISO

International Organization for Standardization. International organization that is responsible for a wide range of standards, including those relevant to networking. ISO developed the OSI reference model, a popular networking reference model.

## ISO 3309

HDLC procedures developed by ISO. ISO 3309:1979 specifies the HDLC frame structure for use in synchronous environments. ISO 3309:1984 specifies proposed modifications to allow the use of HDLC in asynchronous environments as well.

## ISO 9000

Set of international quality-management standards defined by ISO. The standards, which are not specific to any country, industry, or product, allow companies to demonstrate that they have specific processes in place to maintain an efficient quality system.

## ISO development environment

See *ISODE*.

## ISOC

Internet Society. International nonprofit organization, founded in 1992, that coordinates the evolution and use of the Internet. In addition, ISOC delegates authority to other groups related to the Internet, such as the IAB. ISOC is headquartered in Reston, Virginia (United States). See also *ICP cell*.

## isochronous transmission

Asynchronous transmission over a synchronous data link. Isochronous signals require a constant bit rate for reliable transport. Compare with *asynchronous transmission*, *plesiochronous transmission*, and *synchronous transmission*.

## ISODE

ISO development environment. Large set of libraries and utilities used to develop upper-layer OSI protocols and applications.

## ISP

Internet service provider. Company that provides Internet access to other companies and individuals.

## ISR

Intermediate Session Routing. Initial routing algorithm used in APPN. ISR provides node-to-node connection-oriented routing. Network outages cause sessions to fail because ISR cannot provide nondisruptive rerouting around a failure. ISR was replaced by HPR. Compare with *HPR*. See also *APPN*.

## ISSI

Inter-Switching System Interface. Standard interface between SMDS switches.

### ISUP

ISDN User Part. SS7 protocol layer that defines the protocol used to prepare, manage, and release trunks that carry voice and data between calling and called parties.

### isup_console

When the cktint module is running, this process provides management functions for circuits and circuit groups for the SS7 application software in the Cisco VCO/4K.

### ITCM

Integrated Telephony Cable Modem. A DOCSIS CM that enables subscriber VoIP services.

### ITU

International Telecommunication Union. An organization established by the United Nations to set international telecommunications standards and to allocate frequencies for specific uses.

### ITU-T

International Telecommunication Union Telecommunication Standardization Sector. International body that develops worldwide standards for telecommunications technologies. The ITU-T carries out the functions of the former CCITT. See also *CCITT*.

### IV

initialization value. Input parameter that sets the starting state of a cryptographic algorithm or mode.

### IVR

interactive voice response. Term used to describe systems that provide information in the form of recorded messages over telephone lines in response to user input in the form of spoken words or, more commonly, DTMF signaling. Examples include banks that allow you to check your balance from any telephone and automated stock quote systems.

### IXC

inter-exchange carrier. Common carrier providing long distance connectivity between LATAs. The three major IXCs are AT&T, MCI, and Sprint, but several hundred IXCs offer long distance service in the United States.

### jabber

**1.** Error condition in which a network device continually transmits random, meaningless data onto the network.

**2.** In IEEE 802.3, a data packet whose length exceeds that prescribed in the standard.

### JANET

Joint Academic Network. X.25 WAN connecting university and research institutions in the United Kingdom.

### Japan UNIX Network

See *JUNET*.

### Java

Object-oriented programming language developed at Sun Microsystems to solve a number of problems in modern programming practice. The Java language is used extensively on the World Wide Web, particularly for applets.

### JDBC

Java Database Connectivity. Java API that enables Java programs to execute SQL statements. This allows Java programs to interact with any SQL-compliant database. Because nearly all relational database management systems (DBMSs) support SQL, and because Java itself runs on most platforms, JDBC makes it possible to write a single database application that can run on different platforms and can interact with different DBMSs. JDBC is similar to ODBC but is designed specifically for Java programs, whereas ODBC is language-independent. JDBC was developed by JavaSoft, a subsidiary of Sun Microsystems. See also *ODBC*.

### jitter

**1.** The interpacket delay variance; that is, the difference between interpacket arrival and departure. Jitter is an important QoS metric for voice and video applications.

**2.** Analog communication line distortion caused by the variation of a signal from its reference timing positions. Jitter can cause data loss, particularly at high speeds.

**John von Neumann Computer Network**

See *JvNCnet*.

**Joint Academic Network**

See *JANET*.

**JPEG**

Joint Photographics Expert Group. Graphic file format that was adopted as a standard by the ITU-T and the ISO. JPEG most often is used to compress still images using DCT analysis.

**JTAPI**

Java Telephony Application Programming Interface. A call control model developed by Sun Microsystems.

**jumper**

Electrical switch consisting of a number of pins and a connector that can be attached to the pins in a variety of ways. Different circuits are created by attaching the connector to different pins.

**junction**

A junction is a point in the telecommunications network that comprises a switching office or facility cross-connect and/or ADM hardware, a point of connectivity where multiple fiber links come together, and/or a source or destination for a wavelength path.

**JUNET**

Japan UNIX Network. Nationwide, noncommercial network in Japan, designed to promote communication between Japanese and other researchers.

**JvNCnet**

John von Neumann Computer Network. A regional network, owned and operated by Global Enterprise Services, Inc., composed of T1 and slower serial links that provide midlevel networking services to sites in the Northeastern United States.

### KA9Q

Popular implementation of TCP/IP and associated protocols for amateur packet radio systems.

### Karn's algorithm

Algorithm that improves round-trip time estimations by helping transport layer protocols distinguish between good and bad round-trip time samples.

### Kb

kilobit. Approximately 1,000 bits.

### KB

kilobyte. Approximately 1,000 bytes.

### kbps

kilobits per second. A bit rate expressed in thousands of bits per second.

### kBps

kilobytes per second. A bit rate expressed in thousands of bytes per second.

### keepalive interval

Period of time between each keepalive message sent by a network device.

### keepalive message

Message sent by one network device to inform another network device that the virtual circuit between the two is still active.

### KEK

key-encrypting key. Cryptographic key that is used to encrypt other keys, either DEKs or other KEKs, but usually is not used to encrypt application data.

### Kerberos

Developing standard for authenticating network users. Kerberos offers two key benefits: it functions in a multivendor network, and it does not transmit passwords over the network.

### Kermit

Popular file-transfer and terminal-emulation program.

### key distribution

Process that delivers a cryptographic key from the location where it is generated to the locations where it is used in a cryptographic algorithm.

### key establishment (algorithm or protocol)

Process that combines the key generation and key distribution steps needed to set up or install a secure communication association.

### key pair

Set of mathematically related keys—a public key and a private key—that are used for asymmetric cryptography and are generated in a way that makes it computationally infeasible to derive the private key from knowledge of the public key.

### key recovery

**1.** Process for learning the value of a cryptographic key that previously was used to perform some cryptographic operation.

**2.** Techniques that provide an intentional, alternate (that is, secondary) means to access the key used for data confidentiality service in an encrypted association.

### kilobit

Abbreviated Kb.

### kilobits per second

Abbreviated kbps.

### kilobyte

Abbreviated KB.

### kilobytes per second

Abbreviated kBps.

### kVA

kilovoltampere.

### L2F Protocol

Layer 2 Forwarding Protocol. Protocol that supports the creation of secure virtual private dial-up networks over the Internet.

### L2TP session

Communications transactions between the LAC and the LNS that support tunneling of a single PPP connection. There is a one-to-one relationship among the PPP connection, L2TP session, and L2TP call.

### LAA

Longest Available Agent. The agent that has been continuously in the Available state for the longest time. The ICM can examine services or skill groups from different peripherals and route a call to the service or group with the longest available agent. (This feature is not supported on Rockwell ACDs.)

### label

A short fixed-length label that tells switching nodes how the data (packets or cells) should be forwarded.

### label controlled switch

The label switch controller and the controlled ATM switch that it controls, viewed together as a unit.

### label imposition

The act of putting the first label on a packet.

### label swapping

Routing algorithm used by APPN in which each router that a message passes through on its way to its destination independently determines the best path to the next router.

### label switch

A node that forwards units of data (packets or cells) on the basis of labels.

### LAC

L2TP access concentrator. A node that acts as one side of an L2TP tunnel endpoint and is a peer to the L2TP network server (LNS). The LAC sits between an LNS and a remote system and forwards packets to and from each. Packets sent from the LAC to the LNS require tunneling with the L2TP protocol as defined in this document. The connection from the LAC to the remote system is either local or a PPP link.

### laddr

local address. Address of a host on a protected interface.

### lambda

The 11th letter of the Greek alphabet. Lambda is used as the symbol for wavelength in lightwave systems.

### LAN

local-area network. High-speed, low-error data network covering a relatively small geographic area (up to a few thousand meters). LANs connect workstations, peripherals, terminals, and other devices in a single building or other geographically limited area. LAN standards specify cabling and signaling at the physical and data link layers of the OSI model. Ethernet, FDDI, and Token Ring are widely used LAN technologies. Compare with *MAN* and *WAN*.

### LAN emulation

See *LANE*.

### LAN Emulation Client

See *LEC*.

### LAN Emulation Configuration Server

See *LECS*.

### LAN Emulation Server

See *LES*.

### LAN Manager

Distributed NOS, developed by Microsoft, that supports a variety of protocols and platforms. See also *NOS*.

### LAN Manager for UNIX

See *LM/X*.

**LAN Network Manager**

See *LNM*.

**LAN Server**

Server-based NOS developed by IBM and derived from LNM. See also *LNM*.

**LAN switch**

High-speed switch that forwards packets between data-link segments. Most LAN switches forward traffic based on MAC addresses. This variety of LAN switch is sometimes called a frame switch. LAN switches often are categorized according to the method they use to forward traffic: cut-through packet switching or store-and-forward packet switching. Multilayer switches are an intelligent subset of LAN switches. Compare with *multilayer switch*. See also *cut-through packet switching* and *store and forward packet switching*.

**LANE**

LAN emulation. Technology that allows an ATM network to function as a LAN backbone. The ATM network must provide multicast and broadcast support, address mapping (MAC-to-ATM), SVC management, and a usable packet format. LANE also defines Ethernet and Token Ring ELANs. See also *ELAN*.

**LANE UNI**

LANE User-Network Interface.

**LAPB**

Link Access Procedure, Balanced. Data link layer protocol in the X.25 protocol stack. LAPB is a bit-oriented protocol derived from HDLC. See also *HDLC* and *X.25*.

**LAPD**

Link Access Procedure on the D channel. ISDN data link layer protocol for the D channel. LAPD was derived from the LAPB protocol and is designed primarily to satisfy the signaling requirements of ISDN basic access. Defined by ITU-T Recommendations Q.920 and Q.921.

**LAPM**

Link Access Procedure for Modems. ARQ used by modems implementing the V.42 protocol for error correction. See also *ARQ* and *V.42*.

### laser

light amplification by stimulated emission of radiation. Analog transmission device in which a suitable active material is excited by an external stimulus to produce a narrow beam of coherent light that can be modulated into pulses to carry data. Networks based on laser technology are sometimes run over SONET.

### LAT

local-area transport. A network virtual terminal protocol developed by Digital Equipment Corporation.

### LATA

local access and transport area. Geographic telephone dialing area serviced by a single local telephone company. Calls within LATAs are called local calls. There are more than 100 LATAs in the United States.

### latency

**1.** Delay between the time a device requests access to a network and the time it is granted permission to transmit.

**2.** Delay between the time a device receives a frame and the time that frame is forwarded out the destination port.

### Layer 2 Tunnel Protocol (L2TP)

An Internet Engineering Task Force (IETF) standards track protocol defined in RFC 2661 that provides tunneling of PPP. Based upon the best features of L2F and PPTP, L2TP provides an industry-wide interoperable method of implementing VPDN.

### Layer 3 Switching

Emerging Layer 3 switching technology that integrates routing with switching to yield very high routing throughput rates in the millions-of-packets- per-second range. The movement to Layer 3 switching is designed to address the downsides of the current generation of Layer 2 switches, which functionally are equivalent to bridges. These downsides for a large, flat network include being subject to broadcast storms, spanning tree loops, and address limitations.

### LBR

label bit rate. Service category defined by this document for label VC traffic. Link and per-VC bandwidth sharing can be controlled by relative bandwidth configuration at the edge and each switch along a label VC. No ATM traffic-related parameters are specified.

**LC-ATM interface**

label-controlled ATM interface. An MPLS interface in which labels are carried in the VPI or VCI fields of the ATM cells and in which VC connections are established under the control of MPLS software.

**LCD**

liquid crystal display. An alphanumeric display on computers and fax devices using liquid crystal sealed between two pieces of glass.

**LCI**

logical channel identifier. See also *VCN*.

**LCN**

logical channel number. See also *VCN*.

**LCP**

link control protocol. Protocol that establishes, configures, and tests data-link connections for use by PPP. See also *PPP*.

**LCV**

line code violation. Occurrence of a BPV or EXZ error event.

**LDAP**

Lightweight Directory Access Protocol. Protocol that provides access for management and browser applications that provide read/write interactive access to the X.500 Directory.

**LDCELP**

low-delay CELP. CELP voice compression algorithm providing 16 kbps, or 4:1 compression. Standardized in ITU-T Recommendation G.728.

**LDIF**

LDAP Data Interchange Format. An LDAP server interchange format in which each record's field value is on a separate line and records are separated by an empty line.

**LDP**

label distribution protocol. A standard protocol between MPLS-enabled routers to negotiate the labels (addresses) used to forward packets. This protocol is not supported in Cisco IOS Release 12.0. The Cisco proprietary version of this protocol is the Tag Distribution Protocol (TDP).

## LE_ARP

LAN Emulation Address Resolution Protocol. Protocol that provides the ATM address that corresponds to a MAC address.

## leaf internetwork

In a star topology, an internetwork whose sole access to other internetworks in the star is through a core router.

## leaky bucket

In ATM, a metaphor for the GCRA, which is used for conformance checking of cell flows from a user or a network. The hole in the bucket represents the sustained rate at which cells can be accommodated, and the bucket depth represents the tolerance for cell bursts over a period of time. See also *GCRA*.

## learning bridge

Bridge that performs MAC address learning to reduce traffic on the network. Learning bridges manage a database of MAC addresses and the interfaces associated with each address. See also *MAC address learning*.

## leased line

Transmission line reserved by a communications carrier for the private use of a customer. A leased line is a type of dedicated line. See also *dedicated line*.

## LEC

**1.** local exchange carrier. A telephone company that provides customer access to the world-wide public switched network through one of its central offices.

**2.** LAN Emulation Client. Entity in an end system that performs data forwarding, address resolution, and other control functions for a single ES within a single ELAN. An LEC also provides a standard LAN service interface to any higher-layer entity that interfaces to the LEC. Each LEC is identified by a unique ATM address, and is associated with one or more MAC addresses reachable through that ATM address. See also *ELAN* and *LES*.

## LECS

LAN Emulation Configuration Server. Entity that assigns individual LANE clients to particular ELANs by directing them to the LES that corresponds to the ELAN. There is logically one LECS per administrative domain, and this serves all ELANs within that domain. See also *ELAN*.

## LED

light emitting diode. Semiconductor device that emits light produced by converting electrical energy. Status lights on hardware devices are typically LEDs.

## LEN node

low-entry networking node. In SNA, a PU 2.1 that supports LU protocols, but whose CP cannot communicate with other nodes. Because there is no CP-to-CP session between a LEN node and its NN, the LEN node must have a statically defined image of the APPN network.

## LES

LAN Emulation Server. Entity that implements the control function for a particular ELAN. There is only one logical LES per ELAN, and it is identified by a unique ATM address. See also *ELAN*.

## Level 1 router

Device that routes traffic within a single DECnet or OSI area.

## Level 2 router

Device that routes traffic between DECnet or OSI areas. All Level 2 routers must form a contiguous network.

## LFI

low-speed link features.

## LFIB

label forwarding information base. A data structure and way of managing forwarding in which destinations and incoming labels are associated with outgoing interfaces and labels.

## LFSR

linear feedback shift register. Mechanism for generating a sequence of binary bits. The register consists of a series of cells that are set by an initialization vector that is, most often, the secret key. The behavior of the register is regulated by a clock. At each clocking instant, the contents of the cells of the register are shifted right by one position, and the exclusive-or of a subset of the cell contents is placed in the leftmost cell. One bit of output usually is derived during this update procedure.

## LGN

logical group node. The node that represents its peer group in the peer group's parent peer group. See also *parent peer group* and *peer group*.

### license

Purchased right to transmit RF waves over a given BTA for typically periods of 10 years. The license tightly governs the design parameters of an RF system and its use. RF licenses typically are purchased from the FCC on an auction basis.

The FCC provides licenses to ensure maximum competition in a free market (although this is not always obvious in the way the FCC manages the auctions) and spectral efficiency, which is another way of stating efficient use of the RF spectrum.

### light amplification by stimulated emission of radiation

See *laser*.

### light emitting diode

See *LED*.

### limited resource link

Resource defined by a device operator to remain active only when being used.

### limited-route explorer packet

See *spanning explorer packet*.

### line

**1.** In SNA, a connection to the network.

**2.** See *link*.

### line card

Any I/O card that can be inserted in a modular chassis.

### line code type

One of a number of coding schemes used on serial lines to maintain data integrity and reliability. The line code type used is determined by the carrier service provider. See also *AMI*, *B8ZS*, and *HDB3*.

### line code violation

See *LCV*.

### line conditioning

Use of equipment on leased voice-grade channels to improve analog characteristics, thereby allowing higher transmission rates.

### line driver

Inexpensive amplifier and signal converter that conditions digital signals to ensure reliable transmissions over extended distances.

**line of sight**

Characteristic of certain transmission systems, such as laser, microwave, and infrared systems, in which no obstructions in a direct path between transmitter and receiver can exist.

**line printer daemon**

See *LPD*.

**line turnaround**

Time required to change data transmission direction on a telephone line.

**line-terminating equipment**

See *LTE*.

**link**

**1.** Network communications channel consisting of a circuit or transmission path and all related equipment between a sender and a receiver. Most often used to refer to a WAN connection. Sometimes referred to as a line or a transmission link.

**2.** In the context of a transmission network, a link is a point-to-point connection between adjacent nodes, such as two Cisco ONS 15900s. There can be more than one link between adjacent nodes.

**link layer**

See *data-link layer*.

**link-by-link encryption**

Stepwise protection of data that flows between two points in a network, provided by encrypting data separately on each network link, that is, by encrypting data when it leaves a host or subnetwork relay and decrypting when it arrives at the next host or relay. Each link can use a different key or even a different algorithm.

**link-layer address**

See *MAC address*.

**link-state advertisement**

See *LSA*.

**link-state packet**

See *LSA*.

**link-state routing algorithm**

Routing algorithm in which each router broadcasts or multicasts information regarding the cost of reaching each of its neighbors to all nodes in the internetwork. Link state algorithms create a consistent view of the network and therefore are not prone to routing loops; however, they achieve this at the cost of relatively greater computational difficulty and more widespread traffic (compared with distance vector routing algorithms). Compare with *distance vector routing algorithm*. See also *Dijkstra's algorithm*.

**LIS**

logical IP subnet. A group of IP nodes (such as hosts and routers) that connects to a single ATM network and belongs to the same IP subnet.

**listserv**

Automated mailing list distribution system originally designed for the Bitnet/EARN network. Allows users to add or delete themselves from mailing lists without (other) human intervention.

**little-endian**

Method of storing or transmitting data in which the least significant bit or byte is presented first. Compare with *big-endian*.

**LLAP**

LocalTalk Link Access Protocol. Link-level protocol that manages node-to-node delivery of data on a LocalTalk network. LLAP manages bus access, provides a node-addressing mechanism, and controls data transmission and reception, ensuring packet length and integrity. See also *LocalTalk*.

**LLC**

Logical Link Control. The higher of the two data link layer sublayers defined by the IEEE. The LLC sublayer handles error control, flow control, framing, and MAC-sublayer addressing. The most prevalent LLC protocol is IEEE 802.2, which includes both connectionless and connection-oriented variants. See also *data-link layer* and *MAC*.

**LLC2**

Logical Link Control, type 2. Connection-oriented OSI LLC-sublayer protocol. See also *LLC*.

**LM/X**

LAN Manager for UNIX. Monitors LAN devices in UNIX environments.

## LMDS

Local Multipoint Distribution Service; a relatively low power license for broadcasting voice, video, and data. There are typically two licenses granted in three frequencies, each to separate entities within a BTA. These licenses are known as Block A or Block B licenses. Block A licenses operate from 27.5 to 28.35 GHz, 29.10 to 29.25 GHz, and 31.075 to 31.225 GHz for a total of 1.159 MHz of bandwidth. Block B licenses operate from 31.00 to 31.075 GHz and 31.225 to 31.300 for a total of 150 MHz of bandwidth. LMDS systems have a typical maximum transmission range of approximately 3 miles as opposed to the transmission range of an MMDS system, which is typically 25 miles. This difference in range is primarily a function of physics and FCC allocated output power rates.

## LMI

Local Management Interface. Set of enhancements to the basic Frame Relay specification. LMI includes support for a keepalive mechanism, which verifies that data is flowing; a multicast mechanism, which provides the network server with its local DLCI and the multicast DLCI; global addressing, which gives DLCIs global rather than local significance in Frame Relay networks; and a status mechanism, which provides an on-going status report on the DLCIs known to the switch. Known as *LMT* in ANSI terminology.

## LMT

See *LMT* in the "Cisco Systems Terms and Acronyms" section.

## LNM

LAN Network Manager. SRB and Token Ring management package provided by IBM. Typically running on a PC, it monitors SRB and Token Ring devices, and can pass alerts up to NetView.

## LNNI

LAN Emulation Network-to-Network Interface. Supports communication between the server components within a single ELAN. Phase 1 LANE protocols do not allow for the standard support of multiple LESs or BUSs within an ELAN. Phase 2 addresses these limitations.

## LNS

L2TP network server. A node that acts as one side of an L2TP tunnel endpoint and is a peer to the L2TP access concentrator (LAC). The LNS is the logical termination point of a PPP session that is being tunneled from the remote system by the LAC. Analogous to the Layer 2 Forwarding (L2F) home gateway (HGW).

## load balancing

In routing, the capability of a router to distribute traffic over all its network ports that are the same distance from the destination address. Good load-balancing algorithms use both line speed and reliability information. Load balancing increases the use of network segments, thus increasing effective network bandwidth.

## local access and transport area

See *LATA*.

## local acknowledgment

Method whereby an intermediate network node, such as a router, responds to acknowledgments for a remote end host. Use of local acknowledgments reduces network overhead and, therefore, the risk of time-outs. Also known as *local termination*.

## local address

See *laddr*.

## local adjacency

See *local adjacency* in the "Cisco Systems Terms and Acronyms" section.

## local area network

See *LAN*.

## local bridge

Bridge that directly interconnects networks in the same geographic area.

## local exchange carrier

See *LEC*.

## local explorer packet

Packet generated by an end system in an SRB network to find a host connected to the local ring. If the local explorer packet fails to find a local host, the end system produces either a spanning explorer packet or an all-routes explorer packet. See also *all-routes explorer packet*, *explorer packet*, and *spanning explorer packet*.

## local loop

Line from the premises of a telephone subscriber to the telephone company CO.

## Local Management Interface

See *LMDS*.

**local termination**

See *local acknowledgment.*

**local traffic filtering**

Process by which a bridge filters out (drops) frames whose source and destination MAC addresses are located on the same interface on the bridge, thus preventing unnecessary traffic from being forwarded across the bridge. Defined in the IEEE 802.1 standard. See also *IEEE 802.1.*

**LocalTalk**

Apple Computer's proprietary baseband protocol that operates at the data link and physical layers of the OSI reference model. LocalTalk uses CSMA/CD and supports transmissions at speeds of 230.4 kbps.

**LocalTalk Link Access Protocol**

See *LLAP.*

**location server**

A SIP redirect or proxy server uses a location service to get information about the location of a caller. Location services are offered by location servers.

**LOCD**

loss of cell delineation. A SONET port status indicator that activates when an LOCD defect occurs and does not clear for an interval of time equal to the alarm integration period, which is typically 2.5 seconds.

**Lock-and-key**

Lock-and-key is a traffic filtering security feature that dynamically filters IP protocol traffic.

**LOF**

loss of frame. LOF is a generic term with various meanings depending on the signal standards domain in which it's being used.

A SONET port status indicator that activates when an LOF defect occurs and does not clear for an interval of time equal to the alarm integration period, which is typically 2.5 seconds.

**logic bomb**

Malicious logic that activates when specified conditions are met. Usually intended to cause denial of service or otherwise damage system resources.

**logical address**

See *network address*.

**logical channel**

Nondedicated, packet-switched communications path between two or more network nodes. Packet switching allows many logical channels to exist simultaneously on a single physical channel.

**loop**

Route where packets never reach their destination, but simply cycle repeatedly through a constant series of network nodes.

**loop start**

A method of signaling where a DC closure is applied to a phone line (loop), and the start of DC current flow indicates a change from on-hook to off-hook.

**loopback test**

Test in which signals are sent and then directed back toward their source from some point along the communications path. Loopback tests often are used to test network interface usability.

**loop-start trunk**

A two-wire central-office trunk or dial-tone line that recognizes offhook status when a telephone switch hook puts a 1000-ohm short across the tip and ring as the handset is lifted. Also called *POTS line* and *plain-service line*.

**LOP**

loss of pointer. Failure state in the SONET signal where a receiving network cannot identify/lock on the pointer value of the H1 and H2 bytes to show the location of SPE.

**LOS**

**1.** loss of signal. A loss of signal occurs when *n* consecutive zeros is detected on an incoming signal.

**2.** line of sight. Refers to the fact that there must be a clear, unobstructed path between the transmitters and receivers. This is essential for our LMDS products and enhances general performance in every RF deployment as opposed to partial or completely obstructed data paths. The opposite to LOS is NLOS, or Non Line of Sight.

**loss of frame**

See *LOF.*

**loss of pointer**

See *LOP.*

**loss of signal**

See *LOS.*

**lossy**

Characteristic of a network that is prone to lose packets when it becomes highly loaded.

**low-entry networking node**

See *LEN node*.

**LPD**

line printer daemon. Protocol used to send print jobs between UNIX systems.

**LR**

long reach. The distance specification for optical systems that operate effectively from 20 to 100 km (12.5 to 62 mi).

**LSA**

link-state advertisement. Broadcast packet used by link-state protocols that contains information about neighbors and path costs. LSAs are used by the receiving routers to maintain their routing tables. Sometimes called an *LSP.*

**LSB**

least significant bit. Bit zero, the bit of a binary number giving the number of ones, the last or rightmost bit when the number is written in the usual way.

**LSC**

**1.** label switch controller. Controller that creates cross-connects in an ATM switch so that labeled packets are forwarded through the switch, formerly referred to as Tag Switch Controller (TSC).

**2.** link state control. SS7 MTP 2 function that provides the overall coordination of a session.

**LSP**

link-state packet. See also *LSA.*

**LSP tunnel**

label switched path tunnel. A configured connection between two routers that uses MPLS to carry the packets.

**LSR**

label switch router. The role of an LSR is to forward packets in an MPLS network by looking only at the fixed-length label.

**LSSU**

link status signal unit. SS7 message that carries one or two octets (8-bit bytes) of link status information between signalling points at either end of a link. It is used to control link alignment and to provide the status of a signalling point (such as a local processor outage) to the remote signalling point.

**LTE**

line-terminating equipment. Network elements that originate and/or terminate line (OC-*n*) signals. LTEs originate, access, modify, and/or terminate the transport overhead.

**LU**

logical unit. Primary component of SNA, an NAU that enables end users to communicate with each other and to gain access to SNA network resources.

**LU 6.2**

logical unit 6.2. In SNA, an LU that provides peer-to-peer communication between programs in a distributed computing environment. APPC runs on LU 6.2 devices. See also *APPC*.

**LUNI**

LAN Emulation User-to-Network Interface. The ATM Forum standard for LAN emulation on ATM networks. Defines the interface between the LEC and the LAN Emulation Server components. See also *BUS*, *LES*, and *LECS*.

**LVC**

label switched controlled virtual circuit. A virtual circuit (VC) established under the control of MPLS. An LVC is neither a PVC nor an SVC. The LVC must traverse only a single hop in a label-switched path (LSP) but the LVC can traverse several ATM hops only if the LVC exists within a VP tunnel.

## MAC

Media Access Control. Lower of the two sublayers of the data link layer defined by the IEEE. The MAC sublayer handles access to shared media, such as whether token passing or contention will be used. See also *data-link layer* and *LLC*.

## MAC address

Standardized data link layer address that is required for every port or device that connects to a LAN. Other devices in the network use these addresses to locate specific ports in the network and to create and update routing tables and data structures. MAC addresses are 6 bytes long and are controlled by the IEEE. Also known as a *hardware address*, *MAC layer address*, and *physical address*. Compare with *network address*.

## MAC address learning

Service that characterizes a learning bridge, in which the source MAC address of each received packet is stored so that future packets destined for that address can be forwarded only to the bridge interface on which that address is located. Packets destined for unrecognized addresses are forwarded out every bridge interface. This scheme helps minimize traffic on the attached LANs. MAC address learning is defined in the IEEE 802.1 standard. See also *learning bridge* and *MAC address*.

## MacIP

Network layer protocol that encapsulates IP packets in DDP packets for transmission over AppleTalk. MacIP also provides proxy ARP services. See also *DDP* and *proxy ARP*.

## MAC layer address

See *MAC address*.

## MADI

multichannel audio digital interface. MADI is an interface standard described by the Audio Engineering Society (AES) standards AES-10 and AES-10id. It was developed by Neve, Sony, and SSL as an easy way to interface digital multitrack tape recorders to mixing consoles.

## MAE

metropolitan access exchange. One of a number of Internet exchange points. Examples include MAE West and MAE East. See also *CIX*, *FIX*, and *GIX*.

### mail bridge

Mail gateway that forwards e-mail between two or more networks while ensuring that the messages it forwards meet certain administrative criteria. A mail bridge is simply a specialized form of mail gateway that enforces an administrative policy with regard to what mail it forwards.

### mail exchange record

See *MX record*.

### mail exploder

Part of an e-mail delivery system that allows a message to be delivered to a list of addressees. Mail exploders are used to implement mailing lists. Users send messages to a single address (for example, hacks@somehost.edu), and the mail exploder takes care of delivery to the individual mailboxes in the list.

### mail gateway

Machine that connects two or more e-mail systems (especially dissimilar mail systems on two different networks) and transfers messages between them. Sometimes the mapping and translation can be quite complex, and generally it requires a store-and-forward scheme whereby the message is received from one system completely before it is transmitted to the next system after suitable translations.

### Maintenance Operation Protocol

See *MOP*.

### MAN

metropolitan-area network. Network that spans a metropolitan area. Generally, a MAN spans a larger geographic area than a LAN, but a smaller geographic area than a WAN. Compare with *LAN* and *WAN*.

### managed object

In network management, a network device that can be managed by a network management protocol.

### Management Information Base

See *MIB*.

### management services

SNA functions distributed among network components to manage and control an SNA network.

### Manchester encoding

Digital coding scheme, used by IEEE 802.3 and Ethernet, in which a mid–bit-time transition is used for clocking, and a 1 is denoted by a high level during the first half of the bit time.

### man-in-the-middle

Form of active wiretapping attack in which the attacker intercepts and selectively modifies communicated data to masquerade as one or more of the entities involved in a communication association.

### Manufacturing Automation Protocol

See *MAP*.

### MAP

Manufacturing Automation Protocol. Network architecture created by General Motors to meet the specific needs of the factory floor. MAP specifies a token-passing LAN similar to IEEE 802.4. See also *IEEE 802.4*.

### MARS

Multicast Address Resolution Server. Mechanism for supporting IP multicast. A MARS serves a group of nodes (known as a cluster); each node in the cluster is configured with the ATM address of the MARS. The MARS supports multicast through multicast messages of overlaid point-to-multipoint connections or through multicast servers.

### Martian

Humorous term applied to packets that turn up unexpectedly on the wrong network because of bogus routing entries. Also used as a name for a packet that has an altogether bogus (nonregistered or ill-formed) Internet address.

### mask

See *address mask* and *subnet mask*.

### masquerade attack

Type of attack in which one system entity illegitimately poses as (assumes the identity of) another entity.

**master control port**

A physical interface on an MPLS LSC that is connected to one end of a slave control link.

**MATIP**

mapping of airline traffic over IP. A standard defined in RFC 2351 for transporting airline reservation, ticketing, and messaging traffic over TCP/IP.

**MATV**

master antenna TV. A mini cable system relaying the broadcast channels usually to a block of flats or a small housing estate.

**MAU**

media attachment unit. Device used in Ethernet and IEEE 802.3 networks that provides the interface between the AUI port of a station and the common medium of the Ethernet. The MAU, which can be built into a station or can be a separate device, performs physical layer functions, including the conversion of digital data from the Ethernet interface, collision detection, and injection of bits onto the network. Sometimes referred to as a *media access unit* (also breviated *MAU*) or as a *transceiver*. In Token Ring, an MAU is known as a *multistation access unit* and usually is abbreviated *MSAU* to avoid confusion. See also *AUI* and *MSAU*.

**maximum burst**

Specifies the largest burst of data above the insured rate that will be allowed temporarily on an ATM PVC but will not be dropped at the edge by the traffic policing function, even if it exceeds the maximum rate. This amount of traffic will be allowed only temporarily; on average, the traffic source needs to be within the maximum rate. Specified in bytes or cells. Compare with *insured burst*. See also *maximum rate*.

**maximum rate**

Maximum total data throughput allowed on a given virtual circuit, equal to the sum of the insured and uninsured traffic from the traffic source. The uninsured data might be dropped if the network becomes congested. The maximum rate, which cannot exceed the media rate, represents the highest data throughput the virtual circuit will ever deliver, measured in bits or cells per second. Compare with *excess rate* and *insured rate*. See also *maximum burst*.

**maximum transmission unit**

See *MTU*.

**Mb**

megabit. Approximately 1,000,000 bits.

## MB

megabyte. Approximately 1,000,000 bytes.

## MBONE

multicast backbone. Multicast backbone of the Internet. MBONE is a virtual multicast network composed of multicast LANs and the point-to-point tunnels that interconnect them.

## Mbps

megabits per second. A bit rate expressed in millions of binary bits per second.

## MBps

megabits per second. A bit rate expressed in millions of binary bytes per second.

## MBS

maximum burst size. In an ATM signaling message, burst tolerance is conveyed through the MBS, which is coded as a number of cells. The burst tolerance together with the SCR and the GCRA determine the MBS that can be transmitted at the peak rate and still be in conformance with the GCRA. See also *SCP* and *GCRA*.

## MCA

micro channel architecture. Bus interface commonly used in PCs and some UNIX workstations and servers.

## MCDV

maximum cell delay variation. In an ATM network, the maximum two-point CDV objective across a link or a node for the specified service category. One of four link metrics exchanged using PTSPs to determine the available resources of an ATM network. There is one MCDV value for each traffic class. See also *CDV* and *PTSP*.

## MCLR

maximum cell loss ratio. In an ATM network, the maximum ratio of cells that do not successfully transit a link or node compared with the total number of cells that arrive at the link or node. One of four link metrics exchanged using PTSPs to determine the available resources of an ATM network. The MCLR applies to cells in the CBR and VBR traffic classes whose CLP bit is set to zero. See also *CBR*, *CLP*, *PTSP*, and *VBR*.

## MCNS

Multimedia Cable Network System Partners Ltd. Consortium of cable companies providing service to the majority of homes in the United States and Canada. This consortium drives a standard with the goal of having interoperable cable modems.

## MCR

minimum cell rate. Parameter defined by the ATM Forum for ATM traffic management. MCR is defined only for ABR transmissions, and specifies the minimum value for the ACR. See also *ABR (available bit rate)*, *ACOM*, and *PCR*.

## MCTD

maximum cell transfer delay. In an ATM network, the sum of the MCDV and the fixed delay component across the link or node. One of four link metrics exchanged using PTSPs to determine the available resources of an ATM network. There is one MCTD value for each traffic class. See also *MCDV* and *PTSP*.

## MD

mediation device. Device that provides protocol translation and concentration of telemetry information originating from multiple network elements and transport to an OSS. See also *OSS*.

## MD5

Message Digest 5. A one-way hashing algorithm that produces a 128-bit hash. Both MD5 and Secure Hash Algorithm (SHA) are variations on MD4 and are designed to strengthen the security of the MD4 hashing algorithm. Cisco uses hashes for authentication within the IPSec framework. Also used for message authentication in SNMP v.2. MD5 verifies the integrity of the communication, authenticates the origin, and checks for timeliness. See also *SNMP2*.

## MDL

The Cisco Message Definition Language; a high-level language used to specify protocols and protocol conversion operations on the VSC.

## MDN

message disposition notification. Message returned to the originator of an e-mail message indicating that the e-mail message has been opened. Specifications for MDN are described in RFC 2298.

## MDS

Message Delivery Service. The facilities used by ICM nodes to communicate with each other. The MDS plays a key role in keeping duplexed components synchronized.

## media

Plural of medium. Various physical environments through which transmission signals pass. Common network media include twisted-pair, coaxial, and fiber-optic cable, and the atmosphere (through which microwave, laser, and infrared transmission occurs). Sometimes called *physical media*.

**Media Access Control**
See *MAC*.

**media access unit**
See *MAU*.

**media attachment unit**
See *MAU*.

**Media Gateway**
A gateway that supports both bearer traffic and signaling traffic.

**Media Gateway Controller**
Another term for call agent.

**media interface connector**
See *MIC*.

**media rate**
Maximum traffic throughput for a particular media type.

**media stream**
A single media instance, for example, an audio stream.

**medium**
See *media*.

**megabit**
Abbreviated Mb. Approximately 1,000,000 bits.

**megabits per second**
Abbreviated Mbps.

**megabyte**
Abbreviated MB. Approximately 1,000,000 bytes.

**MEL CAS**
Mercury Exchange Limited (MEL) Channel Associated Signaling. A voice signaling protocol used primarily in the United Kingdom.

**mesh**

Network topology in which devices are organized in a manageable, segmented manner with many, often redundant, interconnections strategically placed between network nodes. See also *full mesh* and *partial mesh*.

**message**

Application layer (Layer 7) logical grouping of information, often composed of a number of lower-layer logical groupings, such as packets. The terms *datagram*, *frame*, *packet*, and *segment* alsoare used to describe logical information groupings at various layers of the OSI reference model and in various technology circles.

**Message Digest 5**

See *MDS*.

**message handling system**

See *MHS*.

**Message Queuing Interface**

See *MQI*.

**message switching**

Switching technique involving transmission of messages from node to node through a network. The message is stored at each node until such time as a forwarding path is available. Contrast with *circuit switching* and *packet switching*.

**message unit**

Unit of data processed by any network layer.

**metasignaling**

Process running at the ATM layer that manages signaling types and virtual circuits.

**metering**

See *traffic shaping*.

**metric**

See *routing metric*.

**metropolitan-area network**

See *MAN*.

## MF

Multifrequency tones. Made of 6 frequencies that provide 15 two-frequency combinations for indication digits 0 through 9 and KP/ST signals.

## MFT

multiflex trunk module.

## MG

Media Gateway. The emerging industry standard generic term for a gateway.

## MGC

Media Gateway Controller. The emerging industry standard generic term for the VSC.

## MGC Switchover

The rerouting of signalling traffic by the signalling gateway as required (and requested by the MGCs) between related MGCs in the event of failure or unavailability of the currently used MGC. The traffic is rerouted from the primary MGC to the backup MGC.

## MGCP

Media Gateway Control Protocol. A merging of the IPDC and SGCP protocols.

## MHP

multimedia home platform. A set of common application programming interfaces (API) designed to create an operating system–independent, level playing field for broadcasters and consumer-electronics manufacturers. The goal is to provide all DVB-based terminals (set-tops, TVs, and multimedia PCs) full access to programs and services built on the DVB Java (DVB-J) platform.

## MHS

message handling system. ITU-T X.400 recommendations that provide message handling services for communications between distributed applications. NetWare MHS is a different (though similar) entity that also provides message-handling services. See also *IFIP*.

## MIB

Management Information Base. Database of network management information that is used and maintained by a network management protocol, such as SNMP or CMIP. The value of a MIB object can be changed or retrieved using SNMP or CMIP commands, usually through a GUI network management system. MIB objects are organized in a tree structure that includes public (standard) and private (proprietary) branches.

## MIC

media interface connector. FDDI *de facto* standard connector.

## MICA

Modem ISDN channel aggregation. Modem module and card used in the Cisco AS5300 universal access servers. A MICA modem provides an interface between an incoming or outgoing digital call and an ISDN telephone line; the call does not have to be converted to analog as it does with a conventional modem and an analog telephone line. Each line can accommodate, or aggregate, up to 24 (T1) or 30 (E1) calls.

## micro channel architecture

See *MCA*.

## microcode

Translation layer between machine instructions and the elementary operations of a computer. Microcode is stored in ROM and allows the addition of new machine instructions without requiring that they be designed into electronic circuits when new instructions are needed.

## microfilter

Device that prevents data frequencies (intended for a data device, such as a router) from traveling over the telephone line and interfering with telephone calls.

## microsegmentation

Division of a network into smaller segments, usually with the intention of increasing aggregate bandwidth to network devices.

## microwave

Electromagnetic waves in the range 1 to 30 GHz. Microwave-based networks are an evolving technology gaining favor due to high bandwidth and relatively low cost.

## MID

message identifier. In ATM, used to identify ATM cells that carry segments from the same higher-layer packet.

## mid-level network

Makes up the second level of the Internet hierarchy. They are the transit networks that connect the stub networks to the backbone networks. Also referred to as *regionals*.

**midsplit**

Broadband cable system in which the available frequencies are split into two groups: one for transmission and one for reception.

**MII**

media independent interface. Standard specification for the interface between network controller chips and their associated media interface chip(s). The MII automatically senses 10- and 100-MHz Ethernet speeds.

**Military Network**

See *MILNET*.

**millions of instructions per second**

See *mips*.

**MILNET**

Military Network. Unclassified portion of the DDN. Operated and maintained by the DISA. See also *DDN* and *DISA*.

**MIME**

Multipurpose Internet Mail Extension. Standard for transmitting non-text data (or data that cannot be represented in plain ASCII code) in Internet mail, such as binary, foreign language text (such as Russian or Chinese), audio, or video data. MIME is defined in RFC 2045.

**minimum cell rate**

See *MCR*.

**MIP**

See *MIP* in the "Cisco Systems Terms and Acronyms" section.

**mips**

millions of instructions per second. Number of instructions executed by a processor per second.

**MIX**

multiservice interchange.

**MLP**

Multilink PPP. Method of splitting, recombining, and sequencing datagrams across multiple logical data links.

## MLS

multilayer switching.

## MM fiber

multimode fiber. A fiber-optic medium in which light travels in multiple modes.

## MMDS

Multichannel Multipoint Distribution Service. MMDS is comprised of as many as 33 discrete channels that are transmitted in a pseudo random order between the transmitters and the receivers. The FCC allocated two bands of frequencies for each BTA: 2.15 to 2.161 GHz and 2.5 to 2.686 GHz.

## MMF

multimode fiber. Optical fiber supporting the propagation of multiple frequencies of light. See also *single-mode fiber*.

## MML

Man-Machine Language. Industry standard command line language used to manage telecommunications network elements.

## MMLS-RP

Multicast MLS-Route Processor. Routing platform running Cisco IOS software that supports IP multicast MLS. The MMLS-RP interacts with the IP multicast routing software and updates the MLS cache in the MMLS-SE. When the IP Multicast MLS feature is enabled, the MMLS-RP continues to handle all non–IP-multicast traffic while off-loading IP multicast traffic forwarding to the MMLS-SE.

## MMLS-SE

Multicast MLS-Switching Engine. Catalyst 5000 series switch with hardware that supports IP multicast MLS. The MMLS-SE provides layer 3 LAN-switching services.

## MMoIP

Multimedia Mail over IP.

## MMoIP dial peer

Multimedia Mail over IP dial peer. Dial peer specific to Store and Forward Fax. The MMoIP dial peer is the vehicle you use to assign particular line characteristics (such as a destination telephone number) to the connection between the Cisco router or the access server and the SMTP mail server during on-ramp faxing.

## MMP

Multichassis Multilink PPP. Extends MLP support across multiple routers and access servers. MMP enables multiple routers and access servers to operate as a single, large dial-up pool, with a single network address and an ISDN access number. MMP correctly handles packet fragmenting and reassembly when a user connection is split between two physical access devices.

## modem

modulator-demodulator. Device that converts digital and analog signals. At the source, a modem converts digital signals to a form suitable for transmission over analog communication facilities. At the destination, the analog signals are returned to their digital form. Modems allow data to be transmitted over voice-grade telephone lines.

## modem eliminator

Device allowing the connection of two DTE devices without modems.

## modulation

Process by which the characteristics of electrical signals are transformed to represent information. Types of modulation include AM, FM, and PAM. See also *AM*, *FM*, and *PAM*.

## modulator-demodulator

See *modem*.

## monomode fiber

See *single-mode fiber*.

## MOP

Maintenance Operation Protocol. Digital Equipment Corporation protocol that provides a way to perform primitive maintenance operations on DECnet systems. For example, MOP can be used to download a system image to a diskless station.

## Mosaic

Public-domain WWW browser developed at the NCSA. See also *browser*.

## MOSPF

Multicast OSPF. Intradomain multicast routing protocol used in OSPF networks. Extensions are applied to the base OSPF unicast protocol to support IP multicast routing.

## MOSS

MIME Object Security Services. Internet protocol [RFC 1848] that applies end-to-end encryption and digital signature to MIME message content, using symmetric cryptography for encryption and asymmetric cryptography for key distribution and signature.

## moves, adds, and changes

See *MAC*.

## MPEG

*Motion Picture Experts Group. Standard for compressing video. MPEG1* is a bit stream standard for compressed video and audio optimized to fit into a bandwidth of 1.5 Mbps. *MPEG2 is* intended for higher quality video-on-demand applications and runs at data rates between 4 and 9 Mbps. *MPEG4* is a low–bit-rate compression algorithm intended for 64-kbps connections.

## MPLS

Multiprotocol Label Switching. Switching method that forwards IP traffic using a label. This label instructs the routers and the switches in the network where to forward the packets based on preestablished IP routing information.

## MPOA

Multiprotocol over ATM. ATM Forum standardization effort specifying how existing and future network-layer protocols, such as IP, IPv6, AppleTalk, and IPX, run over an ATM network with directly attached hosts, routers, and multilayer LAN switches.

## MQI

Message Queuing Interface. International standard API that provides functionality similar to that of the RPC interface. In contrast to RPC, MQI is implemented strictly at the application layer. See also *RPC*.

## MR

Modem Registrar. One of the suite of software products included in the Cisco Subscriber Registration Center (CSRC) product. MR is a policy-based cable modem management product that provides dynamic cable modem configuration.

## MRM

Multicast Routing Monitor. A management diagnostic tool that provides network fault detection and isolation in a large multicast routing infrastructure. It is designed to notify a network administrator of multicast routing problems in near real time.

### MRP

Multiservice route processor. A card that acts as a voice-and-data–capable router and that can carry voice traffic over an IP network and can link small-to-medium-size remote Ethernet LANs to central offices (COs) over WAN links. The MRP has two slots that support WAN interface cards (WICs), voice interface cards (VICs), or both in combination.

### MS

mobile station. Refers generically to any mobile device, such as a mobile handset or computer, that is used to access network services. GPRS networks support three classes of MS, which describe the type of operation supported within the GPRS and the GSM mobile wireless networks. For example, a Class A MS supports simultaneous operation of GPRS and GSM services.

### MSAU

multistation access unit. Wiring concentrator to which all end stations in a Token Ring network connect. The MSAU provides an interface between these devices and the Token Ring interface of a router. Sometimes abbreviated *MAU*.

### MSB

most significant bit. Bit n-1 in an *n* bit binary number, the bit with the greatest weight ($2^{(n-1)}$). The first or leftmost bit when the number is written in the usual way.

### MSC

mobile switching center. Provides telephony switching services and controls calls between telephone and data systems.

### MS-CHAP

Microsoft CHAP (Challenge Handshake Authentication Protocol). See *CHAP*.

### MSLT

Minimum Scan Line Time. The time set by the receiving fax machine and sent to the sending machine during the initial handshaking. MSLT defines how much time the receiving machine requires to print a single scan line.

### MSLT adjustment

Minimum Scan Line Time adjustment. An alternative to Scan Line Fix Up meant to eliminate fax failures caused by an excessive number of received page errors because of data loss. MSLT adjustment sets a minimum MSLT value that an ingress gateway communicates to a sending fax machine. This value overrides an MSLT of lesser value that is supplied by a receiving fax machine.

## MSO

multiple service operator. Cable service provider that also provides other services, such as data and/or voice telephony.

## MSU

Message Signal Unit. SS7 message that carries call control, database traffic, network management, and network maintenance data in the signalling information field (SIF).

## MTA

**1.** Message Transfer Agent. OSI application process used to store and forward messages in the X.400 Message Handling System. Equivalent to Internet mail agent.

**2.** Mail Transfer Agent. Software that implements SMTP and provides storage for mail messages to be forwarded or delivered to a local user. MTAs implement SMTP (RFC 821).

## MTBF

mean time between failure.

## MTP

Message Transfer Part. Layers 1 (physical), 2 (data), and 3 (network) of the SS7 signaling protocol.

## MTP1

Message Transfer Part Level 1. SS7 architectural level that defines the physical, electrical, and functional characteristics of the digital signaling link.

## MTP2

Message Transfer Part Level 2. SS7 data link layer protocol. SS7 architectural level that exercises flow control, message sequence validation, error checking, and retransmission.

## MTP3

Message Transfer Part Level 3. S7 architectural level that provides messages between signalling points in the network, helping control traffic when congestion or failures occur.

## MTTR

Mean time to repair. The average time needed to return a failed device or system to service.

**MTU**

maximum transmission unit. Maximum packet size, in bytes, that a particular interface can handle.

**MUD**

multi-user dungeon. Adventure, role playing games, or simulations played on the Internet. Players interact in real time and can change the "world" in the game as they play it. Most MUDs are based on the Telnet protocol.

**mu-law**

North American companding standard used in conversion between analog and digital signals in PCM systems. Similar to the European a-law. See also *a-law* and *companding*.

**multiaccess network**

Network that allows multiple devices to connect and communicate simultaneously.

**multicast**

Single packets copied by the network and sent to a specific subset of network addresses. These addresses are specified in the Destination Address Field. Compare with *broadcast* and *unicast*.

**multicast address**

Single address that refers to multiple network devices. Synonymous with group address. Compare with *broadcast address* and *unicast address*. See also *multicast*.

**multicast backbone**

See *MBONE*.

**multicast forward VCC**

VCC set up by the BUS to the LEC as a leaf in a point-to-multipoint connection. See also *BUS*, *LEC* (LAN Emulation Client), and *VCC*.

**multicast group**

Dynamically determined group of IP hosts identified by a single IP multicast address.

**Multicast OSPF**

See *MOSPF*.

### multicast router

Router used to send IGMP query messages on their attached local networks. Host members of a multicast group respond to a query by sending IGMP reports noting the multicast groups to which they belong. The multicast router takes responsibility for forwarding multicast datagrams from one multicast group to all other networks that have members in the group. See also *IGMP*.

### multicast send VCC

In an ATM network, a bi-directional point-to-point VCC set up by an LEC to a BUS. One of three data connections defined by Phase 1 LANE. Compare with *control distribute VCC* and *control direct VCC*. See also *BUS*, *LEC* (LAN Emulation Client), and *VCC*.

### multicast server

Establishes a one-to-many connection to each device in a VLAN, thus establishing a broadcast domain for each VLAN segment. The multicast server forwards incoming broadcasts only to the multicast address that maps to the broadcast address.

### MultiChannel Interface Processor

See *MIP* in the "Cisco Systems Terms and Acronyms" section.

### multidrop line

Communications line with multiple cable access points. Sometimes called a multipoint line.

### multihomed host

Host attached to multiple physical network segments in an OSI CLNS network.

### multihoming

Addressing scheme in IS-IS routing that supports the assignment of multiple area addresses.

### Multi-instance option

A DOCSIS option that can occur multiple times in an option set.

### multilayer switch

Switch that filters and forwards packets based on MAC addresses and network addresses. A subset of LAN switch. Compare with *LAN switch*.

### Multilink PPP

Multilink Point-to-Point Protocol. This protocol is a method of splitting, recombining, and sequencing datagrams across multiple logical data links.

**multimode fiber**

See *MMF*.

**multiple domain network**

SNA network with multiple SSCPs. See also *SSCP*.

**multiplexer**

See *Mux*.

**multiplexing**

Scheme that allows multiple logical signals to be transmitted simultaneously across a single physical channel. Compare with *demultiplexing*.

**Multipoint**

**1.** Line or channel connecting three or more different service points.

**2.** Circuit that has points served by three or more switches. Single communications channel (typically a leased telephone circuit) to which two or more stations or logical units are attached although only one can transmit at a time. Such arrangements usually require a polling mechanism under the control of a master station to ensure that only one device transmits at a time.

**multipoint control unit**

Endpoint on the LAN that provides the capability for three or more terminals and gateways to participate in a multipoint conference.

**multipoint line**

See *multidrop line*.

**multipoint-unicast**

A process of transferring protocol data units (PDUs) where an endpoint sends more than one copy of a media stream to different endpoints. This might be necessary in networks that do not support multicast.

**multipoint-unicast**

A process of transferring protocol data units (PDUs) where an endpoint sends more than one copy of a media stream to different endpoints. This might be necessary in networks that do not support multicast.

**Multiprotocol over ATM**

See *MPOA*.

**Multipurpose Internet Mail Extension**

See *MIME*.

**Multiservice route processor**

See *MRP*.

**multistation access unit**

See *MSAU*.

**multi-user dungeon**

See *MUD*.

**multivendor network**

Network using equipment from more than one vendor. Multivendor networks pose many more compatibility problems than single-vendor networks. Compare with *single-vendor network*.

**MUX**

multiplexer. Equipment that enables several data streams to be sent over a single physical line. It is also a function by which one connection from an (ISO) layer is used to support more than one connection to the next higher layer. A device for combining several channels to be carried by one line or fiber.

**MX record**

mail exchange record. DNS resource record type indicating which host can handle e-mail for a particular domain.

### NAA

next available agent. A strategy for selecting an agent to handle a call. The strategy seeks to maintain an equal load across skill groups or services.

### NACS

NetWare Asynchronous Communication Services. Novell software that supports Novell's AIO and NASI programming interfaces. NACS promotes the sharing of communications resources, such as modems, asynchronous hosts, and X.25 network services.

### NADF

North American Directory Forum. Collection of organizations that offer, or plan to offer, public directory services in North America based on the ITU-T X.500 Recommendations.

### NADN

nearest active downstream neighbor. In Token Ring or IEEE 802.5 networks, the closest downstream network device from any given device that is still active.

### Nagle's algorithm

Actually two separate congestion control algorithms that can be used in TCP-based networks. One algorithm reduces the sending window; the other limits small datagrams.

### NAK

negative acknowledgment. Response sent from a receiving device to a sending device indicating that the information received contained errors. Compare to *acknowledgment*.

### NAM

network applications management. In a two-tier service bureau architecture, the ICM that receives route requests from the carrier network and forwards them to a Customer ICM (CICM). A NAM usually contains only a small configuration that allows it to directly route a subset of calls and dispatch the other requests to the appropriate CICM. The NAM receives route responses from the CICMs and forwards them to the carrier network.

**Name Binding Protocol**

See *NBP*.

**name caching**

Method by which remotely discovered host names are stored by a router for use in future packet-forwarding decisions to allow quick access.

**name resolution**

Generally, the process of associating a name with a network location.

**name server**

Server connected to a network that resolves network names into network addresses.

**namespace**

Commonly distributed set of names in which all names are unique.

**NANOG**

North American Network Operator's Group. Primary forum for information exchange among U.S. exchange point participants, Internet service providers, and end users.

**NANP**

North American Numbering Plan.

**NAP**

network access point. Location for interconnection of Internet service providers in the United States for the exchange of packets.

**NARP**

NBMA Address Resolution Protocol. Functional subset of NHRP that returns only the address mappings of nodes that are connected directly to the NBMA network. Compare with *NHRP*.

**narrowband**

See *baseband*.

**Narrowband ISDN**

See *N-ISDN*.

### NAS

network access server. Cisco platform (or collection of platforms, such as an AccessPath system) that interfaces between the packet world (for example, the Internet) and the circuit world (for example, the PSTN). See also *access device.*

### NASI

**1.** NetWare Asynchronous Support Interface.

**2.** NetWare Access Server Interface.

### NAT

Network Address Translation. Mechanism for reducing the need for globally unique IP addresses. NAT allows an organization with addresses that are not globally unique to connect to the Internet by translating those addresses into globally routable address space. Also known as *Network Address Translator.*

### National Bureau of Standards

See *NBS.*

### National Institute of Standards and Technology

See *NIST.*

### National Research and Education Network

See *NREN.*

### National Science Foundation

See *NSF.*

### National Science Foundation Network

See *NSFNET.*

### native client interface architecture

See *NCIA* in the "Cisco Systems Terms and Acronyms" section.

### NAU

network addressable unit. SNA term for an addressable entity. Examples include LUs, PUs, and SSCPs. NAUs generally provide upper-level network services. Compare with *path control network.*

### NAUN

nearest active upstream neighbor. In Token Ring or IEEE 802.5 networks, the closest upstream network device from any given device that is still active.

## NBFCP

NetBIOS Frames Control Protocol. Protocol that establishes and configures NetBIOS over PPP. See also *NetBIOS* and *PPP*.

## NBMA

nonbroadcast multiaccess. Term describing a multiaccess network that either does not support broadcasting (such as X.25) or in which broadcasting is not feasible (for example, an SMDS broadcast group or an extended Ethernet that is too large). See also *multiaccess network*.

## NBNS

NetBIOS Name Service.

## NBP

Name Binding Protocol. AppleTalk transport-level protocol that translates a character string name into the DDP address of the corresponding socket client. NBP enables AppleTalk protocols to understand user-defined zones and device names by providing and maintaining translation tables that map names to their corresponding socket addresses.

## NBS

National Bureau of Standards. Organization that was part of the U.S. Department of Commerce. Now known as NIST. See also *NIST*.

## NCB

network control byte. Used by host application developers for debugging communications between a controlling host application and the Cisco VCO/4K.

## NCIA

See *NCIA* (native client interface architecture) in the "Cisco Systems Terms and Acronyms" section.

## NCP

**1.** Network Control Program. In SNA, a program that routes and controls the flow of data between a communications controller (in which it resides) and other network resources.

**2.** Network Control Protocol. Series of protocols for establishing and configuring different network layer protocols, such as for AppleTalk over PPP. See also *PPP*.

**3.** network control point. The process within the AT&T signaling network that sends routing requests to a Customer Routing Point (CRP), such as the network interface controller (NIC) within the ICM.

**NCP/Token Ring Interconnection**

See *NTRI*.

**NCSA**

National Center for Supercomputing Applications.

**NDE**

NetFlow data eport.

**NDIS**

network driver interface specification. Microsoft specification for a generic, hardware- and protocol-independent device driver for NICs.

**NDS**

Netscape Directory Server. An LDAP server.

**NE**

network element. In general, an NE is a combination hardware and software system that is designed primarily to perform a telecommunications service function. For example, an NE is the part of the network equipment where a transport entity (such as a line, a path, or a section) is terminated and monitored.

As defined by wavelength routing, an NE is the originating, transient, or terminating node of a wavelength path.

**nearest active upstream neighbor**

See *NAUN*.

**NEARNET**

Regional network in New England (United States) that links Boston University, Harvard University, and MIT. Now part of BBN Planet. See also *BBN Planet*.

**NEBS**

Network Equipment Building Systems. In OSS, the Bellcore requirement for equipment deployed in a central office environment. Covers spatial, hardware, crafts person interface, thermal, fire resistance, handling and transportation, earthquake and vibration, airborne contaminants, grounding, acoustical noise, illumination, EMC, and ESD requirements.

**negative acknowledgment**

See *NAK*.

**neighborhood**

A grouping of subscribers, computers, and shared or private cable modems associated with an account administered in the User Registrar Admin UI. A neighborhood contains settings for auto-provisioning modems as shared or private through the User Registrar Subscriber UI.

**neighboring routers**

In OSPF, two routers that have interfaces to a common network. On multiaccess networks, neighbors are discovered dynamically by the OSPF Hello protocol.

**NEMS**

Network Element Management Server.

**net**

Short for *network*.

**NET**

network entity title. Network addresses, defined by the ISO network architecture, and used in CLNS-based networks.

**NetBEUI**

NetBIOS Extended User Interface. Enhanced version of the NetBIOS protocol used by network operating systems, such as LAN Manager, LAN Server, Windows for Workgroups, and Windows NT. NetBEUI formalizes the transport frame and adds additional functions. NetBEUI implements the OSI LLC2 protocol. See also *LLC2* and *OSI*.

**NetBIOS**

Network Basic Input/Output System. API used by applications on an IBM LAN to request services from lower-level network processes. These services might include session establishment and termination, and information transfer.

**netflow**

A feature of some routers that allows them to categorize incoming packets into flows. Because packets in a flow often can be treated in the same way, this classification can be used to bypass some of the work of the router and accelerate its switching operation.

**netiquette**

A pun on "etiquette" referring to proper behavior on a network.

**NETscout**

See *NETscout* in the "Cisco Systems Terms and Acronyms" section.

**NetView**

IBM network management architecture and related applications. NetView is a VTAM application used for managing mainframes in SNA networks. See also *VTAM*.

**NetWare**

Popular distributed NOS developed by Novell. Provides transparent remote file access and numerous other distributed network services.

**NetWare Link Services Protocol**

See *NLSP*.

**NetWare Loadable Module**

See *NLM*.

**network**

**1.** Collection of computers, printers, routers, switches, and other devices that can communicate with each other over some transmission medium.

**2.** The highest level of your signaling controller system. You have only one network, within which you create your sites.

**network access point**

See *NAP*.

**network access server**

See *access server* and *NAS*.

**network address**

Network layer address referring to a logical, rather than a physical, network device. Also called a *protocol address*. Compare with *MAC address*.

**Network Address Translation**

See *NAT*.

**network addressable unit**

See *NAU*.

### network administrator

Person responsible for the operation, the maintenance, and the management of a network. See also *network operator*.

### network analyzer

Hardware or software device offering various network troubleshooting features, including protocol-specific packet decodes, specific preprogrammed troubleshooting tests, packet filtering, and packet transmission.

### Network Basic Input/Output System

See *NetBIOS*.

### network byte order

Internet-standard ordering of the bytes corresponding to numeric values.

### Network Control Program

See *NCP*.

### network driver interface specification

See *NDIS*.

### network element

See *NE*.

### network entity title

See *NET*.

### Network File System

See *NFS*.

### Network Indicator

Determines the type of call that is being placed: 0 = international, 1 = reserved, 2= national, and 3 = national spare.

### Network Information Center

See *InterNIC*.

### Network Information Service

See *NIS*.

### network interface

Boundary between a carrier network and a privately owned installation.

**network interface card**

See *NIC*.

**network layer**

Layer 3 of the OSI reference model. This layer provides connectivity and path selection between two end systems. The network layer is the layer at which routing occurs. Corresponds roughly with the *path control layer* of the SNA model. See also *application layer*, *data-link layer*, *physical layer*, *PQ*, *session layer*, and *transport layer*.

**network management**

Generic term used to describe systems or actions that help maintain, characterize, or troubleshoot a network.

**Network Management Processor**

See *NMP*.

**network management system**

See *NMS*.

**network management vector transport**

See *NMVT*.

**network node**

See *NN*.

**network node interface**

See *NNI*.

**Network Node Server**

SNA NN that provides resource location and route selection services for ENs, LEN nodes, and LUs that are in its domain.

**network number**

Part of an IP address that specifies the network to which the host belongs.

**network operating system**

See *NOS*.

**Network Operations Center**

See *NOC*.

### network operator

Person who routinely monitors and controls a network, performing such tasks as reviewing and responding to traps, monitoring throughput, configuring new circuits, and resolving problems. See also *network administrator*.

### network port

In the context of wavelength routing, a network port is a port that tandems through the node; that is, it is a port on the NE that points to another wavelength router.

### network service access point

See *NSAP*.

### Network Time Protocol

See *NTP*.

### Network-to-
### Network Interface

See *NNI*.

### network-visible entity

See *NVE*.

### Next Hop Resolution Protocol

See *NHRP*.

### NFAS

Non-Facility Associated Signaling. A classification of signalling protocols that provide the signalling channel in a separate physical line from the bearer channels.

### NFS

Network File System. As commonly used, a distributed file system protocol suite developed by Sun Microsystems that allows remote file access across a network. In actuality, NFS is simply one protocol in the suite. NFS protocols include NFS, RPC, XDR, and others. These protocols are part of a larger architecture that Sun refers to as ONC. See also *ONC*.

### NHRP

Next Hop Resolution Protocol. Protocol used by routers to dynamically discover the MAC address of other routers and hosts connected to an NBMA network. These systems then can communicate directly without requiring traffic to use an intermediate hop, increasing performance in ATM, Frame Relay, SMDS, and X.25 environments.

### NHS

Next Hop Server. Server defined by the NHRP protocol that maintains next-hop resolution cache tables containing the IP-to-ATM address mappings of associated nodes and nodes that are reachable through routers served by the NHS.

### NIC

**1.** network interface card. Board that provides network communication capabilities to and from a computer system. Also called an *adapter*. See also *AUI*.

**2.** Network Information Center. Organization whose functions have been assumed by the InterNIC. See *InterNIC*.

### NIS

Network Information Service. Protocol developed by Sun Microsystems for the administration of network-wide databases. The service essentially uses two programs: one for finding an NIS server and one for accessing the NIS databases.

### N-ISDN

Narrowband ISDN. Communication standards developed by the ITU-T for baseband networks. Based on 64-kbps B channels and 16- or 64-kbps D channels. Contrast with *BISDN*. See also *BRI*, *ISDN*, and *PRI*.

### NIST

National Institute of Standards and Technology. U.S. government organization that supports and catalogs a variety of standards. Formerly the NBS. See also *NBS*.

### NLC

node line card. One of the component cards used in the Cisco 6400 universal access controller. These cards provide the interfaces for moving data into and out of the Cisco 6400 system. They can be used as either uplink or downlink interfaces. Different types of line cards support different transmission protocols and data rates.

### NLESO

Network-level Extended Security Option. NLESO processing requires that security options be checked against configured allowable information, source, and compartment bit values, and requires that the router be capable of inserting extended security options in the IP header.

### NLM

NetWare Loadable Module. Individual program that can be loaded into memory and can function as part of the NetWare NOS.

## NLOS

non line of sight. Also known as obstructed path or pathway.

## NLRI

Network Layer Reachability Information. BGP sends routing update messages containing NLRI to describe a route and how to get there. In this context, an NLRI is a prefix. A BGP update message carries one or more NLRI prefixes and the attributes of a route for the NLRI prefixes; the route attributes include a BGP next hop gateway address, community values, and other information.

## NLSP

**1.** NetWare Link Services Protocol. Link-state routing protocol based on IS-IS. See also *IS-IS*.

**2.** Network Layer Security Protocol. OSI protocol (ISO 11577) for end-to-end encryption services at the top of OSI layer 3. NLSP is derived from an SDNS protocol, SP3, but is much more complex.

## NMA

Network Management and Analysis. Bellcore OSS providing alarm surveillance and performance monitoring of intelligent network elements.

## NME

Network Management Ethernet. The LAN used to control and manage equipment in a central office and branch locations.

## NMP

See *NMP* (Network Management Processor) in the "Cisco Systems Terms and Acronyms" section.

## NMS

network management system. System responsible for managing at least part of a network. An NMS is generally a reasonably powerful and well-equipped computer, such as an engineering workstation. NMSs communicate with agents to help keep track of network statistics and resources.

## NMVT

network management vector transport. SNA message consisting of a series of vectors conveying network management specific information.

## NN

**1.** National Number. Part of a numbering plan.

**2.** network node. SNA intermediate node that provides connectivity, directory services, route selection, intermediate session routing, data transport, and network management services to LEN nodes and ENs. The NN contains a CP that manages the resources of both the NN itself and those of the ENs and LEN nodes in its domain. NNs provide intermediate routing services by implementing the APPN PU 2.1 extensions. Compare with *EN*. See also *CP*.

## NNI

**1.** Network-to-Network Interface. ATM Forum standard that defines the interface between two ATM switches that are both located in a private network or are both located in a public network. The UNI standard defines the interface between a public switch and a private one. Also, the standard interface between two Frame Relay switches meeting the same criteria. Compare with *UNI*.

**2.** network node interface.

## NNTP

Network News Transfer Protocol. News reader service.

## NOA

nature of address.

## NOC

network operations center. Organization responsible for maintaining a network.

## node

**1.** Endpoint of a network connection or a junction common to two or more lines in a network. Nodes can be processors, controllers, or workstations. Nodes, which vary in routing and other functional capabilities, can be interconnected by links, and serve as control points in the network. Node sometimes is used generically to refer to any entity that can access a network, and frequently is used interchangeably with *device*. See also *host*.

**2.** H.323 entity that uses RAS to communicate with the gatekeeper, for example, an endpoint (such as a terminal, a proxy, or a gateway).

**3.** In SNA, the basic component of a network and the point at which one or more functional units connect channels or data circuits.

**4.** A node is a point of connectivity, or wavelength router, where multiple fiber links come together into one point, and/or a source or a destination for a wavelength path.

**noise**

Undesirable communications channel signals.

**nonbroadcast multiaccess**

See *NBMA*.

**nonce**

Random or non-repeating value that is included in data exchanged by a protocol, usually for the purpose of guaranteeing liveness and thus detecting and protecting against replay attacks.

**none line of sight**

See *NLOS*.

**nonextended network**

AppleTalk Phase 2 network that supports addressing of up to 253 nodes and only 1 zone.

**non-repudiation service**

Security service that provide protection against false denial of involvement in a communication.

**nonreturn to zero**

See *NRZ*.

**nonreturn to zero inverted**

See *NRZI*.

**nonseed router**

In AppleTalk, a router that must first obtain, and then verify, its configuration with a seed router before it can begin operation. See also *seed router*.

**nonstub area**

Resource-intensive OSPF area that carries a default route, static routes, intra-area routes, interarea routes, and external routes. Nonstub areas are the only OSPF areas that can have virtual links configured across them, and are the only areas that can contain an ASBR. Compare with *stub area*. See also *ASAM* and *OSPF*.

**nonvolatile random-access memory**

See *NVRAM*.

**normal response mode**

See *NRM*.

**Northwest Net**

NSF-funded regional network serving the Northwestern United States, Alaska, Montana, and North Dakota. Northwest Net connects all major universities in the region as well as many leading industrial concerns.

**NOS**

network operating system. Generic term used to refer to what are really distributed file systems. Examples of NOSs include LAN Manager, NetWare, NFS, and VINES.

**notification code**

Defines the severity assigned to a given condition under a specific set of circumstances.

**Novell IPX**

See *IPX*.

**NPA**

Numbering Plan Area. The "area code" of a North American Dialing Plan number.

**NPI**

number plan identification.

**NR**

Network Registrar; same as CNR. Network Registrar provides Domain Name Server (DNS) and DHCP services. Network Registrar supplies IP addresses and configuration parameters to DOCSIS cable modems and PCs based on network and service policies, and allocates host names for these devices in DNS.

**NREN**

National Research and Education Network. A component of the HPCC program designed to ensure U.S. technical leadership in computer communications through research and development efforts in state-of-the-art telecommunications and networking technologies. See also *HPCC*.

**NRM**

normal response mode. HDLC mode for use on links with one primary station and one or more secondary stations. In this mode, secondary stations can transmit only if they first receive a poll from the primary station.

### NRZ

nonreturn to zero. Signals that maintain constant voltage levels with no signal transitions (no return to a zero-voltage level) during a bit interval. Compare with *NRZI*.

### NRZI

nonreturn to zero inverted. Signals that maintain constant voltage levels with no signal transitions (no return to a zero-voltage level) but interpret the presence of data at the beginning of a bit interval as a signal transition and the absence of data as no transition. Compare with *NRZ*.

### NSA

non–service-affecting. A category of conditions that do not interrupt payload traffic; see *service affecting*.

### NSAP

network service access point. Network addresses, as specified by ISO. An NSAP is the point at which OSI network service is made available to a transport layer (Layer 4) entity.

### NSB

Network Status Byte. A byte returned by the Cisco VCO/4K to the controlling host to indicate the successful completion or error status of command processing.

### NSF

National Science Foundation. U.S. government agency that funds scientific research in the United States. The now-defunct NSFNET was funded by the NSF. See also *NSFNET*.

### NSFNET

National Science Foundation Network. Large network that was controlled by the NSF and provided networking services in support of education and research in the United States, from 1986 to 1995. NSFNET is no longer in service.

### NT-1

network termination 1. In ISDN, a device that provides the interface between customer premises equipment and central office switching equipment.

### NTP

Network Time Protocol. Protocol built on top of TCP that ensures accurate local time-keeping with reference to radio and atomic clocks located on the Internet. This protocol is capable of synchronizing distributed clocks within milliseconds over long time periods.

## NTRI

NCP/Token Ring Interconnection. Function used by ACF/NCP to support Token Ring–attached SNA devices. NTRI also provides translation from Token Ring–attached SNA devices (PUs) to switched (dial-up) devices.

## NTSC

National Television Systems Committee. A United States TV technical standard, named after the organization that created the standard in 1941. Specifies a 6 MHz–wide modulated signal.

## NULL encryption algorithm

Algorithm [RFC 2410] that does nothing to transform plaintext data; that is, a no-op. It originated because of IPsec ESP, which always specifies the use of an encryption algorithm to provide confidentiality. The NULL encryption algorithm is a convenient way to represent the option of not applying encryption in ESP (or in any other context where this is needed).

## null modem

Small box or cable used to join computing devices directly, rather than over a network.

## NVE

network-visible entity. Resource that is addressable through a network. Typically, an NVE is a socket client for a service available in a node.

## NVRAM

nonvolatile RAM. RAM that retains its contents when a unit is powered off.

## NYSERNet

Network in New York (United States) with a T1 backbone connecting the NSF, many universities, and several commercial concerns.

## NZ-DSF

non zero-dispersion-shifted fiber. A dispersion shifted SM fiber that has the zero dispersion point near the 1550 nm window but outside the window actually used to transmit signals.

### OADM

optical add drop multiplexer. Optical multiplexing equipment that provides interfaces between different signals in a network.

### OAKLEY

Key establishment protocol (proposed for IPsec but superseded by IKE) based on the Diffie-Hellman algorithm and designed to be a compatible component of ISAKMP.

### OAM cell

Operation, Administration, and Maintenance. ATM Forum specification for cells used to monitor virtual circuits. OAM cells provide a virtual circuit–level loopback in which a router responds to the cells, demonstrating that the circuit is up and the router is operational.

### OAM&P

operations, administration, management, and provisioning. Provides the facilities and the personnel required to manage a network.

### OARnet

Ohio Academic Resources Network. Internet service provider that connects a number of U.S. sites, including the Ohio supercomputer center in Columbus, Ohio.

### OBC

out-of-band control. Refers to the standard method of issuing MICA technologies commands on the control channel, versus IBC, on the in-band data channel. Out-of-band commands are passed through the MICA mailbox mechanism.

### object identifier

See *OID*.

### object instance

Network management term referring to an instance of an object type that has been bound to a value.

## OC

optical carrier. Series of physical protocols (OC-1, OC-2, OC-3, and so on), defined for SONET optical signal transmissions. OC signal levels put STS frames onto multimode fiber-optic line at a variety of speeds. The base rate is 51.84 Mbps (OC-1); each signal level thereafter operates at a speed divisible by that number (thus, OC-3 runs at 155.52 Mbps). See also *SONET*, *STS-1*, and *STS-3c*.

## OCC

originating call control.

## OCLC

Online Computer Library Catalog. Nonprofit membership organization offering computer-based services to libraries, educational organizations, and their users.

## OC-n

SONET optical carrier, Level $n$ (such as $n = 3, 12, 48, 192$).

## octet

8 bits. In networking, the term *octet* often is used (rather than byte) because some machine architectures employ bytes that are not 8 bits long.

## ODA

Open Document Architecture. ISO standard that specifies how documents are represented and transmitted electronically. Formerly called *Office Document Architecture*.

## ODBC

Open DataBase Connectivity. Standard application programming interface for accessing data in both relational and nonrelational database management systems. Using this application programming interface, database applications can access data stored in database management systems on a variety of computers even if each database management system uses a different data storage format and programming interface. ODBC is based on the call level interface specification of the X/Open SQL Access Group and was developed by Digitial Equipment Corporation, Lotus, Microsoft, and Sybase. Contrast with *JDBC*.

## ODI

Open Data-Link Interface. Novell specification providing a standardized interface for NICs (network interface cards) that allows multiple protocols to use a single NIC. See also *NIC*.

**OEMI channel**

See *block multiplexer channel*.

**OFA**

optical fiber amplifier. A device that amplifies an optical signal directly, without the need to convert it to an electrical signal, amplify it electrically, and reconvert is to an optical signal.

**off hook**

Call condition in which transmission facilities are already in use. Also known as *busy*.

**Office Document Architecture**

See *ODA*.

**Ohio Academic Resources Network**

See *OARnet*.

**OID**

object identifier. Values are defined in specific MIB modules. The Event MIB allows a user or an NMS to watch over specified objects and to set event triggers based on existence, threshold, and boolean tests. An event occurs when a trigger is fired; this means that a specified test on an object returns a value of true. To create a trigger, a user or an NMS configures a trigger entry in the mteTriggerTable of the Event MIB. This trigger entry specifies the OID of the object to be watched. For each trigger entry type, corresponding tables (existence, threshold, and boolean tables) are populated with the information required for carrying out the test. The MIB can be configured so that when triggers are activated (fired) either an SNMP Set is performed, a notification is sent out to the interested host, or both.

**OIM**

OSI Internet Management. Group tasked with specifying ways in which OSI network management protocols can be used to manage TCP/IP networks.

**OIR**

online insertion and removal. Feature that permits the addition, the replacement, or the removal of cards without interrupting the system power, entering console commands, or causing other software or interfaces to shutdown. Sometimes called *hot swapping* or *power-on servicing*.

**OLO**

other local operator.

### OMG

Object Management Group.

### on hook

**1.** Condition that exists when a receiver or a handset is resting on the switchhook, or is not in use.

**2.** Idle state (open loop) of a single telephone or private branch exchange (PBX) line loop.

### ONC

Open Network Computing. Distributed applications architecture designed by Sun Microsystems, currently controlled by a consortium led by Sun. The NFS protocols are part of ONC. See also *NFS*.

### ones density

Scheme that allows a CSU/DSU to recover the data clock reliably. The CSU/DSU derives the data clock from the data that passes through it. To recover the clock, the CSU/DSU hardware must receive at least one 1 bit value for every 8 bits of data that pass through it. Also called *pulse density*.

### one-way encryption

Irreversible transformation of plaintext to ciphertext, such that the plaintext cannot be recovered from the ciphertext by other than exhaustive procedures even if the cryptographic key is known.

### online insertion and removal

See *OIR*.

### on-the-fly packet switching

See *cut-through packet switching*.

### OOS

**1.** Out-of-Service.

**2.** Telecommunications: Out-of-Service signaling.

### OOTB

out-of-the-box. Default configuration of the product when it is first installed.

### OPC

own point code. Point code of the Cisco SC2200 signaling controller.

### OPI

See *OPI* in the "Cisco Systems Terms and Acronyms" section.

### open architecture

Architecture with which third-party developers legally can develop products and for which public domain specifications exist.

### open circuit

Broken path along a transmission medium. Open circuits usually prevent network communication.

### open database connectivity

See *ODBC*.

### Open Data-Link Interface

See *ODI*.

### Open Document Architecture

See *ODA*.

### Open Group

Group formed in February 1996 by the consolidation of the two leading open systems consortia: X/Open Company Ltd (X/Open) and the Open Software Foundation (OSF).

### Open Network Computing

See *ONC*.

### Open Shortest Path First

See *OSPF*.

### Open System Interconnection

See *OSI*.

### Open System Interconnection reference model

See *OSI reference model*.

### Operation, Administration, and Maintenance cell

See *OAM cell*.

### OPS/INE

Operations Provisioning System/Intelligent Network Element. Bellcore OSS that provides provisioning services for intelligent network elements. See also *OSS*.

## OPT
See *OPT* in the "Cisco Systems Terms and Acronyms" section.

## Optical Carrier
See *OC*.

## optical fiber
See *fiber-optic cable*.

## Optimized Bandwidth Management
Cisco wide-area switches ensure fair and cost-efficient bandwidth utilization using various techniques. ABR and Optimized Banwidth Management are used for ATM and Frame Relay traffic. ABR is a standards-based ATM traffic management mechanism, and ForeSight is Cisco's implementation that mirrors ABR capabilities for Frame Relay traffic. ABR and Optimized Bandwidth Management optimize real-time traffic performance and throughput, and minimize data loss. Bandwidth management for voice is achieved through the use of standards-based voice compression and silence suppression mechanisms for circuit data services. Formerly called ForeSight.

## Organizational Unique Identifier
See *OUI*.

## OSF
Open Software Foundation. Group responsible for the Distributed Computing Environment (DCE) and the Distributed Management Environment (DME). See also *DCE*.

## OSI
Open System Interconnection. International standardization program created by ISO and ITU-T to develop standards for data networking that facilitate multivendor equipment interoperability.

## OSI Internet Management
See *OIM*.

## OSI network address
Address, consisting of up to 20 octets, used to locate an OSI Transport entity. The address is formatted into two parts: an Initial Domain Part that is standardized for each of several addressing domains and a Domain Specific Part that is the responsibility of the addressing authority for that domain.

**OSI presentation address**

Address used to locate an OSI Application entity. It consists of an OSI Network Address and up to three selectors, one each for use by the transport, session, and presentation entities.

**OSI reference model**

Open System Interconnection reference model. Network architectural model developed by ISO and ITU-T. The model consists of seven layers, each of which specifies particular network functions, such as addressing, flow control, error control, encapsulation, and reliable message transfer. The lowest layer (the physical layer) is closest to the media technology. The lower two layers are implemented in hardware and software whereas the upper five layers are implemented only in software. The highest layer (the application layer) is closest to the user. The OSI reference model is used universally as a method for teaching and understanding network functionality. Similar in some respects to *SNA*. See also *application layer*, *data link layer*, *network layer*, *physical layer*, *presentation layer*, *session layer*, and *transport layer*.

**OSINET**

International association designed to promote OSI in vendor architectures.

**OSP**

Open Settlement Protocol. Client/server protocol defined by the ETSI TIPHON to establish authenticated connections between gateways, and to allow gateways and servers to transfer accounting and routing information securely. OSP allows service providers to roll out VoIP services without establishing direct peering agreements with other ITSPs.

**OSPF**

Open Shortest Path First. Link-state, hierarchical IGP routing algorithm proposed as a successor to RIP in the Internet community. OSPF features include least-cost routing, multipath routing, and load balancing. OSPF was derived from an early version of the IS-IS protocol. See also *IGP*, *IS-IS*, and *RIP*. See also *EIGRP* and *IGRP* in the "Cisco Systems Terms and Acronyms" section.

**OSS**

Operations Support System. Network management system supporting a specific management function, such as alarm surveillance and provisioning, in a carrier network. Many OSSs are large centralized systems running on mainframes or minicomputers. Common OSSs used within an RBOC include *NMA*, *OPS/INE*, and *TIRKS*.

### OSSI

operations support system interface. DOCSIS specification. For example, DOCSIS OSSI 1.0 defines the network management requirements for support in a DOCSIS 1.0 environment.

### OUI

Organizational Unique Identifier. Three octets assigned by the IEEE in a block of 48-bit LAN addresses.

### outframe

Maximum number of outstanding frames allowed in an SNA PU 2 server at any time.

### out-of-band signaling

Transmission using frequencies or channels outside the frequencies or channels normally used for information transfer. Out-of-band signaling often is used for error reporting in situations in which in-band signaling can be affected by whatever problems the network might be experiencing. Contrast with *in-band signaling*.

### outpulse rule

Sequence of instructions that define autonomous call processing actions to be completed on outgoing ports in the Cisco VCO/4K switch. See also *answer supervision template* and *inpulse rule*.

### overlap

Mode where call control is waiting for possible additional call information from the preceding PINX because it received acknowledgment that the subsequent PINX can receive additional call information.

## P/F

poll/final bit. Bit in bit-synchronous data link layer protocols that indicates the function of a frame. If the frame is a command, a 1 in this bit indicates a poll. If the frame is a response, a 1 in this bit indicates that the current frame is the last frame in the response.

## p2mp

point-to-multipoint. Communication between a series of receivers and transmitters to a central location. Cisco p2mp typically is set up in three segments to enable frequency re-use. Cisco offers MMDS, U-NII, and LMDS systems in p2mp.

## p2p

point-to-point. Communication between one receiver and one location. P2p has a higher bandwidth than p2mp for reasons including that it has less overhead to manage the data paths and there is only one receiver per transmitter. Cisco offers MMDS, U-NII, and LMDS systems in p2p.

## PABX

private automatic branch exchange. Telephone switch for use inside a corporation. PABX is the preferred term in Europe, whereas PBX is used in the United States.

## pacing

See *flow control*.

## packet

Logical grouping of information that includes a header containing control information and (usually) user data. Packets most often are used to refer to network layer units of data. The terms *datagram*, *frame*, *message*, and *segment* also are used to describe logical information groupings at various layers of the OSI reference model and in various technology circles. See also *PDU*.

## packet buffer

See *buffer*.

**packet internet groper**

See *ping*.

**packet level protocol**

See *PLP*.

**packet of disconnect**

Process that allows a PPP session to be verified and then terminated by the network access server. It terminates connections on the network access server when particular session attributes are identified. The POD client, residing on a UNIX workstation, sends disconnect packets to the POD server running on the network access server using session information obtained from AAA. The network access server terminates any inbound user session with one or more matching key attributes. It rejects requests that do not have the required fields or where an exact match is not found.

**packet per second**

See *PPS*.

**packet switch**

WAN device that routes packets along the most efficient path and allows a communications channel to be shared by multiple connections. Formerly called an IMP. See also *IMP*.

**packet switch exchange**

See *PSE*.

**packet switching**

Networking method in which nodes share bandwidth with each other by sending packets. Compare with *circuit switching* and *message switching*. See also *PSN*.

**packet-switched data network**

See *PSN*.

**packet-switched network**

See *PSN*.

**packet-switching node**

See *packet switch*.

### PAD

packet assembler/disassembler. Device used to connect simple devices (like character-mode terminals) that do not support the full functionality of a particular protocol to a network. PADs buffer data and assemble and disassemble packets sent to such end devices.

### PAgP

port aggregation protocol.

### PAL

Phase Alternating Line. TV system used in most of Europe in which the color carrier phase definition changes in alternate scan lines. Utilizes an 8 MHz–wide modulated signal.

### Palo Alto Research Center

See *PARC*.

### PAM

Port to Application Mapping. PAM allows you to customize TCP or UDP port numbers for network services or applications.

### PAM

pulse amplitude modulation. Modulation scheme where the modulating wave is caused to modulate the amplitude of a pulse stream. Compare with *AM* and *FM*. See also *modulation*.

### PAP

Password Authentication Protocol. Authentication protocol that allows PPP peers to authenticate one another. The remote router attempting to connect to the local router is required to send an authentication request. Unlike CHAP, PAP passes the password and the host name or username in the clear (unencrypted). PAP does not itself prevent unauthorized access but merely identifies the remote end. The router or access server then determines whether that user is allowed access. PAP is supported only on PPP lines. Compare with *CHAP*.

### parabolic antenna

Dish-like antenna that sends RF waves in a highly focused manner. Such antennas provide very large power gains and are highly efficient. This antenna is typical to Cisco's LMDS, U-NII, and MMDS systems but is not the only design available or appropriate for those frequencies.

**parallel channel**

Channel that uses bus and tag cables as a transmission medium. Compare with *ESCON channel*. See also *bus and tag channel*.

**parallel transmission**

Method of data transmission in which the bits of a data character are transmitted simultaneously over a number of channels. Compare with *serial transmission*.

**parallelism**

Indicates that multiple paths exist between two points in a network. These paths might be of equal or unequal cost. Parallelism is often a network design goal: If one path fails, there is redundancy in the network to ensure that an alternate path to the same point exists.

**PARC**

Palo Alto Research Center. Research and development center operated by XEROX. A number of widely used technologies were originally conceived at PARC, including the first personal computers and LANs.

**PARC Universal Protocol**

See *PUP*.

**parent peer group**

In ATM, a peer group that acts as a "parent" to a subordinate peer group. Organizing peer groups hierarchically reduces the exchange of PTSPs. See also *child peer group*, *peer group*, and *PTSP*.

**parity check**

Process for checking the integrity of a character. A parity check involves appending a bit that makes the total number of binary 1 digits in a character or word (excluding the parity bit) either odd (for *odd parity*) or even (for *even parity*).

**partial mesh**

Network in which devices are organized in a mesh topology with some network nodes organized in a full mesh but others that are connected only to one or two other nodes in the network. A partial mesh does not provide the level of redundancy of a full mesh topology but is less expensive to implement. Partial mesh topologies generally are used in the peripheral networks that connect to a fully meshed backbone. See also *full mesh* and *mesh*.

**password**

Secret data value, usually a character string, that is used as authentication information.

**Password Authentication Protocol**

See *PAP*.

**password sniffing**

Passive wiretapping, usually on a local-area network, to gain knowledge of passwords.

**path control layer**

Layer 3 in the SNA architectural model. This layer performs sequencing services related to proper data reassembly. The path control layer also is responsible for routing. Corresponds roughly with the *network layer* of the OSI model. See also *data flow control layer*, *data-link control layer*, *physical control layer*, *presentation services layer*, *transaction services layer*, and *transmission control layer*.

**path control network**

SNA concept that consists of lower-level components that control the routing and data flow through an SNA network and handle physical data transmission between SNA nodes. Compare with *NAU*.

**path cost**

See *cost*.

**path discovery**

For a digital certificate, the process of finding a set of public-key certificates that comprise a certification path from a trusted key to that specific certificate.

**path loss**

Power loss that occurs when RF waves are transmitted through the air. This loss occurs because the atmosphere provides a filtering effect to the signal. Certain electromagnetic frequencies (very high and non-commercial) are completely blocked or filtered by the atmosphere.

**path name**

Full name of a DOS, Mac OS, or UNIX file or directory, including all directory and subdirectory names. Consecutive names in a path name typically are separated by a backslash (\) for DOS, a colon (:) for Mac OS, and a forward slash (/) for UNIX.

**path state block**

Block maintained by RSVP to store a path.

**path validation**

Process of validating (a) all the digital certificates in a certification path and (b) the required relationships between those certificates, thus validating the contents of the last certificate on the path.

**payload**

Portion of a cell, frame, or packet that contains upper-layer information (data).

**payload type identifier**

See *PTI*.

**PBX**

private branch exchange. Digital or analog telephone switchboard located on the subscriber premises and used to connect private and public telephone networks.

**PCI**

protocol control information. Control information added to user data to comprise an OSI packet. The OSI equivalent of the term *header*. See also *header*.

**PCM**

pulse code modulation. Technique of encoding analog voice into a 64-kbit data stream by sampling with eight-bit resolution at a rate of 8000 times per second.

**PCR**

peak cell rate. Parameter defined by the ATM Forum for ATM traffic management. In CBR transmissions, PCR determines how often data samples are sent. In ABR transmissions, PCR determines the maximum value of the ACR. See also *ABR (available bit rate)*, *ACOM*, and *CBR*.

**PCS**

**1.** Personal Communications Service. Advanced network architecture that provides personal, terminal, and service mobility. In the United States, PCS spectrum has been allocated for broadband, narrowband, and unlicensed services.

**2.** port concentrator switch.

**PCU**

packet control unit. Network component that normally resides in a BSC and directs packet traffic to the SGSN for processing by the GPRS network.

### PDN

**1.** public data network. Network operated either by a government (as in Europe) or by a private concern to provide computer communications to the public, usually for a fee. PDNs enable small organizations to create a WAN without the equipment costs of long-distance circuits.

**2.** public/private/packet data network. Represents a public or private packet-based network, such as an IP or X.25 network.

### PDP context

packet data protocol. Network protocol used by external packet data networks that communicate with a GPRS network. IP is an example of a PDP supported by GPRS. Refers to a set of information (such as a charging ID) that describes a mobile wireless service call or session, which is used by mobile stations and GSNs in a GPRS network to identify the session.

### PDU

protocol data unit. OSI term for packet. See also *Bpdu* and *packet*.

### peak cell rate

See *PCR*.

### peak rate

Maximum rate, in kilobits per second, at which a virtual circuit can transmit.

### peer

Router or device that participates as an endpoint in IPSec and IKE.

### peer group

Collection of ATM nodes that share identical topological databases and exchange full link state information with each other. Peer groups are arranged hierarchically to prevent excessive PTSP traffic. See also *parent peer group* and *PTSP*.

### peer group leader

See *PGL*.

### peer-to-peer computing

Calls for each network device to run both client and server portions of an application. Also describes communication between implementations of the same OSI reference model layer in two different network devices. Compare with *client/server computing*.

### PEM

privacy enhanced mail. Internet e-mail that provides confidentiality, authentication, and message integrity using various encryption methods. Not widely deployed in the Internet.

### penetration

Successful, repeatable, unauthorized access to a protected system resource.

### performance management

One of five categories of network management defined by ISO for management of OSI networks. Performance management subsystems are responsible for analyzing and controlling network performance, including network throughput and error rates. See also *accounting management, configuration management, fault management,* and *security management.*

### peripheral node

In SNA, a node that uses local addresses and therefore is not affected by changes to network addresses. Peripheral nodes require boundary function assistance from an adjacent subarea node.

### permanent calls

Private line calls used for fixed point-to-point calls, for connections between PBXs (E&M to E&M), or for remote telephone extensions (FXO to FXS).

### permanent virtual circuit

See *PVC.*

### permanent virtual circuit interface priority queueing

Interface-level priority queueing scheme in which prioritization is based on destination PVC rather than packet contents.

### permanent virtual connection

See *PVC.*

### permanent virtual path

See *PVP.*

### permit processing

See *traffic policing.*

### Personal Communications Service

See *PCS.*

### Personal Computer Memory Card International Association

Standard used for credit-card–sized computer peripherals. Type I devices are very thin memory cards, Type 2 devices include most modems and interfaces, and Type 3 devices are used for disk drives and thicker components.

### PFS

perfect forward secrecy. Cryptographic characteristic associated with a derived shared secret value. With PFS, if one key is compromised, previous and subsequent keys are not compromised because subsequent keys are not derived from previous keys.

### PG

peripheral gateway. Computer and process within the ICM system that communicates directly with the ACD, the PBX, or the VRU at the call center. The PG reads status information from the peripheral and sends it to the Central Controller. In a private network configuration, the PG sends routing requests to the Central Controller and receives routing information in return.

### PGL

peer group leader. In ATM, a node in a peer group that performs the functions of the LGN. Peer group leaders exchange PTSPs with peer nodes in the parent peer group to inform those nodes of the peer group's attributes and reachability and to propagate information about the parent group and the parent group's parents to the nodes in the peer group. See also *peer group* and *PTSP*.

### PGM

Pragmatic General Multicast. Reliable multicast transport protocol for multicast applications that require reliable, ordered, duplicate-free multicast data delivery from multiple sources to multiple receivers.

### PGP

Pretty Good Privacy. Public-key encryption application that allows secure file and message exchanges. There is some controversy over the development and the use of this application, in part due to U.S. national security concerns.

### phase

Location of a position on an alternating wave form.

### phase shift

Situation in which the relative position in time between the clock and data signals of a transmission becomes unsynchronized. In systems using long cables at higher transmission speeds, slight variances in cable construction, temperature, and other factors can cause a phase shift, resulting in high error rates.

### PHY

**1.** physical sublayer. One of two sublayers of the FDDI physical layer. See also *PMD*.

**2.** physical layer. In ATM, the physical layer provides for the transmission of cells over a physical medium that connects two ATM devices. The PHY is comprised of two sublayers: PMD and TC. See also *PMD* and *TC*.

### physical address

See *MAC address*.

### physical control layer

Layer 1 in the SNA architectural model. This layer is responsible for the physical specifications for the physical links between end systems. Corresponds to the *physical layer* of the OSI model. See also *data flow control layer*, *data-link control layer*, *path control layer*, *presentation services layer*, *transaction services layer*, and *transmission control layer*.

### physical layer

Layer 1 of the OSI reference model. The physical layer defines the electrical, mechanical, procedural, and functional specifications for activating, maintaining, and deactivating the physical link between end systems. Corresponds with the *physical control layer* in the SNA model. See also *application layer*, *data-link layer*, *network layer*, *presentation layer*, *session layer*, and *transport layer*.

### physical layer convergence procedure

See *PLCP*.

### physical layer interface module

See *PLIM* in the "Cisco Systems Terms and Acronyms" section.

### physical media

See *media*.

### physical medium

See *media*.

**physical medium dependent**
See *PMD*.

**physical sublayer**
See *PHY*.

**physical unit**
See *PU*.

**Physical Unit 2**
See *PU 2*.

**Physical Unit 2.1**
See *PU 2.1*.

**Physical Unit 4**
See *PU 4*.

**Physical Unit 5**
See *PU 5*.

**Physics Network**
See *PHYSNET*.

**PHYSNET**
Physics Network. Group of many DECnet-based physics research networks, including HEPnet. See also *HEPnet*.

**PIAFS**
Personal Handyphone Internet Access Forum Standard. PHS Internet Access Forum Standard. ITU-T standard for support by ISDN of data terminal equipment with V-series type interfaces.

**PIC**
**1.** point in call. Phase within a call. Examples of PIC are Answered, Long Duration, Released, and so on.

**2.** pre-subscribed inter-exchange carrier.

**piggyback attack**
Form of active wiretapping in which the attacker gains access to a system via intervals of inactivity in another user's legitimate communication connection. Sometimes called a "between-the-lines" attack.

**piggybacking**

Process of carrying acknowledgments within a data packet to save network bandwidth.

**PIM**

See *PIM* in the "Cisco Systems Terms and Acronyms" section.

**PIM**

Protocol Independent Multicast. Multicast routing architecture that allows the addition of IP multicast routing on existing IP networks. PIM is unicast routing protocol independent and can be operated in two modes: dense and sparse. See also *PIM dense mode* and *PIM sparse mode*.

**PIM dense mode**

One of the two PIM operational modes. PIM dense mode is data-driven and resembles typical multicast routing protocols. Packets are forwarded on all outgoing interfaces until pruning and truncation occurs. In dense mode, receivers are densely populated, and it is assumed that the downstream networks want to receive and will probably use the datagrams that are forwarded to them. The cost of using dense mode is its default flooding behavior. Sometimes called dense mode PIM or PIM DM. Contrast with *PIM sparse mode*. See also *PIM*.

**PIM DM**

See *PIM dense mode*.

**PIM SM**

See *PIM sparse mode*.

**PIM sparse mode**

One of the two PIM operational modes. PIM sparse mode tries to constrain data distribution so that a minimal number of routers in the network receive it. Packets are sent only if they are explicitly requested at the RP (rendezvous point). In sparse mode, receivers are widely distributed, and the assumption is that downstream networks will not necessarily use the datagrams that are sent to them. The cost of using sparse mode is its reliance on the periodic refreshing of explicit join messages and its need for RPs. Sometimes called sparse mode PIM or PIM SM. Contrast with *PIM dense mode*. See also *PIM* and *rendezvous point*.

**ping**

packet internet groper. ICMP echo message and its reply. Often used in IP networks to test the reachability of a network device.

## ping of death

Attack that sends an improperly large ICMP [R0792] echo request packet (a "ping") with the intent of overflowing the input buffers of the destination machine and causing it to crash.

## ping sweep

Attack that sends ICMP [RFC 0792] echo requests ("pings") to a range of IP addresses with the goal of finding hosts that can be probed for vulnerabilities.

## ping-ponging

Phrase used to describe the actions of a packet in a two-node routing loop.

## PINX

private integrated services network exchange. A PBX or key system which, in a BRI voice application, uses QSIG signaling.

## PKCS

Public-Key Cryptography Standards. Series of specifications published by RSA Laboratories for data structures and algorithm usage for basic applications of asymmetric cryptography.

## PKI

public-key infrastructure. System of CAs (and, optionally, RAs and other supporting servers and agents) that perform some set of certificate management, archive management, key management, and token management functions for a community of users in an application of asymmetric cryptography.

## PKI

public key infrastructure.

## plain old telephone service

See *POTS*.

## plaintext

Data that is input to and transformed by an encryption process, or that is output by a decryption process.

## PLAR

private line, automatic ringdown. Leased voice circuit that connects two single endpoints together. When either telephone handset is taken off-hook, the remote telephone automatically rings.

### plar-opx

Specifies a PLAR Off-Premises eXtension connection. Using this option, the local voice port provides a local response before the remote voice port receives an answer. On FXO interfaces, the voice port will not answer until the remote side answers.

### PLCP

physical layer convergence procedure. Specification that maps ATM cells into physical media, such as T3 or E3, and defines certain management information.

### plesiochronous transmission

Term describing digital signals that are sourced from different clocks of comparable accuracy and stability. Compare with *asynchronous transmission, isochronous transmission,* and *synchronous transmission.*

### PLIM

See *PLIM* in the "Cisco Systems Terms and Acronyms" section.

### PLMN

public land mobile network. Generic name for all mobile wireless networks that use earth-based stations rather than satellites. PLMN is the mobile equivalent of the PSTN.

### PLP

packet level protocol. Network layer protocol in the X.25 protocol stack. Sometimes called X.25 Level 3 and X.25 Protocol. See also *X.25.*

### PLSP

PNNI link state packets.

### PLU

Primary Logical Unit. The LU that is initiating a session with another LU. See also *LU.*

### PM

performance monitoring. Provides a variety of automatic functions to aid in the maintenance and operation of the network. PM is continuous, in-service monitoring of transmission quality that uses software-provisionable performance parameters. Performance parameters are measured for all four layers of the SONET signal: physical, section, line, and STS path.

## PMD

**1.** polarization mode dispersion. An inherent property of all optical media, caused by the difference in the propagation velocities of light in the orthogonal principal polarization states of the transmission medium.

**2.** physical medium dependent. Sublayer of the FDDI physical layer that interfaces directly with the physical medium and performs the most basic bit transmission functions of the network. See also *PHY*.

## PNNI

**1.** Private Network-Network Interface. ATM Forum specification for distributing topology information between switches and clusters of switches that is used to compute paths through the network. The specification is based on well-known link-state routing techniques and includes a mechanism for automatic configuration in networks in which the address structure reflects the topology.

**2.** *Private Network Node Interface*. ATM Forum specification for signaling to establish point-to-point and point-to-multipoint connections across an ATM network. The protocol is based on the ATM Forum UNI specification with additional mechanisms for source routing, crankback, and alternate routing of call setup requests.

## PNNI Link State Packets

See *PLSP*.

## PNNI topology state element

See *PTSE*.

## PNO

Public Network Operator. See also *PTT*.

## POET

packet over E3/T3.

## point of presence

See *POP*.

## point-to-multipoint

See *p2mp*.

### point-to-multipoint connection

One of two fundamental connection types. In ATM, a point-to-multipoint connection is a unidirectional connection in which a single source end-system (known as a root node) connects to multiple destination end-systems (known as leaves). Compare with *point-to-point connection*.

### point-to-point

See *p2p*.

### point-to-point connection

One of two fundamental connection types. In ATM, a point-to-point connection can be a unidirectional or bidirectional connection between two ATM end-systems. Compare with *point-to-multipoint connection*.

### Point-to-Point Protocol

See *PPP*.

### poison reverse updates

Routing updates that explicitly indicate that a network or a subnet is unreachable, rather than implying that a network is unreachable by not including it in updates. Poison reverse updates are sent to defeat large routing loops.

### POL

Provisioning Object Library.

### policy

Any defined rule that determines the use of resources within the network. A policy can be based on a user, a device, a subnetwork, a network, or an application.

### policy decision point

Server that makes policy decisions. It has global knowledge of network policies, and is consulted by network devices (like routers) that enforce the policies.

### policy enforcement point

Device on which policy decisions are carried out. Usually a network node like a router or a switch.

### policy routing

Routing scheme that forwards packets to specific interfaces based on user-configured policies. Such policies might specify that traffic sent from a particular network should be forwarded out one interface, and all other traffic should be forwarded out another interface.

**policy server**

Server (at least one in each QoS domain) that holds policies for reference by and decision over client routers and switches.

**policy-based routing**

See *policy routing*.

**poll/final bit**

See *P/F*.

**polling**

Access method in which a primary network device inquires, in an orderly fashion, whether secondaries have data to transmit. The inquiry occurs in the form of a message to each secondary that gives the secondary the right to transmit.

**POM**

Provisioning Object Manager.

**POP**

**1.** point of presence. In OSS, a physical location where an interexchange carrier installed equipment to interconnect with a *local exchange carrier (LEC)*.

**2.** Post Office Protocol. Protocol that client e-mail applications use to retrieve mail from a mail server.

**port**

**1.** Interface on an internetworking device (such as a router).

**2.** In IP terminology, an upper-layer process that receives information from lower layers. Ports are numbered, and each numbered port is associated with a specific process. For example, SMTP is associated with port 25. A port number is also called a well-known address.

**3.** To rewrite software or microcode so that it runs on a different hardware platform or in a different software environment than that for which it was originally designed.

**port address translation**

Translation method that allows the user to conserve addresses in the global address pool by allowing source ports in TCP connections or UDP conversations to be translated. Different local addresses then map to the same global address, with port translation providing the necessary uniqueness. When translation is required, the new port number is picked out of the same range as the original following the convention of Berkeley Standard Distribution (SD).

This prevents end stations from seeing connection requests with source ports apparently corresponding to the Telnet, HTTP, or FTP daemon, for example. As a result, Cisco IOS PAT supports about 4000 local addresses that can be mapped to the same global address.

### port concentrator switch

See *PCS*.

### port scan

Attack that sends client requests to a range of server port addresses on a host with the goal of finding an active port and exploiting a known vulnerability of that service.

### port snooping

See *circuit steering*.

### portware

Software running on a MICA technology HMM or DMM.

### POSI

Promoting Conference for OSI. Group of executives from the six major Japanese computer manufacturers and Nippon Telephone and Telegraph that sets policies and commits resources to promote OSI.

### POST

power-on self test. Set of hardware diagnostics that runs on a hardware device when that device is powered up.

### Post Office Protocol

See *POP*.

### Post, Telephone, and Telegraph

See *PTT*.

### POTS

plain old telephone service. See *PSTN*.

### POTS dial peer

Dial peer connected via a traditional telephony network. POTS peers point to a particular voice port on a voice network device.

**POTS splitter**

A device (or one part of a larger device) that enables both a DSL data device (for example, a Cisco 1400 series router) and a standard analog device (such as a telephone) to share the same ADSL line.

**power-on self test**

See *POST*.

**power-on servicing**

Feature that allows faulty components to be diagnosed, removed, and replaced while the rest of the device continues to operate normally. Sometimes abbreviated POS. Sometimes called hot swapping. See also *OIR*.

**PPP**

Point-to-Point Protocol. Successor to SLIP that provides router-to-router and host-to-network connections over synchronous and asynchronous circuits. Whereas SLIP was designed to work with IP, PPP was designed to work with several network layer protocols, such as IP, IPX, and ARA. PPP also has built-in security mechanisms, such as CHAP and PAP. PPP relies on two protocols: LCP and NCP. See also *CHAP*, *LCP*, *NCP*, *PAP*, and *SLIP*.

**PPS**

packet per second.

**PPTP**

Point-to-Point Tunneling Protocol. RFC 2637 describes the PPTP protocol.

**PQ**

priority queuing.

**PQ/CBWFQ**

priority queueing/class-based weighted fair queueing (PQ/CBWFQ). Feature that brings strict priority queueing to CBWFQ. Strict priority queueing allows delay-sensitive data, such as voice, to be dequeued and sent first (before packets in other queues are dequeued), giving delay-sensitive data preferential treatment over other traffic.

**precedence order**

Determines which value of an option is applied to a cable modem. Options defined in the most specific option set scopings take precedence over the same options defined in more general scopings. Within an option set, common options always have a lower precedence order than a specific service tuple if the cable modem has an associated service package. If a service package is not associated with the cable modem, the TFTP server uses the common options.

**precloning**

Cloning a specified number of virtual access interfaces from a virtual template at system startup or when the command is configured.

**presentation layer**

Layer 6 of the OSI reference model. This layer ensures that information sent by the application layer of one system will be readable by the application layer of another. The presentation layer also is concerned with the data structures used by programs and therefore negotiates data transfer syntax for the application layer. Corresponds roughly with the *presentation services layer* of the SNA model. See also *application layer*, *data-link layer*, *network layer*, *physical layer*, *session layer*, and *transport layer*.

**presentation services layer**

Layer 6 of the SNA architectural model. This layer provides network resource management, session presentation services, and some application management. Corresponds roughly with the *PQ* of the OSI model. See also *data flow control layer*, *data-link control layer*, *path control layer*, *physical control layer*, *transaction services layer*, and *transmission control layer*.

**preshared key**

Shared secret key that is used during IKE authentication.

**Pretty Good Privacy**

See *PGP*.

**PRI**

Primary Rate Interface. ISDN interface to primary rate access. Primary rate access consists of a single 64-kbps D channel plus 23 (T1) or 30 (E1) B channels for voice or data. Compare with *BRI*. See also *BISDN*, *ISDN*, and *N-ISDN*.

**primary**

See *primary station*.

**Primary LU**

See *PLU*.

**Primary Rate Interface**

See *PRI*.

**primary ring**

One of the two rings that make up a FDDI or CDDI ring. The primary ring is the default path for data transmissions. Compare with *secondary ring*.

**primary station**

In bit-synchronous data link layer protocols, such as HDLC and SDLC, a station that controls the transmission activity of secondary stations and performs other management functions, such as error control through polling or other means. Primary stations send commands to secondary stations and receive responses. Also called, simply, a primary. See also *secondary station*.

**print server**

Networked computer system that fields, manages, and executes (or sends for execution) print requests from other network devices.

**priority queue**

Routing feature in which frames in an output queue are prioritized based on various characteristics, such as packet size and interface type.

**Privacy Enhanced Mail**

See *PEM*.

**private branch exchange**

See *PBX*.

**private cable modem**

Each subscriber/account pair is associated with a single cable modem, which services one or more CPEs also associated with the subscriber/account.

**private key**

Secret component of a pair of cryptographic keys used for asymmetric cryptography.

**Private Network Node Interface**

See *PNNI*.

**Private Network-Network Interface**

See *PNNI*.

**privilege**

Authorization or set of authorizations to perform security-relevant functions, especially in the context of a computer operating system.

**privileged process**

Computer process that is authorized (and, therefore, trusted) to perform some security-relevant functions that ordinary processes are not.

**PRMD**

Private Management Domain. X.400 Message Handling System private organization mail system (for example, NASAmail).

**probe**

Probe is an intrusive analysis technique that uses the information obtained during scanning to more fully interrogate each network device. The probe uses well known exploitation techniques to fully confirm each suspected vulnerability as well as to detect any vulnerabilities that cannot be found using nonintrusive techniques.

**process switching**

See *process switching* in the "Cisco Systems Terms and Acronyms" section.

**programmable read-only memory**

See *PROM*.

**PROM**

programmable read-only memory. ROM that can be programmed using special equipment. PROMs can be programmed only once. Compare with *EPROM*.

**propagation delay**

Time required for data to travel over a network from its source to its ultimate destination.

**proprietary**

Refers to information (or other property) that is owned by an individual or an organization and for which the use is restricted by that entity.

**protected checksum**

Checksum that is computed for a data object by means that protect against active attacks that would attempt to change the checksum to make it match changes made to the data object.

**protected distribution system**

Wireline or fiber-optic system that includes sufficient safeguards (acoustic, electric, electromagnetic, and physical) to permit its use for unencrypted transmission of (cleartext) data.

**protection ring**

One of a hierarchy of privileged operation modes of a system that gives certain access rights to processes authorized to operate in that mode.

**protocol**

Formal description of a set of rules and conventions that govern how devices on a network exchange information.

**protocol address**

See *network address*.

**protocol control information**

See *PCI*.

**protocol converter**

Enables equipment with different data formats to communicate by translating the data transmission code of one device to the data transmission code of another device.

**protocol data unit**

See *PDU*.

**Protocol Independent Multicast**

See *PIM*.

**protocol stack**

Set of related communications protocols that operate together and, as a group, address communication at some or all of the seven layers of the OSI reference model. Not every protocol stack covers each layer of the model, and often a single protocol in the stack addresses a number of layers at once. TCP/IP is a typical protocol stack.

**protocol suite**

Complementary collection of communication protocols used in a computer network.

**protocol translator**

Network device or software that converts one protocol into another similar protocol.

**provider edge router**

Router that is part of a service provider's network and is connected to a customer edge (CE) router.

**provisioning**

Creation of an active subscriber account, or modification of parameters for an existing subscriber account. Provisioning of a subscriber account includes subscriber account registration and device activation.

**proxy**

**1.** Entity that, in the interest of efficiency, essentially stands in for another entity.

**2.** Special gateways that relay one H.323 session to another.

**proxy Address Resolution Protocol**

See *proxy ARP*.

**proxy ARP**

proxy Address Resolution Protocol. Variation of the ARP protocol in which an intermediate device (for example, a router) sends an ARP response on behalf of an end node to the requesting host. Proxy ARP can lessen bandwidth use on slow-speed WAN links. See also *ARP*.

**proxy explorer**

Technique that minimizes exploding explorer packet traffic propagating through an SRB network by creating an explorer packet reply cache, the entries of which are reused when subsequent explorer packets need to find the same host.

**proxy polling**

See *proxy polling* in the "Cisco Systems Terms and Acronyms" section.

**proxy server**

Intermediary program that acts as both a server and a client for the purpose of making requests on behalf of other clients. Requests are serviced internally or by passing them on, possibly after translation, to other servers. A proxy interprets, and, if necessary, rewrites a request message before forwarding it.

**PSDN**

packet-switched data network. See *PSN*.

### PSE

packet switch exchange. Essentially, a switch. The term PSE generally is used in reference to a switch in an X.25 packet switch. See also *switch*.

### PSN

packet-switched network. Network that uses packet-switching technology for data transfer. Sometimes called a PSDN. See also *packet switching*.

### PSTN

public switched telephone network. General term referring to the variety of telephone networks and services in place worldwide. Sometimes called *POTS*.

### PTI

payload type identifier. 3-bit descriptor in the ATM cell header indicating the type of payload that the cell contains. Payload types include user and management cells; one combination indicates that the cell is the last cell of an AAL5 frame.

### PTSE

PNNI topology state element. Collection of PNNI information that is flooded among all logical nodes within a peer group. See also *peer group* and *PNNI*.

### PTSP

PNNI topology state packet. Type of PNNI routing packet used to exchange reachability and resource information among ATM switches to ensure that a connection request is routed to the destination along a path that has a high probability of meeting the requested QoS. Typically, PTSPs include bidirectional information about the transit behavior of particular nodes (based on entry and exit ports) and current internal state. See also *PNNI* and *QoS*.

### PTT

Post, Telephone, and Telegraph. Government agency that provides telephone services. PTTs exist in most areas outside North America and provide both local and long-distance telephone services.

### PU

physical unit. SNA component that manages and monitors the resources of a node, as requested by an SSCP. There is one PU per node.

### PU 2

Physical Unit 2. SNA peripheral node that can support only DLUs that require services from a VTAM host and that are capable only of performing the secondary LU role in SNA sessions.

## PU 2.1

Physical Unit type 2.1. SNA network node used for connecting peer nodes in a peer-oriented network. PU 2.1 sessions do not require that one node reside on VTAM. APPN is based upon PU 2.1 nodes, which also can be connected to a traditional hierarchical SNA network.

## PU 4

Physical Unit 4. Component of an IBM FEP capable of full-duplex data transfer. Each such SNA device employs a separate data and control path into the transmit and receive buffers of the control program.

## PU 5

Physical Unit 5. Component of an IBM mainframe or host computer that manages an SNA network. PU 5 nodes are involved in routing within the SNA path control layer.

## public data network

See *PDN*.

## public key

Publicly disclosable component of a pair of cryptographic keys used for asymmetric cryptography.

## Public Switched Telephone Network

See *PSTN*.

## public-key certificate

Digital certificate that binds a system entity's identity to a public key value, and possibly to additional data items; a digitally signed data structure that attests to the ownership of a public key.

## Public-Key Cryptography Standards

See *PKCS*.

## pulse amplitude modulation

See *PAM*.

## pulse code modulation

See *PCM*.

## pulse density

See *ones density*.

## PUP

PARC Universal Protocol. Protocol similar to IP developed at PARC.

## PVC

permanent virtual circuit (or connection). Virtual circuit that is permanently established. PVCs save bandwidth associated with circuit establishment and tear down in situations where certain virtual circuits must exist all the time. In ATM terminology, called a permanent virtual connection. Compare with *SVC*. See also *virtual circuit*.

## PVP

permanent virtual path. Virtual path that consists of PVCs. See also *PVC* and *virtual path*.

## PVP tunneling

permanent virtual path tunneling. Method of linking two private ATM networks across a public network using a virtual path. The public network transparently trunks the entire collection of virtual channels in the virtual path between the two private networks.

## PVST+

per-VLAN spanning tree. Support for Dot1q trunks to map multiple spanning trees to a single spanning tree.

# Q

## Q.2931

ITU-T specification, based on Q.931, for establishing, maintaining, and clearing network connections at the B-ISDN user-network interface. The UNI 3.1 specification is based on Q.2931. See also *Q.931* and *UNI*.

## Q.920/Q.921

ITU-T specifications for the ISDN UNI data link layer. See also *UNI*.

## Q.922A

ITU-T specification for Frame Relay encapsulation.

## Q.931

ITU-T specification for signaling to establish, maintain, and clear ISDN network connections. See also *Q.93B*.

## Q.93B

ITU-T specification for signaling to establish, maintain, and clear BISDN network connections. An evolution of ITU-T recommendation Q.931. See also *Q.931*.

## QAM

quadrature amplitude modulation. Method for encoding digital data in an analog signal in which each combination of phase and amplitude represents one of sixteen four-bit patterns. This is required for fax transmission at 9600 bits per second.

## QLLC

Qualified Logical Link Control. Data link layer protocol defined by IBM that allows SNA data to be transported across X.25 networks.

## QoS

quality of service. Measure of performance for a transmission system that reflects its transmission quality and service availability.

### QoS parameters

quality of service parameters. Parameters that control the amount of traffic the source in an ATM network sends over an SVC. If any switch along the path cannot accommodate the requested QoS parameters, the request is rejected and a rejection message is forwarded back to the originator of the request.

### QoS Policy Propagation on BGP

See *QPPB*.

### QPPB

QoS Policy Propagation on BGP. Feature that classifies packets by IP precedence based on BGP community lists, BGP autonomous system paths, and access lists. After a packet is classified, other quality of service features such as committed access rate (CAR) and Weighted Random Early Detection (WRED) can specify and enforce policies to fit a business model.

### QPM

See *QPM* in the "Cisco Systems Terms and Acronyms" section.

### QPSK

quaternary phase shift keying. Digital frequency modulation technique used for sending data over coaxial cable networks. Because it's both easy to implement and fairly resistant to noise, QPSK is used primarily for sending data from the cable subscriber upstream to the Internet.

### QRSS

quasi-random signal sequence. A test pattern widely used to simulate voice signals.

### QSIG

Q (point of the ISDN model) Signaling. Signaling standard. Common channel signaling protocol based on ISDN Q.931 standards and used by many digital PBXs.

### Qualified Logical Link Control

See *QLLC*.

### quality of service

See *QoS*.

### quartet signaling

Signaling technique used in 100VG-AnyLAN networks that allows data transmission at 100 Mbps over four pairs of UTP cable at the same frequencies used in 10BaseT networks. See also *100VG-AnyLAN*.

**query**

Message used to inquire about the value of some variable or set of variables.

**queue**

**1.** Generally, an ordered list of elements waiting to be processed.

**2.** In routing, a backlog of packets waiting to be forwarded over a router interface.

**queuing delay**

Amount of time that data must wait before it can be transmitted onto a statistically multiplexed physical circuit.

**queuing theory**

Scientific principles governing the formation or lack of formation of congestion on a network or at an interface.

**QUIPU**

Pioneering software package developed to study the OSI Directory and to provide extensive pilot capabilities.

**QWP**

query with permission.

### RA

registration authority. Optional PKI entity (separate from the CAs) that does not sign either digital certificates or CRLs but has responsibility for recording or verifying some or all of the information (particularly the identities of subjects) needed by a CA to issue certificates and CRLs and to perform other certificate management functions.

### RACE

Research on Advanced Communications in Europe. Project sponsored by the EC for the development of broadband networking capabilities.

### race condition ranging

The process of acquiring the correct timing offset such that the transmissions of a cable modem are aligned with the correct mini-slot boundary.

### radio frequency

Generally refers to wireless communications with frequencies below 300 GHz.

### RADIUS

Remote Authentication Dial-In User Service. Database for authenticating modem and ISDN connections and for tracking connection time.

### RAM

random-access memory. Volatile memory that can be read and written by a microprocessor.

### random early detection

Congestion avoidance algorithm in which a small percentage of packets are dropped when congestion is detected and before the queue in question overflows completely.

### ranging

Process of acquiring the correct timing offset such that the transmissions of a cable access router are aligned with the correct minislot boundary.

## RARE

Réseaux Associés pour la Recherche Européenne. Association of European universities and research centers designed to promote an advanced tele-communications infrastructure in the European scientific community. RARE merged with EARN to form TERENA. See also *EARN* and *TERENA*.

## RARP

Reverse Address Resolution Protocol. Protocol in the TCP/IP stack that provides a method for finding IP addresses based on MAC addresses. Compare with *ARP*.

## RAS

**1.** Registration, Admission, and Status Protocol. Protocol that is used between endpoints and the gatekeeper to perform management functions. RAS signalling function performs registration, admissions, bandwidth changes, status, and disengage procedures between the VoIP gateway and the gatekeeper.

**2.** remote access server.

## rate enforcement

See *traffic policing*.

## rate queue

In ATM, a value associated with one or more virtual circuits that defines the speed at which an individual virtual circuit transmits data to the remote end. Each rate queue represents a portion of the overall bandwidth available on an ATM link. The combined bandwidth of all configured rate queues should not exceed the total available bandwidth.

## raw mode

MICA technologies interface mode in which no framing takes place. The other interface modes are PPP and SLIP. In raw mode, data is forwarded immediately without interpretation of individual characters.

## RBAC

role-based access control. Form of identity-based access control where the system entities that are identified and controlled are functional positions in an organization or process.

## RBHC

regional Bell holding company. One of seven regional telephone companies formed by the breakup of AT&T. RBHCs differ from RBOCs in that RBHCs cross state boundaries.

### RBOC

regional Bell operating company. Seven regional telephone companies formed by the breakup of AT&T. RBOCs differ from RBHCs in that RBOCs do not cross state boundaries.

### rcp

remote copy protocol. Protocol that allows users to copy files to and from a file system residing on a remote host or server on the network. The rcp protocol uses TCP to ensure the reliable delivery of data.

### rcp server

Router or other device that acts as a server for rcp. See also *rcp*.

### RCV

receive. Direction of signal moving from the high-speed receiver to the low- to medium-speed interface.

### RD

Request Disconnect.

### RDI

remote defect indication.

**1.** Indication that a failure has occurred at the far end of the network. Unlike FERF (far-end remote failure), the RDI alarm indication does not identify the specific circuit in a failure condition.

**2.** In ATM, when the physical layer detects loss of signal or cell synchronization, RDI cells are used to report a VPC/VCC failure. RDI cells are sent upstream by a VPC/VCC endpoint to notify the source VPC/VCC endpoint of the downstream failure.

### re-activation

Process of re-enabling network access and privileges for a subscriber device and reclaiming device attributes for other subscriber devices.

### reassembly

The putting back together of an IP datagram at the destination after it has been fragmented either at the source or at an intermediate node. See also *fragmentation*.

### recovery

The way that a system or a device resumes operation after overcoming a hardware or software problem.

**R**

**Redialer**

Interface hardware device that interconnects between a fax device and a Public Switched Telephone Network (PSTN). A redialer forwards a dialed number to another destination. Redialers contain a database of referral telephone numbers. When the user dials a specific number, the redialer collects the dialed digits and matches them to a listing in its database. If there is a match, the redialer dials the referral number (transparent to the user) and forwards the call to the referral number.

**redirect**

Part of the ICMP and ES-IS protocols that allows a router to tell a host that using another router would be more effective.

**redirect server**

A server that accepts a SIP request, maps the address into zero or more new addresses, and returns these addresses to the client. It does not initiate its own SIP request nor does it accept calls.

**redirector**

Software that intercepts requests for resources within a computer and analyzes them for remote access requirements. If remote access is required to satisfy the request, the redirector forms an RPC and sends the RPC to lower-layer protocol software for transmission through the network to the node that can satisfy the request.

**redistribution**

Allowing routing information discovered through one routing protocol to be distributed in the update messages of another routing protocol. Sometimes called route redistribution.

**redundancy**

**1.** In internetworking, the duplication of devices, services, or connections so that, in the event of a failure, the redundant devices, services, or connections can perform the work of those that failed. See also *redundant system*.

**2.** In telephony, the portion of the total information contained in a message that can be eliminated without loss of essential information or meaning.

**redundant system**

Computer, router, switch, or other system that contains two or more of each of the most important subsystems, such as two disk drives, two CPUs, or two power supplies.

### Reed-Solomon encoder

Device that takes a block of digital data and adds extra "redundant" bits. When errors occur during transmission or storage, the Reed-Solomon decoder processes each block and attempts to correct errors and recover the original data. The number and type of errors that can be corrected depends on the characteristics of the Reed-Solomon code. Reed-Solomon codes are used in storage devices (including tape, compact disc, DVD), barcodes, wireless or mobile communications (including cellular telephones, microwave links, and so on), satellite communications, digital television/DVB, and high-speed modems (such as ADSL, xDSL, and so on).

### reflection attack

Type of replay attack in which transmitted data is sent back to its originator.

### reflexive access list

Reflexive access lists contain condition statements (entries) that define criteria for permitting IP packets. These entries are evaluated in order, and when a match occurs, no more entries are evaluated.

### registrar

Server that accepts REGISTER requests. A registrar typically is colocated with a proxy ora redirect server and might offer location services.

### registration

Administrative act or process whereby an entity's name and other attributes are established for the first time at a CA, prior to the CA issuing a digital certificate that has the entity's name as the subject.

### Registration, Admission, and Status protocol

See *RAS*.

### regrade

Deliberately change the classification level of information in an authorized manner.

### rekey

Change the value of a cryptographic key that is being used in an application of a cryptographic system.

### relay

OSI terminology for a device that connects two or more networks or network systems. A data link layer (Layer 2) relay is a bridge; a network layer (Layer 3) relay is a router. See also *bridge* and *router*.

### reliability

**1.** Total number of system failures, regardless of whether a given failure results in system down time. Compare with *availability*.

**2.** Ratio of expected to received keepalives from a link. If the ratio is high, the line is reliable. Used as a routing metric.

### Reliable SAP Update Protocol

See *RSUP* in the "Cisco Systems Terms and Acronyms" section.

### reload

The event of a Cisco router rebooting, or the command that causes the router to reboot.

### remote alarm indication

yellow alarm.

### remote ATM switch driver

Set of interfaces that allows Cisco IOS software to control the operation of a remote ATM switch through a control protocol, such as a VSI.

### remote bridge

Bridge that connects physically disparate network segments via WAN links.

### remote copy protocol

See *rcp*.

### remote defect identification

See *RDI*.

### remote job entry

See *RJE*.

### remote login

See *rlogin*.

### Remote Monitoring

See *RMON*.

### Remote Operations Service Element

See *ROSE*.

**remote shell protocol**

See *rsh*.

**remote source-route bridging**

See *RSRB*.

**remote system**

End system or router that is attached to a remote access network and that is either the initiator or the recipient of a call.

**remote-procedure call**

See *RPC*.

**rendezvous point**

Router specified in PIM sparse mode implementations to track membership in multicast groups and to forward messages to known multicast group addresses. See also *PIM sparse mode*.

**repeater**

Device that regenerates and propagates electrical signals between two network segments. See also *segment*.

**replay attack**

Attack in which a valid data transmission is maliciously or fraudulently repeated, either by the originator or by an adversary who intercepts the data and retransmits it, possibly as part of a masquerade attack.

**replication**

Process of keeping a copy of data, either through shadowing or caching. See also *caching* and *shadowing*.

**repository**

System for storing and distributing digital certificates and related information (including CRLs, CPSs, and certificate policies) to certificate users.

**repudiation**

Denial by a system entity that was involved in an association (especially an association that transfers information) of having participated in the relationship.

**Request For Comments**

See *RFC*.

**Request To Send**

See *RTS*.

**request/response unit**

See *RU*.

**required visual inspection**

See *RVI*.

**Research on Advanced Communications in Europe**

See *RACE*.

**Réseaux Associés pour la Recherche Européenne**

See *RARE*.

**reservation state block**

Block maintained by RSVP to store a reservation.

**residential gateway**

Customer premises equipment running XGCP that has connections to the VoIP network and connections to user telephony equipment.

**residual risk**

Risk that remains after countermeasures have been applied.

**Resource Reservation Protocol**

See *RSVP*.

**Reverse Address Resolution Protocol**

See *RARP*.

**Reverse Path Forwarding**

See *RPF*.

**RF**

radio frequency. Generic term referring to frequencies that correspond to radio transmissions, that is wireless communications with frequencies below 300 GHz. Cable TV and broadband networks use RF technology.

## RFC

Request For Comments. Document series used as the primary means for communicating information about the Internet. Some RFCs are designated by the IAB as Internet standards. Most RFCs document protocol specifications, such as Telnet and FTP, but some are humorous or historical. RFCs are available online from numerous sources.

## RFI

radio frequency interference. Radio frequencies that create noise that interferes with information being transmitted across unshielded copper cable.

## RFP

request for proposal.

## RFS

Remote File System. Distributed file system, similar to NFS, developed by AT&T and distributed with their UNIX System V operating system.

## RHC

regional holding company.

## RIF

Routing Information Field. Field in the IEEE 802.5 header that is used by a source-route bridge to determine through which Token Ring network segments a packet must transit. A RIF is made up of ring and bridge numbers as well as other information.

## RII

Routing Information Identifier. Bit used by SRT bridges to distinguish between frames that should be transparently bridged and frames that should be passed to the SRB module for handling.

## RIM

Request Initialization Mode.

## ring

Connection of two or more stations in a logically circular topology. Information is passed sequentially between active stations. Token Ring, FDDI, and CDDI are based on this topology.

### ring group

Collection of Token Ring interfaces on one or more routers that is part of a one-bridge Token Ring network.

### ring latency

Time required for a signal to propagate once around a ring in a Token Ring or IEEE 802.5 network.

### ring monitor

Centralized management tool for Token Ring networks based on the IEEE 802.5 specification. See also *active monitor* and *standby monitor*.

### ring topology

Network topology that consists of a series of repeaters connected to one another by unidirectional transmission links to form a single closed loop. Each station on the network connects to the network at a repeater. Although logically a ring, ring topologies most often are organized in a closed-loop star. Compare with *bus topology*, *star topology*, and *tree topology*.

### RIP

Routing Information Protocol. IGP supplied with UNIX BSD systems. The most common IGP in the Internet. RIP uses hop count as a routing metric. See also *hop count*, *IGP*, and *OSPF*. See also *EIGRP* and *IGRP* in the "Cisco Systems Terms and Acronyms" section.

### RIPE

Réseaux IP Européennes. Group formed to coordinate and promote TCP/IP-based networks in Europe.

### RISC

reduced instruction set computing.

### risk assessment

Process that systematically identifies valuable system resources and threats to those resources, quantifies loss exposures (that is, loss potential) based on estimated frequencies and costs of occurrence, and (optionally) recommends how to allocate resources to countermeasures so as to minimize total exposure.

### risk management

Process of identifying, controlling, and eliminating or minimizing uncertain events that might affect system resources.

**RJ connector**

registered jack connector. Standard connectors originally used to connect telephone lines. RJ connectors are now used for telephone connections and for 10BaseT and other types of network connections. RJ-11, RJ-12, and RJ-45 are popular types of RJ connectors.

**RJE**

remote job entry. Application that is batch-oriented, as opposed to interactive. In RJE environments, jobs are submitted to a computing facility, and output is received later.

**RLM**

Redundant Link Manager.

**rlogin**

remote login. Terminal emulation program, similar to Telnet, offered in most UNIX implementations.

**RM**

resource management. Management of critical resources in an ATM network. Two critical resources are buffer space and trunk bandwidth. Provisioning can be used to allocate network resources in order to separate traffic flows according to service characteristics.

**RMON**

remote monitoring. MIB agent specification described in RFC 1271 that defines functions for the remote monitoring of networked devices. The RMON specification provides numerous monitoring, problem detection, and reporting capabilities.

**roaming service**

Dial service for cable subscribers that require access away from their cable modems.

**ROLC**

routing over large clouds. Working group in IETF created to analyze and propose solutions to problems that arise when performing IP routing over large, shared media networks, such as ATM, Frame Relay, SMDS, and X.25.

**ROM**

read-only memory. Nonvolatile memory that can be read, but not written, by the microprocessor.

**root account**

Privileged account on UNIX systems used exclusively by network or system administrators.

**root bridge**

Exchanges topology information with designated bridges in a spanning-tree implementation to notify all other bridges in the network when topology changes are required. This prevents loops and provides a measure of defense against link failure.

**root CA**

Ultimate CA, which signs the certificates of the subordinate CAs. The root CA has a self-signed certificate that contains its own public key.

**root certificate**

Certificate for which the subject is a root. Hierarchical PKI usage: The self-signed public-key certificate at the top of a certification hierarchy.

**root key**

Public key for which the matching private key is held by a root.

**ROSE**

Remote Operations Service Element. OSI RPC mechanism used by various OSI network application protocols.

**rotary groups**

Several contiguous lines that allow a connection to be made to the next free line in the group. Also called a hunt group.

**round-trip time**

See *RTT*.

**route**

Path through an internetwork.

**route distinguisher**

An 8-byte value that is concatenated with an IPv4 prefix to create a unique VPN IPv4 prefix.

**route extension**

In SNA, a path from the destination subarea node through peripheral equipment to an NAU.

## route map

Method of controlling the redistribution of routes between routing domains.

## Route Processor

See *RP* in the "Cisco Systems Terms and Acronyms" section.

## route redistribution

See *redistribution*.

## route summarization

Consolidation of advertised addresses in OSPF and IS-IS. In OSPF, this causes a single summary route to be advertised to other areas by an area border router.

## Route/Switch Processor

See *RSP* in the "Cisco Systems Terms and Acronyms" section.

## routed bridge encapsulation

The process by which a stub-bridged segment is terminated on a point-to-point routed interface. Specifically, the router is routing on an IEEE 802.3 or Ethernet header carried over a point-to-point protocol, such as PPP, RFC 1483 ATM, or RFC 1490 Frame Relay.

## routed protocol

Protocol that can be routed by a router. A router must be able to interpret the logical internetwork as specified by that routed protocol. Examples of routed protocols include AppleTalk, DECnet, and IP.

## router

Network layer device that uses one or more metrics to determine the optimal path along which network traffic should be forwarded. Routers forward packets from one network to another based on network layer information. Occasionally called a gateway (although this definition of gateway is becoming increasingly outdated). Compare with *gateway*. See also *relay*.

## routing

Process of finding a path to a destination host. Routing is very complex in large networks because of the many potential intermediate destinations a packet might traverse before reaching its destination host.

### routing domain

Group of end systems and intermediate systems operating under the same set of administrative rules. Within each routing domain is one or more areas, each uniquely identified by an area address.

### Routing Information Field

See *RIF*.

### Routing Information Identifier

See *RII*.

### Routing Information Protocol

See *RIP*.

### routing metric

Method by which a routing algorithm determines that one route is better than another. This information is stored in routing tables. Metrics include bandwidth, communication cost, delay, hop count, load, MTU, path cost, and reliability. Sometimes referred to simply as a *metric*. See also *cost*.

### routing over large clouds

See *ROLC*.

### routing protocol

Protocol that accomplishes routing through the implementation of a specific routing algorithm. Examples of routing protocols include IGRP, OSPF, and RIP.

### routing table

Table stored in a router or some other internetworking device that keeps track of routes to particular network destinations and, in some cases, metrics associated with those routes.

### Routing Table Maintenance Protocol

See *RTMP*.

### Routing Table Protocol

See *RTP*.

### routing update

Message sent from a router to indicate network reachability and associated cost information. Routing updates typically are sent at regular intervals and after a change in network topology. Compare with *flash update*.

## RP

See *RP* in the "Cisco Systems Terms and Acronyms" section.

## RPC

remote-procedure call. Technological foundation of client/server computing. RPCs are procedure calls that are built or specified by clients and are executed on servers, with the results returned over the network to the clients. See also *client/server computing*.

## RPF

Reverse Path Forwarding. Multicasting technique in which a multicast datagram is forwarded out of all but the receiving interface if the receiving interface is the one used to forward unicast datagrams to the source of the multicast datagram.

## RPR

Restore Path request. The RPR is a WaRP request sent using a Restore Path packet that is used to establish a virtual path between two nodes. The request is sent by a source node, or a proxy source node, to establish an intra-zone path for a VWP. The packet usually is sent during failure recovery procedures but also can be used for provisioning new VWPs. The node that sends the request is called the *originating node*. The node that terminates the request is called the *target node*.

## RR

relative rate. In ATM, one of the congestion feedback modes provided by ABR service. In RR mode, switches set a bit in forward and backward RM cells to indicate congestion. See also *ABR* and *RLM*.

## RRJ

registration rejection. RAS message sent as a registration rejection.

## RRQ

registration request. RAS message sent as a registration request.

## RS-232

Popular physical layer interface. Now known as EIA/TIA-232. See also *EIA/TIA-232*.

## RS-422

Balanced electrical implementation of EIA/TIA-449 for high-speed data transmission. Now referred to collectively with RS-423 as EIA-530. See also *EIA-530* and *RS-423*.

## RS-423

Unbalanced electrical implementation of EIA/TIA-449 for EIA/TIA-232 compatibility. Now referred to collectively with RS-422 as EIA-530. See also *EIA-530* and *RS-422*.

## RS-449

Popular physical layer interface. Now known as *EIA/TIA-449*. See also *EIA/TIA-449*.

## RSA

Acronym stands for Rivest, Shamir, and Adelman, the inventors of the technique. Public-key cryptographic system that can be used for encryption and authentication.

## rsh

remote shell protocol. Protocol that allows a user to execute commands on a remote system without having to log in to the system. For example, rsh can be used to remotely examine the status of a number of access servers without connecting to each communication server, executing the command, and then disconnecting from the communication server.

## RSIP

ReStart In Progress. MGCP command used to indicate that a span (or collection of spans) has come into service, has gone out of service, or is about to go out of service.

## RSM

Route Switch Module.

## RSP

See *RSP* in the "Cisco Systems Terms and Acronyms" section.

## RSRB

remote source-route bridging. SRB over WAN links. See also *SRB*.

## RSUP

See *RSUP* in the "Cisco Systems Terms and Acronyms" section.

## RSVP

Resource Reservation Protocol. Protocol that supports the reservation of resources across an IP network. Applications running on IP end systems can use RSVP to indicate to other nodes the nature (bandwidth, jitter, maximum burst, and so on) of the packet streams they want to receive. RSVP depends on IPv6. Also known as Resource Reservation Setup Protocol. See also *IPv6*.

## RTCP

RTP Control Protocol. Protocol that monitors the QOS of an IPv6 RTP connection and conveys information about the on-going session. See also *RTP (Real-Time Transport Protocol)*.

## RTFM

read the fantastic manual. Acronym often used when someone asks a simple or common question.

## RTMP

Routing Table Maintenance Protocol. Apple Computer's proprietary routing protocol. RTMP establishes and maintains the routing information that is required to route datagrams from any source socket to any destination socket in an AppleTalk network. Using RTMP, routers dynamically maintain routing tables to reflect changes in topology. RTMP was derived from RIP. See also *RTP (Routing Table Protocol)*.

## RTP

**1.** Routing Table Protocol. VINES routing protocol based on RIP. Distributes network topology information and aids VINES servers in finding neighboring clients, servers, and routers. Uses delay as a routing metric. See also *SRTP*.

**2.** Rapid Transport Protocol. Provides pacing and error recovery for APPN data as it crosses the APPN network. With RTP, error recovery and flow control are done end-to-end rather than at every node. RTP prevents congestion rather than reacts to it.

**3.** Real-Time Transport Protocol. Commonly used with IP networks. RTP is designed to provide end-to-end network transport functions for applications transmitting real-time data, such as audio, video, or simulation data, over multicast or unicast network services. RTP provides such services as payload type identification, sequence numbering, timestamping, and delivery monitoring to real-time applications.

## RTP Control Protocol

See *RTCP*.

## RTS

Request To Send. EIA/TIA-232 control signal that requests a data transmission on a communications line.

## RTSC

read the source code.

## RTSP

Real Time Streaming Protocol. Enables the controlled delivery of real-time data, such as audio and video. Sources of data can include both live data feeds, such as live audio and video, and stored content, such as pre-recorded events. RTSP is designed to work with established protocols, such as RTP and HTTP.

## RTT

round-trip time. Time required for a network communication to travel from the source to the destination and back. RTT includes the time required for the destination to process the message from the source and to generate a reply. RTT is used by some routing algorithms to aid in calculating optimal routes.

## RU

request/response unit. Request and response messages exchanged between NAUs in an SNA network.

## RUDP

Reliable User Data Protocol.

## run-time memory

Memory accessed while a program runs.

## RVI

required visual inspection.

## SA

**1.** service affecting. Category of conditions that interrupt payload traffic. See also *non-service affecting*.

**2.** security association. Instance of security policy and keying material applied to a data flow.

## SAC

single-attached concentrator. FDDI or CDDI concentrator that connects to the network by being cascaded from the master port of another FDDI or CDDI concentrator.

## sampling rate

Rate at which samples of a particular waveform amplitude are taken.

## SAN

storage area networking. An emerging data communications platform that interconnects servers and storage at Gigabaud speeds. By combining LAN networking models with the core building blocks of server performance and mass storage capacity, SAN eliminates the bandwidth bottlenecks and scalability limitations imposed by previous SCSI bus-based architectures.

## SAP

**1.** service access point. Field defined by the IEEE 802.2 specification that is part of an address specification. Thus, the destination plus the DSAP define the recipient of a packet. The same applies to the SSAP. See also *DSAP* and *SSAP*.

**2.** Service Advertising Protocol. IPX protocol that provides a means of informing network clients, via routers and servers, of available network resources and services. See also *IPX*.

## SAR

segmentation and reassembly. One of the two sublayers of the AAL CPCS, responsible for dividing (at the source) and reassembling (at the destination) the PDUs passed from the CS. The SAR sublayer takes the PDUs processed by the CS and, after dividing them into 48-byte pieces of payload data, passes them to the ATM layer for further processing. See also *AAL*, *ATM*, *CPCS*, *CS*, and *SSCS*.

## SAS

**1.** single attachment station. Device attached only to the primary ring of a FDDI ring. Also known as a Class B station. Compare with *DAS*. See also *FDDI*.

**2.** statically assigned socket. Socket that is permanently reserved for use by a designated process. In an AppleTalk network, SASs are numbered 1 to 127; they are reserved for use by specific socket clients and for low-level built-in network services.

## satellite communication

Use of orbiting satellites to relay data between multiple earth-based stations. Satellite communications offer high bandwidth and a cost that is not related to distance between earth stations, long propagation delays, or broadcast capability.

## SBus

Bus technology used in Sun SPARC-based workstations and servers. The SBus specification was adopted by the IEEE as a new bus standard.

## SCA

subordinate certification authority. CA whose public-key certificate is issued by another (superior) CA.

## scan

Scan is a nonintrusive analysis technique that identifies the open ports found on each live network device and collects the associated port banners found as each port is scanned. Each port banner is compared against a table of rules to identify the network device, its operating system, and all potential vulnerabilities.

## scan line fix up

Mechanism used for non-ECM calls meant to eliminate fax failures caused by an excessive number of received page errors because of data loss. If data loss is detected, the data of the current scan line is discarded and replaced with the previous line or white space.

## SCCP

Signaling Connection Control Part. Trillium software that supports routing and translation and management functions and data transfer without logical signaling connections.

## SCP

Service Control Point. An element of an SS7-based Intelligent Network that performs various service functions, such as number translation, call setup and teardown, and so on.

## SCR

sustainable cell rate. Parameter defined by the ATM Forum for ATM traffic management. For VBR connections, SCR determines the long-term average cell rate that can be transmitted. See also *VBR*.

## SCTE

serial clock transmit external. Timing signal that DTE echoes to DCE to maintain clocking. SCTE is designed to compensate for clock phase shift on long cables. When the DCE device uses SCTE instead of its internal clock to sample data from the DTE, it is better able to sample the data without error even if there is a phase shift in the cable. See also *phase shift*.

## SDH

Synchronous Digital Hierarchy. European standard that defines a set of rate and format standards that are transmitted using optical signals over fiber. SDH is similar to SONET, with a basic SDH rate of 155.52 Mbps, designated at STM-1. See also *SONET* and *STM-1*.

## SDLC

Synchronous Data Link Control. SNA data link layer communications protocol. SDLC is a bit-oriented, full-duplex serial protocol that has spawned numerous similar protocols, including HDLC and LAPB. See also *HDLC* and *LAPB*.

## SDLC broadcast

See *SDLC broadcast* in the "Cisco Systems Terms and Acronyms" section.

## SDLC Transport

See *SDLC Transport* in the "Cisco Systems Terms and Acronyms" section.

## SDLLC

See *SDLLC* in the "Cisco Systems Terms and Acronyms" section.

### SDP

**1.** Session Definition Protocol. An IETF protocol for the definition of Multimedia Services. SDP messages can be part of SGCP and MGCP messages.

**2.** Session Data Protocol. SDP is intended for describing multimedia sessions for the purposes of session announcement, session invitation, and other forms of multimedia session initiation. [RFC 2327]

### SDSL

single-line digital subscriber line. One of four DSL technologies. SDSL delivers 1.544 Mbps both downstream and upstream over a single copper twisted pair. The use of a single twisted pair limits the operating range of SDSL to 10,000 feet (3048.8 meters). Compare with *ADSL*, *HDSL*, and *VDSL*.

### SDSU

SMDS DSU. DSU for access to SMDS via HSSIs and other serial interfaces.

### SDU

service data unit. Unit of information from an upper-layer protocol that defines a service request to a lower-layer protocol.

### SEAL

simple and efficient AAL. Scheme used by AAL5 in which the SAR sublayer segments CS PDUs without adding additional fields. See also *AAL*, *AAL5*, *CS*, and *SAR*.

### SECAM

TV system used in France and elsewhere, utilizing an 8 MHz–wide modulated signal.

### secondary

See *secondary station*.

### secondary ring

One of the two rings making up an FDDI or CDDI ring. The secondary ring usually is reserved for use in the event of a failure of the primary ring. Compare with *primary ring*.

### secondary station

In bit-synchronous data link layer protocols, such as HDLC, a station that responds to commands from a primary station. Sometimes referred to simply as a *secondary*. See also *primary station*.

**section**

Portion of a transmission facility, including terminating points between a terminal NE and a regenerator or two regenerators. A terminating point is the point after signal regeneration at which performance is monitored or can be monitored.

**section data communications channel**

A SONET-embedded operations channel that is processed by each STE node in a network. It provides many data channels for maintenance and operations functions, such as orderwire, performance monitoring, and craft/OS data communication channel (DCN) extension.

**Section DCC**

Section Data Communications Channel. In OSS, a 192-kbps data communications channel embedded in the section overhead for OAM&P traffic between two SONET network elements. See also *OAM&P* and *SONET*.

**Secure Shell Protocol**

Protocol that provides a secure remote connection to a router through a Transmission Control Protocol (TCP) application.

**secure state**

System condition in which no subject can access any object in an unauthorized manner.

**security association**

An instance of security policy and keying material applied to a data flow. Both IKE and IPSec use SAs, although SAs are independent of one another. IPSec SAs are unidirectional and are unique in each security protocol. An IKE SA is used by IKE only, and unlike the IPSec SA, it is bidirectional. IKE negotiates and establishes SAs on behalf of IPSec. A user also can establish IPSec SAs manually. A set of SAs are needed for a protected data pipe, one per direction per protocol. For example, if you have a pipe that supports ESP between peers, one ESP SA is required for each direction. SAs are identified uniquely by destination (IPSec endpoint) address, security protocol (AH or ESP), and security parameter index (SPI).

**security management**

One of five categories of network management defined by ISO for the management of OSI networks. Security management subsystems are responsible for controlling access to network resources. See also *accounting management*, *configuration management*, *fault management*, and *performance management*.

## security parameter index

See SPI. This is a number that, together with a destination IP address and a security protocol, uniquely identifies a particular security association. When using IKE to establish the security associations, the SPI for each security association is a pseudo-randomly derived number. Without IKE, the SPI is specified manually for each security association.

## seed router

Router in an AppleTalk network that has the network number or cable range built in to its port descriptor. The seed router defines the network number or cable range for other routers in that network segment and responds to configuration queries from nonseed routers on its connected AppleTalk network, allowing those routers to confirm or modify their configurations accordingly. Each AppleTalk network must have at least one seed router. See also *nonseed router*.

## SEFS

severely errored framing second. A PM parameter that counts out-of-frame seconds.

## segment

**1.** Section of a network that is bounded by bridges, routers, or switches.

**2.** In a LAN using a bus topology, a segment is a continuous electrical circuit that often is connected to other such segments with repeaters.

**3.** Term used in the TCP specification to describe a single transport layer unit of information. The terms *datagram*, *frame*, *message*, and *packet* also are used to describe logical information groupings at various layers of the OSI reference model and in various technology circles.

## segmentation and reassembly

See *SAR*.

## selector

Identifier (octet string) used by an OSI entity to distinguish among multiple SAPs at which it provides services to the layer above.

## sequence number protection

See *SNAP*.

## Sequenced Packet Exchange

See *SPX*.

**Sequenced Packet Protocol**

See *SPP*.

**Sequenced Routing Update Protocol**

See *SRTP*.

**serial clock transmit external**

See *SCTE*.

**Serial Line Internet Protocol**

See *SLIP*.

**serial transmission**

Method of data transmission in which the bits of a data character are transmitted sequentially over a single channel. Compare with *parallel transmission*.

**serial tunnel**

See *STUN* in the "Cisco Systems Terms and Acronyms" section.

**server**

Node or software program that provides services to clients. See also *back end, client,* and *FRF.11*.

**Server Message Block**

See *SMB*.

**service access point**

See *SAP*.

**Service Advertising Protocol**

See *SAP*.

**service class**

Collection of service types required for a specific service offered. Each service class includes the attributes and values that define the type or quality of service associated with a given class. For example, data connectivity is a service class you might define that includes the service type data-bandwidth.

**service data unit**

See *SDU*.

### service level

Various levels and quality of services defined for each service type. For example, the service type called quality of sound might have service levels defined for telephone, broadcast, and digital CD.

### service package

Quality of service that a cable provider offers subscribers. For example, Basic Student, Family Plus, and Internet are possible service packages. Subscribers may choose one or more service packages. A service class is selected for each service package, defining which service types make up the service package.

### service point

Interface between non-SNA devices and NetView that sends alerts from equipment unknown to the SNA environment.

### service profile identifier

See *SPID*.

### Service Specific Connection Oriented Protocol

See *SSCOP*.

### service specific convergence sublayer

See *SSCS*.

### service tuple

Service type and level pair. For example, the service tuple data-bandwidth=45 Mbps consists of the service type data-bandwidth and the service level 45 Mbps.

### service type

A component of a service that cable providers offer subscribers. For example, devices-supported might be a service type defined for the home networking service, indicating the number of computers the subscriber can connect to the cable network from home. One or more service levels is defined for each service type.

### SES

severely errored second. Second during which the bit error ratio is greater than a specified limit and transmission performance is significantly degraded. A PM parameter is measured on a per-channel basis.

### session

**1.** Related set of communications transactions between two or more network devices.

**2.** In SNA, a logical connection enabling two NAUs to communicate.

**session group**

Logically ordered list of sessions based on priority of the sessions. All the sessions in the session group should be configured to connect the same physical machines.

**session layer**

Layer 5 of the OSI reference model. This layer establishes, manages, and terminates sessions between applications and manages the data exchange between presentation layer entities. Corresponds to the *data flow control layer* of the SNA model. See also *application layer*, *data-link layer*, *network layer*, *physical layer*, *PQ*, and *transport layer*.

**session manager**

Manages all the sessions in a specific client.

**session set**

Collection of session groups.

**SET**

Secure Electronic Transactions. SET specification developed to allow for secure credit card and off-line debit card (check card) transactions over the World Wide Web.

**SF**

Super Frame. Common framing type used on T1 circuits. SF consists of 12 frames of 192 bits each, with the 193rd bit providing error checking and other functions. SF is superseded by ESF but is still widely used. Also called D4 framing. See also *ESP*.

**S-frame**

Supervisory frame. One of three SDLC frame formats. See also *I-frame* and *U-frame*.

**SG**

signaling gateway. Gateway that supports only signaling traffic (no bearer traffic.) For example, a gateway that terminates SS7 A-links is a signaling gateway.

**SGCP**

Simple Gateway Control Protocol. Controls Voice over IP gateways by an external call control element (called a call-agent). This has been adapted to allow SGCP to control switch ATM Circuit Emulation Service circuits (called endpoints in SGCP). The resulting system (call-agents and gateways) allows for the call-agent to engage in Common Channel Signalling (CCS) over a 64-kbps CES circuit, governing the interconnection of bearer channels on the CES interface.

### SGML

Standardized Generalized Markup Language. International standard for the definition of system-independent, device-independent methods of representing text in electronic form.

### SGMP

Simple Gateway Monitoring Protocol. Network management protocol that was considered for Internet standardization and later evolved into SNMP. Documented in RFC 1028. See also *SNMP*.

### SHA-1

Secure Hash Algorithm 1. Algorithm that takes a message of less than 264 bits in length and produces a 160-bit message digest. The large message digest provides security against brute-force collision and inversion attacks. SHA-1 [NIS94c] is a revision to SHA that was published in 1994.

### shadowing

Form of replication in which well-defined units of information are copied to several DSAs.

### shaping

See *traffic shaping*.

### shared cable modem

Single cable modem servicing multiple CPEs is associated with multiple subscriber/accounts and is administered in the User Registrar Admin UI through a neighborhood.

### shielded cable

Cable that has a layer of shielded insulation to reduce EMI.

### shielded twisted-pair

See *STP*.

### ships in the night mode

Capability to support both MPLS functions and ATM Forum protocols on the same physical interface, or on the same router or switch platform. In this mode, the two protocol stacks operate independently.

### shortest path first algorithm

See *SPF*.

### shortest-path routing

Routing that minimizes distance or path cost through the application of an algorithm.

### SID

Service ID. A number that defines (at the MAC sublayer) a particular mapping between a cable modem (CM) and the CMTS. The SID is used for the purpose of upstream bandwidth allocation and class-of-service management.

### Signal path

Route of a signal channel that carries signaling data.

### signal quality error

See *SQE*.

### signal unit error rate monitor

SS7 MTP 2 function that provides monitoring of signal unit events.

### signaling

**1.** Process of sending a transmission signal over a physical medium for the purposes of communication.

**2.** In telephony, a term that refers to sending call information across a telephone connection. This information can be transmitted by many techniques, such as opening and closing a loop to stop and start the flow of DC loop current (used to indicate on-hook and off-hook state and to transmit dial-pulsing of digits), sending of ringing voltage to alert the other side of an incoming call, sending digit information in the form of DTMF or MF tones, or sending call state information on a DS0 timeslot by using robbed-bits.

### Signaling Connection Control Part

SS7 protocol level that provides connectionless and connection-oriented network services and addressing services. The transport layer for TCAP-based services.

### Signaling Gateway

It sends and receives PSTN signalling at the edge of IP/ATM network. It backhauls the signalling to a Media Gateway Controller. The Signaling Gateway function may be coresident with the Media Gateway function to process signaling associated with line or trunk terminations controlled by the Media Gateway.

**signaling packet**

Generated by an ATM-connected device that wants to establish a connection with another such device. The signaling packet contains the ATM NSAP address of the desired ATM endpoint, as well as any QoS parameters required for the connection. If the endpoint can support the desired QoS, it responds with an accept message, and the connection is opened. See also *QoS*.

**Signaling System 7**

See *SS7*.

**signal-to-noise**

S/N (also SNR). The difference in amplitude between a baseband signal and the noise in a portion of the spectrum.

**Silicon Switch Processor**

See *SSP* in the "Cisco Systems Terms and Acronyms" section.

**silicon switching**

See *silicon switching* in the "Cisco Systems Terms and Acronyms" section.

**silicon switching engine**

See *SSE* in the "Cisco Systems Terms and Acronyms" section.

**SIM**

**1.** subscriber identity module. Component of an MS in a GSM network that contains all the subscriber information.

**2.** Set Initialization Mode.

**simple and efficient AAL**

See *SEAL*.

**Simple Gateway Monitoring Protocol**

See *SGMP*.

**Simple Mail Transfer Protocol**

See *SMRP*.

**Simple Multicast Routing Protocol**

See *SMRP*.

**Simple Network Management Protocol**

See *SNMP*.

**simplex**

Capability for transmission in only one direction between a sending station and a receiving station. Broadcast television is an example of a simplex technology. Compare with *full duplex* and *half duplex*.

**single attachment station**

See *SAS*.

**single in-line memory module**

Module that is commonly used for internal Flash memory.

**single-attached concentrator**

See *SAC*.

**single-mode fiber**

Fiber-optic cabling with a narrow core that allows light to enter only at a single angle. Such cabling has higher bandwidth than multimode fiber, but requires a light source with a narrow spectral width (for example, a laser). Also called monomode fiber. See also *multimode fiber*.

**single-route explorer packet**

See *spanning explorer packet*.

**single-vendor network**

Network using equipment from only one vendor. Single-vendor networks rarely suffer compatibility problems. See also *multivendor network*.

**SINR**

The ratio of the received strength of the desired signal to the received strength of undesired signals (noise and interference).

**SIP**

**1.** SMDS Interface Protocol. Used in communications between CPE and SMDS network equipment. Allows the CPE to use SMDS service for high-speed WAN internetworking. Based on the IEEE 802.6 DQDB standard. See also *DQDB*.

**2.** serial interface processor.

**3.** session initiation protocol. Protocol developed by the IETF MMUSIC Working Group as an alternative to H.323. SIP features are compliant with IETF RFC 2543, published in March 1999. SIP equips platforms to signal the setup of voice and multimedia calls over IP networks.

### Site

Group of closely related configuration data. It can be the name of a physical location or it can be a name you choose to give to one segment of your overall system.

### SLAC

Stanford Linear Accelerator Center.

### SLC

Signaling link code. Code that identifies a linkset.

### sliding window flow control

Method of flow control in which a receiver gives the transmitter permission to transmit data until a window is full. When the window is full, the transmitter must stop transmitting until the receiver advertises a larger window. TCP, other transport protocols, and several data link layer protocols use this method of flow control.

### SLIP

Serial Line Internet Protocol. Standard protocol for point-to-point serial connections using a variation of TCP/IP. Predecessor of PPP. See also *CSI* and *PPP*.

### slotted ring

LAN architecture based on a ring topology in which the ring is divided into slots that circulate continuously. Slots can be either empty or full, and transmissions must start at the beginning of a slot.

### SM fiber

single-mode fiber. Fiber with a relatively low diameter through which only one mode can propagate.

### SMAC

source MAC. MAC address specified in the Source Address field of a packet. Compare with *DMAC*. See also *MAC address*.

### SMATV

satellite master antenna television. Transmission of television programming to a Satellite Master Antenna installed on top of an apartment building, a hotel, or at another central location from where it serves a private group of viewers. The transmission usually is done in C-band to 1.5 or 2 meter dishes.

### SMB

Server Message Block. File-system protocol used in LAN manager and similar NOSs to package data and exchange information with other systems.

## SMDS

Switched Multimegabit Data Service. High-speed, packet-switched, datagram-based WAN networking technology offered by the telephone companies. See also *CBDS*.

## SMDS Interface Protocol

See *SIP*.

## SMF

single-mode fiber.

## SMG

Wireless—Special Mobile Group. A standards body within ETSI that develops specifications related to mobile networking technologies, such as GSM and GPRS.

## SMI

Structure of Management Information. Document (RFC 1155) specifying rules used to define managed objects in the MIB. See also *MIB*.

## SMO

state machine object.

## smoothing

See *traffic shaping*.

## SMRP

Simple Multicast Routing Protocol. Specialized multicast network protocol for routing multimedia data streams on enterprise networks. SMRP works in conjunction with multicast extensions to the AppleTalk protocol.

## SMT

Station Management. ANSI FDDI specification that defines how ring stations are managed.

## SMTP

Simple Mail Transfer Protocol. Internet protocol providing e-mail services.

## SNA

Systems Network Architecture. Large, complex, feature-rich network architecture developed in the 1970s by IBM. Similar in some respects to the OSI reference model but with a number of differences. SNA essentially is composed of seven layers. See also *data flow control layer*, *data-link control layer*, *path control layer*, *physical control layer*, *presentation services layer*, *transaction services layer*, and *transmission control layer*.

**SNA Distribution Services**

See *SNADS*.

**SNA Network Interconnection**

See *SNI*.

**SNADS**

SNA Distribution Services. Consists of a set of SNA transaction programs that interconnect and cooperate to provide asynchronous distribution of information between end users. One of three SNA transaction services. See also *DDM* and *DIA*.

**SNAP**

Subnetwork Access Protocol. Internet protocol that operates between a network entity in the subnetwork and a network entity in the end system. SNAP specifies a standard method of encapsulating IP datagrams and ARP messages on IEEE networks. The SNAP entity in the end system makes use of the services of the subnetwork and performs three key functions: data transfer, connection management, and QoS selection.

**SNI**

**1.** Subscriber Network Interface. Interface for SMDS-based networks that connects CPE and an SMDS switch. See also *UNI*.

**2.** SNA Network Interconnection. IBM gateway connecting multiple SNA networks.

**SNMP**

Simple Network Management Protocol. Network management protocol used almost exclusively in TCP/IP networks. SNMP provides a means to monitor and control network devices, and to manage configurations, statistics collection, performance, and security. See also *SGMP* and *SNMP2*.

**SNMP communities**

Authentication scheme that enables an intelligent network device to validate SNMP requests.

**SNMP2**

SNMP Version 2. Version 2 of the popular network management protocol. SNMP2 supports centralized as well as distributed network management strategies, and includes improvements in the SMI, protocol operations, management architecture, and security. See also *SNMP*.

**SNP**

sequence number protection.

### SNPA

subnetwork point of attachment. Data link layer address (such as an Ethernet address, X.25 address, or Frame Relay DLCI address). SNPA addresses are used to configure a CLNS route for an interface.

### SNR

signal-to-noise ratio. SNR is the ratio of usable signal being transmitted to the undesired signal (noise). It is a measure of transmission quality.
The ratio of good data (signal) to bad (noise) on a line, expressed in decibels (dB).

### SNRM

Set Normal Response.

### SNRME

Set Normal Response. Mode Exchange.

### socket

**1.** Software structure operating as a communications end point within a network device.

**2.** Addressable entity within a node connected to an AppleTalk network; sockets are owned by software processes known as socket clients. AppleTalk sockets are divided into two groups: SASs, which are reserved for such clients as AppleTalk core protocols, and DASs, which are assigned dynamically by DDP upon request from clients in the node. An AppleTalk socket is similar in concept to a TCP/IP port.

### socket client

Software process or function implemented in an AppleTalk network node.

### socket listener

Software provided by a socket client to receive datagrams addressed to the socket. See also *socket client*.

### socket number

8-bit number that identifies a socket. A maximum of 254 different socket numbers can be assigned in an AppleTalk node.

### software generic

The system operating software release for general availability.

### SOHO

small office, home office. Networking solutions and access technologies for offices that are not directly connected to large corporate networks.

### SONET

Synchronous Optical Network. A standard format for transporting a wide range of digital telecommunications services over optical fiber. SONET is characterized by standard line rates, optical interfaces, and signal formats.

High-speed (up to 2.5 Gbps) synchronous network specification developed by Bellcore and designed to run on optical fiber. STS-1 is the basic building block of SONET. Approved as an international standard in 1988. See also *SDH*, *STS-1*, and *STS-3c*.

### SONET multiplexing

SONET multiplexing byte interlaces the lower-rate payloads, which creates a high-rate synchronous signal.

### source address

Address of a network device that is sending data. See also *destination address*.

### source MAC

See *SMAC*.

### source node

A source node is the originating node of an end-to-end channel or virtual wavelength path (VWP).

### source service access point

See *SSAP*.

### source-route bridging

See *SRP*.

### source-route translational bridging

See *SR/TLB*.

### source-route transparent bridging

See *SRT*.

### Southeastern Universities Research Association Network

See *SURAnet*.

### SP

**1.** Signaling Processor, Signaling Point.

**2.** See *SP* in the "Cisco Systems Terms and Acronyms" section.

### SPA

See *SPA* in the "Cisco Systems Terms and Acronyms" section.

### SPAG

Standards Promotion and Application Group. Group of European OSI manufacturers that chooses option subsets and publishes these in the "Guide to the Use of Standards" (GUS).

### spam

Term used to describe unsolicited e-mail or newsgroup posts, often in the form of commercial announcements. The act of sending a spam is called, naturally, spamming.

### span

Full-duplex digital transmission line between two digital facilities.

### SPAN

See *SPAN* (Switched Port Analyzer) in the "Cisco Systems Terms and Acronyms" section.

### spanning explorer packet

Follows a statically configured spanning tree when looking for paths in an SRB network. Also known as a limited-route explorer packet or a single-route explorer packet. See also *all-routes explorer packet*, *explorer packet*, and *local explorer packet*.

### spanning tree

Loop-free subset of a network topology. See also *spanning-tree algorithm* and *Spanning-Tree Protocol*.

### spanning-tree algorithm

Algorithm used by the Spanning-Tree Protocol to create a spanning tree. Sometimes abbreviated as STA. See also *spanning tree* and *Spanning-Tree Protocol*.

### Spanning-Tree Protocol

See *STP*.

### sparse mode PIM

See *PIM sparse mode*.

## SPC

Service Platform Card. Provides call processing services, such as tone receivers and conference ports, within the Cisco VCO/4K switch. Available resources include DTMF detection, call progress analysis, MF reception, MFCR2 reception and transmission, tone generation, DTMF and MF outpulsing, and call conferencing.

## SPE

**1.** synchronous payload envelope. The payload carrying portion of the STS signal in SONET. The SPE is used to transport a tributary signal across the synchronous network. In most cases, this signal is assembled at the point of entry to the synchronous network and is disassembled at the point of exit from the synchronous network. Within the synchronous network, the SPE is passed on intact between NEs on its route through the network.

**2.** system processing engine. A card that acts as a single-board computer and that runs system software applications, such as Cisco ICS 7750 System Manager and Cisco CallManager.

## spectrum reuse

CATV's most fundamental concept. Historically, the over-the-air spectrum has been assigned to many purposes other than that of carrying TV signals. This has resulted in an inadequate supply of spectrum to serve the needs of viewers. Cable can reuse spectrum that is sealed in its aluminum tubes.

## speed matching

Feature that provides sufficient buffering capability in a destination device to allow a high-speed source to transmit data at its maximum rate, even if the destination device is a lower-speed device.

## SPF

shortest path first algorithm. Routing algorithm that iterates on length of path to determine a shortest-path spanning tree. Commonly used in link-state routing algorithms. Sometimes called Dijkstra's algorithm. See also *link-state routing algorithm*.

## SPI

security parameter index. This is a number that, together with a destination IP address and security protocol, uniquely identifies a particular security association. When using IKE to establish the security associations, the SPI for each security association is a pseudo-randomly derived number. Without IKE, the SPI is manually specified for each security association.

### SPID

service profile identifier. Number that some service providers use to define the services to which an ISDN device subscribes. The ISDN device uses the SPID when accessing the switch that initializes the connection to a service provider.

### split-horizon updates

Routing technique in which information about routes is prevented from exiting the router interface through which that information was received. Split-horizon updates are useful in preventing routing loops.

### SPNNI connection

See *SPNNI connection* in the "Cisco Systems Terms and Acronyms" section.

### spoofing

**1.** Scheme used by routers to cause a host to treat an interface as if it were up and supporting a session. The router spoofs replies to keepalive messages from the host in order to convince that host that the session still exists. Spoofing is useful in routing environments, such as DDR, in which a circuit-switched link is taken down when there is no traffic to be sent across it in order to save toll charges. See also *DDR*.

**2.** The act of a packet illegally claiming to be from an address from which it was not actually sent. Spoofing is designed to foil network security mechanisms, such as filters and access lists.

### spooler

Application that manages requests or jobs submitted to it for execution. Spoolers process the submitted requests in an orderly fashion from a queue. A print spooler is a common example of a spooler.

### SPP

Sequenced Packet Protocol. Provides reliable, connection-based, flow-controlled packet transmission on behalf of client processes. Part of the XNS protocol suite.

### SPX

Sequenced Packet Exchange. Reliable, connection-oriented protocol that supplements the datagram service provided by network layer (Layer 3) protocols. Novell derived this commonly used NetWare transport protocol from the SPP of the XNS protocol suite.

### SQE

signal quality error. Transmission sent by a transceiver back to the controller to let the controller know whether the collision circuitry is functional. Also called *heartbeat*.

## SQL

Structured Query Language. International standard language for defining and accessing relational databases.

## SR

short reach. The distance specification for optical systems that operate effectively up to 3 km (1.8 mi).

## SR/TLB

source-route translational bridging. Method of bridging where source-route stations can communicate with transparent bridge stations with the help of an intermediate bridge that translates between the two bridge protocols. Compare with *SRT*.

## SRAM

Type of RAM that retains its contents for as long as power is supplied. SRAM does not require constant refreshing, like DRAM. Compare with *DRAM*.

## SRB

source-route bridging. Method of bridging originated by IBM and popular in Token Ring networks. In an SRB network, the entire route to a destination is predetermined, in real time, prior to the sending of data to the destination. Contrast with *transparent bridging*.

## SRCP

Simple Resource Control Protocol. Set of extensions to MGCP to allow the VSC to poll the gateway about its current configuration.

## SRP

spatial reuse protocol.

## SRT

source-route transparent bridging. IBM bridging scheme that merges the two most prevalent bridging strategies: SRB and transparent bridging. SRT employs both technologies in one device to satisfy the needs of all ENs. No translation between bridging protocols is necessary. Compare with *SR/TLB*.

## SRTP

Sequenced Routing Update Protocol. Protocol that assists VINES servers in finding neighboring clients, servers, and routers. See also *RTP (Routing Table Protocol)*.

### SRVTAB

Password that a network service shares with the KDC. The network service authenticates an encrypted service credential by using the SRVTAB (also known as a KEYTAB) to decrypt it.

### SS7

Signaling System 7. Standard CCS system used with BISDN and ISDN. Developed by Bellcore. See also *CCS*.

### SSAP

source service access point. SAP of the network node designated in the Source field of a packet. Compare to *DSAP*. See also *SAP (service access point)*.

### SSCOP

Service Specific Connection Oriented Protocol. Data link protocol that guarantees the delivery of ATM signaling packets.

### SSCP

system services control points. Focal points within an SNA network for managing network configuration, coordinating network operator and problem determination requests, and providing directory services and other session services for network end users.

### SSCP-PU session

Session used by SNA to allow an SSCP to manage the resources of a node through the PU. SSCPs can send requests to, and receive replies from, individual nodes in order to control the network configuration.

### SSCS

service specific convergence sublayer. One of the two sublayers of any AAL. SSCS, which is service dependent, offers assured data transmission. The SSCS can be null as well, in classical IP over ATM or LAN emulation implementations. See also *AAL*, *ATM layer*, *CPCS*, *CS*, and *SAR*.

### SSD server

Service Selection Dashboard server. Customizable Web-based application that works with the Cisco SSG to allow end customers to login to and disconnect from proxy and passthrough services through a standard Web browser. After the customer logs in to the network of the service provider, an HTML Dashboard is populated with the services authorized for that user.

**SSE**

See *SSE* in the "Cisco Systems Terms and Acronyms" section.

**SSG**

Service Selection Gateway. Gateway that offers service providers a means for menu-based service selection. End users can select services from the Dashboard menu, and the Cisco SSG can set up and tear down proxy and passthrough network connections based on a selection of a user. The Cisco SSG accounts for the services selected so that service providers can bill for individual services.

**SSL**

Secure Socket Layer. Encryption technology for the Web used to provide secure transactions, such as the transmission of credit card numbers for e-commerce.

**SSM**

Source Specific Multicast. A datagram delivery model that best supports one-to-many applications, also known as broadcast applications. SSM is the core networking technology for the Cisco implementation of the IP Multicast Lite suite of solutions targeted for audio and video broadcast application environments.

**SSN**

Subsystem number.

**SSO**

system security officer. Person responsible for enforcement or administration of the security policy that applies to the system.

**SSP**

**1.** system switch processor. A card that acts as an Ethernet switch and passes data between all system cards and to any other switches connected to the system.

**2.** service switching point. Element of an SS7-based Intelligent Network that performs call origination, termination, or tandem switching.

**3.** Switch-to-Switch Protocol. Protocol specified in the DLSw standard that routers use to establish DLSw connections, locate resources, forward data, and handle flow control and error recovery. See also *DLSw*.

**4.** Silicon Switch Processor. See *SSP* in the "Cisco Systems Terms and Acronyms" section.

## SSRP

Simple Server Redundancy Protocol. The LANE simple server redundancy feature creates fault-tolerance using standard LANE protocols and mechanisms. Also called SSRP. See also *FSSRP*.

## STA

See *spanning-tree algorithm*.

## stack

See *protocol stack*.

## standard

Set of rules or procedures that are either widely used or officially specified. See also *de facto standard* and *de jure standard*.

## standby monitor

Device placed in standby mode on a Token Ring network in case an active monitor fails. See also *active monitor* and *ring monitor*.

## star topology

LAN topology in which end points on a network are connected to a common central switch by point-to-point links. A ring topology that is organized as a star implements a unidirectional closed-loop star, instead of point-to-point links. Compare with *bus topology*, *ring topology*, and *tree topology*.

## StarLAN

CSMA/CD LAN, based on IEEE 802.3, developed by AT&T.

## start-stop transmission

See *asynchronous transmission*.

## startup range

Range of values (from 65280 to 65534) from which an AppleTalk node selects the network number part of its provisional address if it has not saved another network number.

## stat mux

See *statistical multiplexing*.

## static route

Route that is explicitly configured and entered into the routing table. Static routes take precedence over routes chosen by dynamic routing protocols.

**statically assigned socket**

See *SAS*.

**Station Management**

See *SMT*.

**statistical multiplexing**

Technique whereby information from multiple logical channels can be transmitted across a single physical channel. Statistical multiplexing dynamically allocates bandwidth only to active input channels, making better use of available bandwidth and allowing more devices to be connected than with other multiplexing techniques. Also referred to as *statistical time-division multiplexing* or *stat mux*. Compare with *ATDM*, *FDM*, and *TDM*.

**statistical time-division multiplexing**

See *statistical multiplexing*.

**STD**

Subseries of RFCs that specify Internet standards. The official list of Internet standards is in STD 1.

**STM-1**

Synchronous Transport Module level 1. One of a number of SDH formats that specifies the frame structure for the 155.52-Mbps lines used to carry ATM cells. See also *SDH*.

**store and forward**

Function whereby a message is transmitted to some intermediate relay point and temporarily stored before forwarding to the next relay point.

**store and forward packet switching**

Packet-switching technique in which frames are completely processed before being forwarded out the appropriate port. This processing includes calculating the CRC and checking the destination address. In addition, frames must be stored temporarily until network resources (such as an unused link) are available to forward the message. Contrast with *cut-through packet switching*.

**STP**

**1.** shielded twisted-pair. Two-pair wiring medium used in a variety of network implementations. STP cabling has a layer of shielded insulation to reduce EMI. Compare with *UTP*. See also *twisted pair*.

**2.** Spanning-Tree Protocol. Bridge protocol that uses the spanning-tree algorithm, enabling a learning bridge to dynamically work around loops in a network topology by creating a spanning tree. Bridges exchange BPDU messages with other bridges to detect loops, and then remove the loops by shutting down selected bridge interfaces. Refers to both the IEEE 802.1 Spanning-Tree Protocol standard and the earlier Digital Equipment Corporation Spanning-Tree Protocol upon which it is based. The IEEE version supports bridge domains and allows the bridge to construct a loop-free topology across an extended LAN. The IEEE version generally is preferred over the Digital version. Sometimes abbreviated as STP. See also *Bpdu*, *learning bridge*, *MAC address learning*, *spanning tree*, and *spanning-tree algorithm*.

**3.** signal transfer point. Element of an SS7-based Intelligent Network that performs routing of the SS7 signaling.

## Stratum

Hierarchical clock reference in the PSTN network, where 1 represents the highest possible quality of clocking.

## Stratum 3

Precision timing reference that provides a free-run accuracy of plus or minus 4.6 parts per million (PPM), pull-in capability of 4.6 PPM, and holdover stability of fewer than 255 slips during first day. Thorough descriptions can be found in ANSI T1.101-1994 and the Bellcore document GR-1244-CORE.

## stream-oriented

Type of transport service that allows its client to send data in a continuous stream. The transport service guarantees that all data will be delivered to the other end in the same order as sent and without duplicates.

## Structure of Management Information

See *SMI*.

## STS-1

Synchronous Transport Signal level 1. Basic building block signal of SONET, operating at 51.84 Mbps. Faster SONET rates are defined as STS-*n*, where *n* is a multiple of 51.84 Mbps. See also *SONET*.

## STS-3c

Synchronous Transport Signal level 3, concatenated. SONET format that specifies the frame structure for the 155.52-Mbps lines used to carry ATM cells. See also *SONET*.

**stub area**

OSPF area that carries a default route, intra-area routes, and interarea routes, but does not carry external routes. Virtual links cannot be configured across a stub area, and they cannot contain an ASBR. Compare with *nonstub area*. See also *ASAM* and *OSPF*.

**stub network**

Network that has only a single connection to a router.

**STUN**

See *STUN* in the "Cisco Systems Terms and Acronyms" section.

**SU**

**1.** signaling unit. Another name for the TransPath product.

**2.** service unit or signaling unit.

**subarea**

Portion of an SNA network that consists of a subarea node and any attached links and peripheral nodes.

**subarea node**

SNA communication controller or host that handles complete network addresses.

**subchannel**

In broadband terminology, a frequency-based subdivision creating a separate communications channel.

**subinterface**

One of a number of virtual interfaces on a single physical interface.

**subnet**

See *subnetwork*.

**subnet address**

Portion of an IP address that is specified as the subnetwork by the subnet mask. See also *IP address*, *subnet mask*, and *subnetwork*.

**subnet mask**

32-bit address mask used in IP to indicate the bits of an IP address that are being used for the subnet address. Sometimes referred to simply as mask. See also *address mask* and *IP address*.

**subnetwork**

**1.** In IP networks, a network sharing a particular subnet address. Subnetworks are networks arbitrarily segmented by a network administrator in order to provide a multilevel, hierarchical routing structure while shielding the subnetwork from the addressing complexity of attached networks. Sometimes called a subnet. See also *IP address*, *subnet address*, and *subnet mask*.

**2.** In OSI networks, a collection of ESs and ISs under the control of a single administrative domain and using a single network access protocol.

**Subnetwork Access Protocol**

See *SNAP*.

**subnetwork point of attachment**

See *SNPA*.

**Subscriber Network Interface**

See *SNI*.

**subvector**

Data segment of a vector in an SNA message. A subvector consists of a length field, a key that describes the subvector type, and subvector specific data.

**Super Frame**

See *SF*.

**superencryption**

Encryption operation for which the plaintext input to be transformed is the ciphertext output of a previous encryption operation.

**Super-JANET**

Latest phase in the development of JANET, the UK educational and research network run by UKERNA. It uses SMDS and ATM to provide multiservice network facilities for many new applications, including multimedia conferencing.

**supernet**

Aggregation of IP network addresses advertised as a single classless network address. For example, given four Class C IP networks—192.0.8.0, 192.0.9.0, 192.0.10.0, and 192.0.11.0—each having the intrinsic network mask of 255.255.255.0, one can advertise the address 192.0.8.0 with a subnet mask of 255.255.252.0.

### SURAnet

Southeastern Universities Research Association Network. Network connecting universities and other organizations in the Southeastern United States. SURAnet, originally funded by the NSF and a part of the NSFNET, is now part of BBN Planet. See also *BBN Planet*, *NSF*, and *NSFNET*.

### survivability

Capability of a system to remain in operation or existence despite adverse conditions, including natural occurrences, accidental actions, and attacks on the system.

### sustainable cell rate

See *SCP*.

### SVC

switched virtual circuit. Virtual circuit that is dynamically established on demand and is torn down when transmission is complete. SVCs are used in situations where data transmission is sporadic. See also *virtual circuit*. Called a switched virtual connection in ATM terminology. Compare with *PVC*.

### switch

**1.** Network device that filters, forwards, and floods frames based on the destination address of each frame. The switch operates at the data link layer of the OSI model.

**2.** General term applied to an electronic or mechanical device that allows a connection to be established as necessary and terminated when there is no longer a session to support.

**3.** In telephony, a general term for any device, such as a PBX, that connects individual phones to phone lines. See also *PBX* and *PSTN*.

### switch hook

Plunger or switch where a telephone handset sits when the telephone is on hook, or hung up. When the handset is lifted, the switch hook goes up and the telephone is off hook. Also called hook switch.

### Switch Processor

See *SP* in the "Cisco Systems Terms and Acronyms" section.

### switched calls

Normal telephone calls in which a user picks up a phone, hears a dial tone, and enters the destination phone number to reach the other phone. Switched calls also can be private line auto-ringdown (PLAR) calls, or tie-line calls for fixed point-to-point connections. See also *PLAR*.

### switched LAN

LAN implemented with LAN switches. See also *LAN switch*.

### Switched Multimegabit Data Service

See *SMDS*.

### Switched Port Analyzer

See *SPAN* in the "Cisco Systems Terms and Acronyms" section.

### switched virtual circuit

See *SVC*.

### switched virtual connection

See *SVC*.

### Switching

Process of taking an incoming frame from one interface and delivering it through another interface. Routers use Layer 3 switching to route a packet, and Layer 2 switches use Layer 2 switching to forward frames. See also *Layer 2 switching* and *Layer 3 switching*.

### Switch-to-Switch Protocol

See *SSP*.

### symbol

Phase range of a sine wave.

### symmetric cryptography

Branch of cryptography involving algorithms that use the same key for two different steps of the algorithm (such as encryption and decryption, or signature creation and signature verification).

### symmetric key

Cryptographic key that is used in a symmetric cryptographic algorithm.

### SYN flood

Denial of service attack that sends a host more TCP SYN packets (request to synchronize sequence numbers, used when opening a connection) than the protocol implementation can handle.

### synchronization

Establishment of common timing between sender and receiver.

**Synchronous Data Link Control**

See *SDLC*.

**Synchronous Digital Hierarchy**

See *SDH*.

**Synchronous Optical Network**

See *SONET*.

**synchronous transmission**

Term describing digital signals that are transmitted with precise clocking. Such signals have the same frequency, with individual characters encapsulated in control bits (called start bits and stop bits) that designate the beginning and the end of each character. Compare with *asynchronous transmission*, *isochronous transmission*, and *plesiochronous transmission*.

**Synchronous Transport Module level 1**

See *STM-1*.

**Synchronous Transport Signal level 1**

See *STS-1*.

**Synchronous Transport Signal level 3, concatenated**

See *STS-3c*.

**synthetic operation**

Packets sent into the network that appear to be user data traffic but actually measure network performance. Formerly known as a probe. Also referred to as operation.

**sysgen**

system generation. Process of defining network resources in a network.

**system entity**

Active element of a system—for example, an automated process, a subsystem, a person or a group of persons—that incorporates a specific set of capabilities.

**system generation**

See *sysgen*.

**system high**

The highest security level supported by a system at a particular time or in a particular environment.

**system high security mode**

Mode of operation of an information system, wherein all users having access to the system possess a security clearance or authorization, but not necessarily a need-to-know, for all data handled by the system.

**system integrity service**

Security service that protects system resources in a verifiable manner against unauthorized or accidental change, loss, or destruction.

**system low**

The lowest security level supported by a system at a particular time or in a particular environment.

**system services control points**

See *SSCP*.

**Systems Network Architecture**

See *SNA*.

## T.120

ITU standard that describes data conferencing. H.323 provides for the capability to establish T.120 data sessions inside an existing H.323 session.

## T.30

Describes the overall procedure for establishing and managing communication between two fax machines.

## T.38

Defines procedures for real-time Group 3 facsimile communication over IP networks.

## T1

Digital WAN carrier facility. T1 transmits DS-1–formatted data at 1.544 Mbps through the telephone-switching network, using AMI or B8ZS coding. Compare with *E1*. See also *AMI*, *B8ZS*, and *DS-1*.

## T3

Digital WAN carrier facility. T3 transmits DS-3-formatted data at 44.736 Mbps through the telephone switching network. Compare with *E3*. See also *DS-3*.

## TABS

Telemetry Asynchronous Block Serial. AT&T polled point-to-point or multipoint communication protocol that supports moderate data transfer rates over intra-office wire pairs.

## TAC

**1.** Terminal Access Controller. Internet host that accepts terminal connections from dial-up lines.

**2.** Cisco Technical Assistance Center. See *TAC* and *TACACS+* in the "Cisco Systems Terms and Acronyms" section.

## TACACS

Terminal Access Controller Access Control System. Authentication protocol, developed by the DDN community, that provides remote access authentication and related services, such as event logging. User passwords are administered in a central database rather than in individual routers, providing an easily scalable network security solution. See also *TACACS+* in the "Cisco Systems Terms and Acronyms" section.

## TACACS+

See *TACACS+* in the "Cisco Systems Terms and Acronyms" section.

## tag

Identification information, including a number plus other information.

## tag switching

High-performance, packet-forwarding technology that integrates network layer (Layer 3) routing and data link layer (Layer 2) switching and provides scalable, high-speed switching in the network core. Tag switching is based on the concept of label swapping, in which packets or cells are assigned short, fixed-length labels that tell switching nodes how data should be forwarded.

## tagged traffic

ATM cells that have their CLP bit set to 1. If the network is congested, tagged traffic can be dropped to ensure the delivery of higher-priority traffic. Sometimes called DE traffic. See also *CLP*.

## tail-end

The downstream, receive end of a tunnel.

## Tandem switching

Dynamic switching of voice calls between VoFR, VoATM, or VoHDLC PVCs and subchannels; also called tandeming. Tandem switching often is encountered in multi-hop VoFR call connection paths.

## TAPI

Telephony Application Programming Interface. A call control model developed by Microsoft and Intel.

## TARP

TID Address Resolution Protocol. In OSS, a protocol that resolves a TL-1 TID to a CLNP address (NSAP).

## TAXI 4B/5B

Transparent Asynchronous Transmitter/Receiver Interface 4-byte/5-byte. Encoding scheme used for FDDI LANs as well as for ATM. Supports speeds of up to 100 Mbps over multimode fiber. TAXI is the chipset that generates 4B/5B encoding on multimode fiber. See also *4B/5B local fiber*.

## TB

transparent bridging. This feature supports connectivity for multiple VLANs bridged between Dot1q interfaces and other interface encapsulations or other types of interface media.

## TBOS protocol

Telemetry Byte Oriented Serial protocol. Protocol that transmits alarm, status, and control points between NE and OSS. TBOS defines one physical interface for direct connection between the telemetry equipment and the monitored equipment.

## TC

**1.** Telephony Controller. A new generic term for the Signaling Controller (SC) and the Virtual Switch Controller (VSC).

**2.** transmission convergence. Sublayer of the ATM physical layer that transforms the flow of cells into a steady flow of bits for transmission over the physical medium. When transmitting, the TC sublayer maps the cells into the frame format, generates the HEC, and sends idle cells when there is nothing to send. When receiving, the TC sublayer delineates individual cells in the received bit stream and uses HEC to detect and correct errors. See also *HEC* and *PHY*.

## TCA

telecommunications access method.

## TCAP

transaction capabilities applications part. SS7 protocol layer that helps exchange noncircuit-related data between applications.

## T-carrier

TDM transmission method usually referring to a line or a cable carrying a DS-1 signal.

## TCC

terminating call control.

### T-CCS

Transparent Common Channel Signaling. Feature that allows the connection of two PBXs with digital interfaces that use a proprietary or unsupported CCS protocol without the need for interpretation of CCS signalling for call processing. T1/E1 traffic is transported transparently through the data network and the feature preserves proprietary signalling. From the PBX standpoint, this is accomplished through a point-to-point connection. Calls from the PBXs are not routed, but follow a preconfigured route to the destination.

### TCL

Toolkit Command Language. A scripting language used for gateway products both internally and externally to Cisco IOS software code.

### TCL Interface

tool command line interface.

### Tcl/Tk

Toolkit Command Language windowing toolkit. A combination of a scripting language (Tcl) with a windowing toolkit (Tk). Used for rapid prototyping and application development.

### TCP

Transmission Control Protocol. Connection-oriented transport layer protocol that provides reliable full-duplex data transmission. TCP is part of the TCP/IP protocol stack. See also *TCP/IP*.

### TCP/IP

Transmission Control Protocol/Internet Protocol. Common name for the suite of protocols developed by the U.S. DoD in the 1970s to support the construction of worldwide internetworks. TCP and IP are the two best-known protocols in the suite. See also *IP* and *TCAP*.

### TCU

trunk coupling unit. In Token Ring networks, a physical device that enables a station to connect to the trunk cable.

### TDM

time-division multiplexing. Technique in which information from multiple channels can be allocated bandwidth on a single wire based on preassigned time slots. Bandwidth is allocated to each channel regardless of whether the station has data to transmit. Compare with *ATDM*, *FDM*, and *statistical multiplexing*.

## TDM Cross-Connect

Allows DSO channels from one T1 or E1 facility to be cross-connected digitally to DS0 channels on another T1 or E1. By using this method, channel traffic is sent between a PBX and CO PSTN switch or other telephony device, so that some PBX channels are directed for long-distance service through the PSTN while the router compresses others for interoffice VoIP calls. In addition, Drop and Insert can cross-connect a telephony switch (from the CO or PSTN) to a channel bank for external analog connectivity. Also called *drop and insert.*

## TDMA

time division multiplex access. Type of multiplexing where two or more channels of information are transmitted over the same link by allocating a different time interval ("slot" or "slice") for the transmission of each channel, that is, the channels take turns to use the link. Some kind of periodic synchronizing signal or distinguishing identifier usually is required so that the receiver can tell which channel is which. See also *TDM.*

## TDR

time domain reflectometer. Device capable of sending signals through a network medium to check cable continuity and other attributes. TDRs are used to find physical layer network problems.

## TE

terminal equipment. Any ISDN-compatible device that can be attached to the network, such as a telephone, a fax, or a computer.

## Technical Assistance Center

See *TAC.*

## Technical Office Protocol

See *TOP.*

## Technology prefix

Discriminators used to distinguish between gateways having specific capabilities within a given zone. In the exchange between the gateway and the gatekeeper, the technology prefix is used to select a gateway after the zone has been selected. Technology prefixes can be used to tell the gatekeeper that a certain technology is associated with a particular call (for example, 15# could mean a fax transmission), or it can be used like an area code for more generic routing. No standard defines what the numbers in a technology prefix mean; by convention, technology prefixes are designated by a pound (#) symbol as the last character.

### TEI

terminal endpoint identifier. Field in the LAPD address that identifies a device on an ISDN interface. See also *TE*.

### telco

Abbreviation for telephone company.

### Telco-Return CM

A cable modem that uses the cable plant only for subscriber downstream traffic, and uses the PSTN for subscriber upstream traffic (which is necessary in older cable plants); DOCSIS has issued specifications for telco-return CMs that include dialup with PPP/IPCP and RADIUS, as well as booting with DHCP, Time, and TFTP service.

### Telecommunication Management Network

See *TMN*.

### telecommunications

Term referring to communications (usually involving computer systems) over the telephone network.

### Telecommunications Industry Association

See *TIA*.

### telemetry

Capability of transmitting or retrieving data over long distance communication links, such as satellite or telephone.

### Telemetry Asynchronous Block Serial

See *TABS*.

### telephony

Science of converting sound to electrical signals and transmitting it between widely removed points.

### TeleRouter

An optional software overlay product for the Cisco VCO/4K switch. TeleRouter uses its own database to parse dialed digit strings from inbound calls and routes calls based on this information.

### telex

Teletypewriter service allowing subscribers to send messages over the PSTN.

### Telnet

Standard terminal emulation protocol in the TCP/IP protocol stack. Telnet is used for remote terminal connection, enabling users to log in to remote systems and use resources as if they were connected to a local system. Telnet is defined in RFC 854.

### Tempest

U.S. military standard. Electronic products adhering to the Tempest specification are designed to withstand EMP. See also *EMP*.

### TERENA

Trans-European Research and Education Networking Association. Organization that promotes information and telecommunications technologies development in Europe. Formed by the merger of EARN and RARE. See also *EARN* and *RARE*.

### termid

SNA cluster controller identification for switched lines only. Also called Xid.

### terminal

Simple device at which data can be entered or retrieved from a network. Generally, terminals have a monitor and a keyboard, but no processor or local disk drive.

### Terminal Access Controller

See *TAC*.

### Terminal Access Controller Access System

See *TACACS*.

### terminal adapter

Device used to connect ISDN BRI connections to existing interfaces, such as EIA/TIA-232. Essentially, an ISDN modem.

### terminal emulation

Network application in which a computer runs software that makes it appear to a remote host as a directly attached terminal.

### terminal endpoint identifier

See *TEI*.

### terminal equipment

See *TE*.

**terminal server**

Communications processor that connects asynchronous devices, such as terminals, printers, hosts, and modems, to any LAN or WAN that uses TCP/IP, X.25, or LAT protocols. Terminal servers provide the internetwork intelligence that is not available in the connected devices.

**termination point**

See *TP.*

**terminator**

Device that provides electrical resistance at the end of a transmission line to absorb signals on the line, thereby keeping them from bouncing back and being received again by network stations.

**TESS**

The Exponential Encryption System. A system of separate but cooperating cryptographic mechanisms and functions for the secure authenticated exchange of cryptographic keys, the generation of digital signatures, and the distribution of public keys. TESS employs asymmetric cryptography, based on discrete exponentiation, and a structure of self-certified public keys.

**TEST**

test.

**Texas Higher Education Network**

See *THEnet.*

**TFN**

Tribe Flood Network. A common type of denial-of-service (DoS) attack that can take advantage of forged or rapidly changing source IP addresses to allow attackers to thwart efforts to locate or filter the attacks.

**TFTP**

Trivial File Transfer Protocol. Simplified version of FTP that allows files to be transferred from one computer to another over a network, usually without the use of client authentication (for example, username and password).

**TGT**

Ticket granting ticket. A credential that the key distribution center (KDC) issues to authenticated users.

### TGW

Trunking Gateway. A gateway that supports only bearer traffic (no signaling traffic). For example, a gateway that terminates T1s (or greater) with no signaling control is a trunking gateway.

### TH

transmission header. SNA header that is appended to the SNA basic information unit (BIU). The TH uses one of a number of available SNA header formats. See also *FID0*, *FID1*, *FID2*, *FID3*, and *FID4*.

### THC over X.25

See *THC over X.25* in the "Cisco Systems Terms and Acronyms" section.

### The Exponential Encryption System

See *TESS*.

### THEnet

Texas Higher Education Network. Regional network comprising over 60 academic and research institutions in the Texas (United States) area.

### Thinnet

Term used to define a thinner, less expensive version of the cable specified in the IEEE 802.3 10Base2 standard. Compare with *Cheapernet*. See also *10Base2*, *EtherChannel*, and *IEEE 802.3*.

### three-way handshake

Process whereby two protocol entities synchronize during connection establishment.

### threshold

Each PM parameter has a provisionable threshold that defines the autonomous message trigger point. Thresholds usually are defined in terms of either a specific BER value or a specific number of events counted during a set time period.

### throughput

Rate of information arriving at, and possibly passing through, a particular point in a network system.

### TIA

Telecommunications Industry Alliance. Organization that develops standards relating to telecommunications technologies. Together, the TIA and the EIA have formalized standards, such as EIA/TIA-232, for the electrical characteristics of data transmission. See also *EIA*.

## TIC

Token Ring interface coupler. Controller through which an FEP connects to a Token Ring.

## TID

**1.** tunnel identifier. Used to identify a GTP tunnel between two GSNs in a GPRS network. Contains an MM Context ID and an NSAPI. A tunnel is created whenever an SGSN sends a Create PDP Context Request in a GPRS network. See also *GTP tunnel*.

A two-octet value that denotes a tunnel between an L2TP access concentrator (LAC) and an L2TP Network Server (LNS). An L2TP device that the client directly connects to and whereby PPP frames are tunneled to the L2TP network server (LNS). The LAC need only implement the media over which L2TP is to operate to pass traffic to one or more LNSs. It may tunnel any protocol carried within PPP. The LAC initiates incoming calls and receives outgoing calls. Analogous to the Layer 2 Forwarding (L2F) network access server (NAS).

**2.** Terminal Identifier.

## tie-line

Specifies a connection that emulates a temporary tie-line trunk to a private branch exchange (PBX). A tie-line connection is set up automatically for each call and is torn down when the call ends.

## tie-line trunk

PBX trunk that is *tied* to a line, which leads to a remote PBX; typically used for private telephone networks, although the tie-line connection often is carried on telco-provided lines.

## Tier 1 Authentication

Call authentication using DNIS and CLID.

## Tier 2 Authentication

User authentication using User ID and Password.

## Time

Time Protocol (RFC 868). Time clients obtain the current time-of-day within one-second resolution from Time servers.

## time domain reflectometer

See *TDM Cross-Connect*.

**time-division multiplexing**

See *TDM*.

**timeout**

Event that occurs when one network device expects to hear from another network device within a specified period of time, but does not. The resulting timeout usually results in a retransmission of information or the dissolving of the session between the two devices.

**TINA-C**

Telecommunications Information Networking Architecture. Services applications built in C and corresponding to TINA guidelines.

**TIOS**

Transpath Input Output Subsystem.

**tip and ring**

Pair of wires that provide the electrical connection between a telephone set and the local CO. The more electrically positive side of a POTS (Plain Old Telephone Service) telephone line (0 V) is the tip. It is designated internationally as black, but in the U.S. it often is designated green. It's counterpart is the ring (the more negative side, 52 v), which is designated red internationally and in the U.S. When tip and ring are terminated on a connecting block, tip usually goes on top (left) and ring usually goes on the bottom (right).

**TIRKS**

Trunk Information Record Keeping System. Bellcore OSS that provides record keeping for interoffice trunk facilities. See also *OSS*.

**TL-1**

Transaction Language One. Bellcore term for intelligent network elements.

**TLAP**

TokenTalk Link Access Protocol. Link-access protocol used in a TokenTalk network. TLAP is built on top of the standard Token Ring data-link layer.

**TLS**

Transport Layer Security. A future IETF protocol to replace SSL.

**TM**

traffic management.

### TMN

Telecommunication Management Network. ITU-T generic model for transporting and processing OAM&P information for a telecommunications network. See also *OAM&P*.

### TMSI

Wireless—temporary mobile subscriber identity. A temporary code used to identify an MS, which is assigned using encryption after the MS is identified to the HLR.

### TN3270

Terminal emulation software that allows a terminal to appear to an IBM host as a 3278 Model 2 terminal.

### TNotify

Time Notify. Specifies how often SMT initiates neighbor notification broadcasts. See also *SMT*.

### token

Frame that contains control information. Possession of the token allows a network device to transmit data onto the network. See also *token passing*.

### token bucket

A formal definition of a rate of transfer. A token bucket has three components: a burst size, a mean rate, and a time interval (Tc). A token bucket is used to manage a device that regulates the of a flow.

### token bus

LAN architecture using token passing access over a bus topology. This LAN architecture is the basis for the IEEE 802.4 LAN specification. See also *IEEE 802.4*.

### token passing

Access method by which network devices access the physical medium in an orderly fashion based on possession of a small frame called a token. Contrast with *circuit switching* and *contention*. See also *token*.

### Token Ring

Token-passing LAN developed and supported by IBM. Token Ring runs at 4 or 16 Mbps over a ring topology. Similar to IEEE 802.5. See also *IEEE 802.5*, *ring topology*, and *token passing*.

**token storage key**

Cryptography key used to protect data that is stored on a security token.

**TokenTalk**

Apple Computer's data-link product that allows an AppleTalk network to be connected by Token Ring cables.

**TOP**

Technical Office Protocol. OSI-based architecture developed for office communications.

**top CA**

The highest-level CA (that is, the most trusted CA) in a certification hierarchy.

**topology**

Physical arrangement of network nodes and media within an enterprise networking structure.

**ToS**

type of service. See *CoS*.

**TP**

termination point. A termination point is a transmission line or path that terminates or originates on an NE, such as the Line Card unit on the Cisco ONS 15900.

**TP0**

Transport Protocol Class 0. OSI connectionless transport protocol for use over reliable subnetworks. Defined by ISO 8073.

**TP4**

Transport Protocol Class 4. OSI connection-based transport protocol. Defined by ISO 8073.

**TPD**

Mechanism used by some ATM switches that allows the remaining cells supporting an AAL5 frame to be discarded when one or more cells of that AAL5 frame are dropped. This avoids sending partial AAL5 frames through the ATM network when they have to be retransmitted by the sender. Compare with *EPD*.

**TPPMD**

twisted-pair physical medium dependent.

### TR VLAN

Token Ring virtual LAN.

### traceroute

Program available on many systems that traces the path a packet takes to a destination. It is used mostly to debug routing problems between hosts. A traceroute protocol is also defined in RFC 1393.

### traffic analysis

Inference of information from observable characteristics of data flow(s), even when the data is encrypted or otherwise not directly available. Such characteristics include the identities and locations of the source(s) and destination(s), and the presence, amount, frequency, and duration of occurrence.

### traffic engineering

Techniques and processes that cause routed traffic to travel through the network on a path other than the one that would have been chosen if standard routing methods were used.

### traffic engineering tunnel

A label-switched tunnel that is used for traffic engineering. Such a tunnel is set up through means other than normal Layer 3 routing; it is used to direct traffic over a path different from the one that Layer 3 routing could cause the tunnel to take.

### traffic flow confidentiality

Data confidentiality service to protect against traffic analysis.

### traffic management

Techniques for avoiding congestion and shaping and policing traffic. Allows links to operate at high levels of utilization by scaling back lower-priority, delay-tolerant traffic at the edge of the network when congestion begins to occur.

### Traffic path

Route of a bearer channel that carries voice traffic.

### traffic policing

Process used to measure the actual traffic flow across a given connection and compare it to the total admissible traffic flow for that connection. Traffic outside of the agreed upon flow can be tagged (where the CLP bit is set to 1) and can be discarded en route if congestion develops. Traffic policing is used in ATM, Frame Relay, and other types of networks. Also known as admission control, permit processing, rate enforcement, and UPC. See also *tagged traffic*.

**traffic profile**

Set of CoS attribute values assigned to a given port on an ATM switch. The profile affects numerous parameters for data transmitted from the port, including rate, cell drop eligibility, transmit priority, and inactivity timer. See also *CoS*.

**traffic shaping**

Use of queues to limit surges that can congest a network. Data is buffered and then sent into the network in regulated amounts to ensure that the traffic fits within the promised traffic envelope for the particular connection. Traffic shaping is used in ATM, Frame Relay, and other types of networks. Also known as metering, shaping, and smoothing.

**trail**

In the context of wavelength routing, a trail is the physical connection of two network ports. A single trail is equal to either an OC-48 or OC-192 wavelength between two Cisco ONS 15900s.

**trailer**

Control information appended to data when encapsulating the data for network transmission. Compare with *header*.

**transaction**

Result-oriented unit of communication processing.

**transaction services layer**

Layer 7 in the SNA architectural model. Represents user application functions, such as spreadsheets, word-processing, or e-mail, by which users interact with the network. Corresponds roughly with the *application layer* of the OSI reference model. See also *data flow control layer*, *data link control layer*, *path control layer*, *physical control layer*, *presentation services layer*, and *transaction services layer*.

**transceiver**

See *MAU*.

**transceiver cable**

See *AUI*.

**transfer syntax**

Description on an instance of a data type that is expressed as a string of bits.

**transform**

The list of operations done on a dataflow to provide data authentication, data confidentiality, and data compression. For example, one transform is the ESP protocol with the HMAC-MD5 authentication algorithm; another transform is the AH protocol with the 56-bit DES encryption algorithm and the ESP protocol with the HMAC-SHA authentication algorithm.

**transit bridging**

Bridging that uses encapsulation to send a frame between two similar networks over a dissimilar network.

**transit node**

A transit node interfaces with other nodes and transfers packet data.

**translational bridging**

Bridging between networks with dissimilar MAC sublayer protocols. MAC information is translated into the format of the destination network at the bridge. Contrast with *encapsulation bridging*.

**transmission control layer**

Layer 4 in the SNA architectural model. This layer is responsible for establishing, maintaining, and terminating SNA sessions, sequencing data messages, and controlling session level flow. Corresponds to the *transport layer* of the OSI model. See also *data flow control layer*, *data-link control layer*, *path control layer*, *physical control layer*, *presentation services layer*, and *transaction services layer*.

**Transmission Control Protocol**

See *TCAP*.

**transmission group**

In SNA routing, one or more parallel communications links treated as one communications facility.

**transmission link**

See *link*.

**TRANSPAC**

Major packet data network run by France Telecom.

**transparent bridging**

Bridging scheme often used in Ethernet and IEEE 802.3 networks in which bridges pass frames along one hop at a time based on tables associating end nodes with bridge ports. Transparent bridging is so named because the presence of bridges is transparent to network end nodes. Contrast with *SRB*.

**TransPath component**

The part of your signaling controller system where signals are identified, converted, and routed.

**transport layer**

Layer 4 of the OSI reference model. This layer is responsible for reliable network communication between end nodes. The transport layer provides mechanisms for the establishment, maintenance, and termination of virtual circuits, transport fault detection and recovery, and information flow control. Corresponds to the *transmission control layer* of the SNA model. See also *application layer*, *data link layer*, *network layer*, *physical layer*, *PQ*, and *session layer*.

**trap**

Message sent by an SNMP agent to an NMS, a console, or a terminal to indicate the occurrence of a significant event, such as a specifically defined condition or a threshold that was reached. See also *alarm* and *event*.

**trap door**

Hidden computer flaw known to an intruder, or a hidden computer mechanism (usually software) installed by an intruder, who can activate the trap door to gain access to the computer without being blocked by security services or mechanisms.

**TRBRF**

Token Ring Bridge Relay Function. Internal multiport bridge function used to interconnect rings to form a domain.

**TRCRF**

Token Ring Concentrator Relay Function. A logical ring domain formed by defining groups of ports that have the same ring number.

**tree topology**

LAN topology similar to a bus topology, except that tree networks can contain branches with multiple nodes. Transmissions from a station propagate the length of the medium and are received by all other stations. Compare with *bus topology*, *ring topology*, and *star topology*.

**TRIP**

See *TRIP* (Token Ring Interface Processor) in the "Cisco Systems Terms and Acronyms" section.

**triple-wrapped**

In S/MIME, data that has been signed with a digital signature, and then encrypted, and then signed again. [RFC 2634]

**TRISL**

Token Ring Inter-Switch Link.

**Trojan horse**

Computer program that appears to have a useful function but also has a hidden and potentially malicious function that evades security mechanisms, sometimes by exploiting legitimate authorizations of a system entity that invokes the program.

**trunk**

**1.** Physical and logical connection between two switches across which network traffic travels. A backbone is composed of a number of trunks.

**2.** In telephony, a phone line between two COs or between a CO and a PBX.

**trust level**

Characterization of a standard of security protection to be met by a computer system.

**trusted certificate**

Certificate upon which a certificate user relies as being valid without the need for validation testing; especially a public-key certificate that is used to provide the first public key in a certification path.

**trusted key**

Public key upon which a user relies; especially a public key that can be used as the first public key in a certification path.

**trusted process**

System process that has privileges that enable it to affect the state of system security and that can, therefore, through incorrect or malicious execution, violate the system's security policy.

### trusted subnetwork

Subnetwork containing hosts and routers that trust each other not to engage in active or passive attacks. (There also is an assumption that the underlying communication channels—for example, telephone lines or a LAN—are protected from attack by some means.)

### trust-file PKI

Non-hierarchical PKI in which each certificate user has a local file (which is used by application software) of public-key certificates that the user trusts as starting points (that is, roots) for certification paths.

### TSAPI

Telephony Services Application Programming Interface. A call control model developed by Lucent and Novell.

### TSI

**1.** transport session identifier. Unique identifier used by both the PGM Host and PGM Router Assist features to identify each individual session.

**2.** transmitting subscriber information. Frame that can be sent by the caller with the caller's telephone number that can be used to screen calls.

### TUD

trunk up-down. Protocol used in ATM networks that monitors trunks and detects when one goes down or comes up. ATM switches send regular test messages from each trunk port to test trunk line quality. If a trunk misses a given number of these messages, TUD declares the trunk down. When a trunk comes back up, TUD recognizes that the trunk is up, declares the trunk up, and returns it to service. See also *trunk*.

### TULIP

TCP and UDP over Lightweight IP. Proposed protocol for running TCP and UDP applications over ATM.

### TUNIP

TCP and UDP over Nonexistent IP. Proposed protocol for running TCP and UPD applications over ATM.

### tunnel

Secure communication path between two peers, such as two routers.

**tunneling**

Architecture that is designed to provide the services necessary to implement any standard point-to-point encapsulation scheme. See also *encapsulation*.

**TUV**

German test agency that certifies products to European safety standards.

**twisted pair**

Relatively low-speed transmission medium consisting of two insulated wires arranged in a regular spiral pattern. The wires can be shielded or unshielded. Twisted pair is common in telephony applications and is increasingly common in data networks. See also *STP* and *UTP*.

**two-way simultaneous**

See *TWS* in the "Cisco Systems Terms and Acronyms" section.

**TYMNET**

See *XStream*.

**Type 1 operation**

IEEE 802.2 (LLC) connectionless operation.

**Type 2 operation**

IEEE 802.2 (LLC) connection-oriented operation.

**Type A traffic**

Transactional traffic. Typically, this is conversational traffic exchanged between a host and its ASCUs for terminal queries and responses for another form of Type A traffic is called host-to-host traffic.

**Type B traffic**

Messaging traffic. Typically, this is e-mail application traffic in IATA-compliant format.

**type of service**

See *ToS*.

### U interface

The interface between the telco and the user, also known as the local digital subscriber line (DSL) loop.

### UA

unnumbered acknowledgement.

### UAC

user agent client. A client application that initiates the SIP request.

### UART

Universal Asynchronous Receiver/Transmitter. Integrated circuit, attached to the parallel bus of a computer, used for serial communications. The UART translates between serial and parallel signals, provides transmission clocking, and buffers data sent to or from the computer.

### UAS

**1.** unavailable seconds. The PM parameter that measures the duration in seconds for which the path is unavailable; the time interval in seconds, starting with the first of 10 or more consecutive Severely Errored Seconds (SESs) and ending at the beginning of 10 consecutive non–SESs.

**2.** user agent server. A server application that contacts the user when a SIP request is received, and then returns a response on behalf of the user. The response accepts, rejects, or redirects the request.

### uauth

user authentication.

### UB Net/One

Ungermann-Bass Net/One. Routing protocol, developed by UB Networks, that uses hello packets and a path-delay metric, with end nodes communicating using the XNS protocol. There are a number of differences between the manner in which Net/One uses the XNS protocol and the usage common among other XNS nodes.

## uBR

Universal Broadband Router. The uBR7246 and uBR7223 are DOCSIS-compliant cable modem termination systems (CMTSs). The uBR900, uBR904, and uBR924 are DOCSIS-certified cable modems.

## UBR

unspecified bit rate. QoS class defined by the ATM Forum for ATM networks. UBR allows any amount of data up to a specified maximum to be sent across the network but there are no guarantees in terms of cell loss rate and delay. Compare with *ABR*, *CBR*, and *VBR*.

## UBR+

unspecified bit rate plus. UBR service complemented by ATM switches that use intelligent packet discard mechanisms, such as EPD or TPD. See also *EPD* and *TPD*.

## UCM

universal call model. Used interchangeably with LCM.

## UCP

User Control Point. Cisco UCP is a carrier-class service policy administration system that enables personalized IP services. The Cisco UCP distributed, fault-tolerant architecture integrates authentication, authorization, and accounting (AAA); roaming; and address management services into operations support systems of a service provider.

## UDLP

UniDirectional Link Protocol. Protocol used by inexpensive, receive-only antennas to receive data via satellite.

## UDP

User Datagram Protocol. Connectionless transport layer protocol in the TCP/IP protocol stack. UDP is a simple protocol that exchanges datagrams without acknowledgments or guaranteed delivery, requiring that error processing and retransmission be handled by other protocols. UDP is defined in RFC 768.

## U-frame

Unnumbered frame. One of three SDLC frame formats. See also *I-frame* and *S-frame*.

## UI

unnumbered information.

## UI-frame

Unnumbered information frame. See also *I-frame*, *S-frame*, and *U-frame*.

## UIO

Universal I/O serial port (Cisco router).

## UKERNA

UK Education and Research Networking Association.

## UL

Underwriters Laboratories. Independent agency within the United States that tests product safety.

## U-law

Companding technique commonly used in North America. U-law is standardized as a 64-kbps CODEC in ITU-T G.711.

## ULP

upper-layer protocol. Protocol that operates at a higher layer in the OSI reference model, relative to other layers. ULP is sometimes used to refer to the next-highest protocol (relative to a particular protocol) in a protocol stack.

## UMTS

Universal Mobile Telephone Service. A 3G mobile wireless telecommunications system whose standards are being developed by the Third Generation Partnership Project (3GPP).

## unbalanced configuration

HDLC configuration with one primary station and multiple secondary stations.

## UNI

User-Network Interface. ATM Forum specification that defines an interoperability standard for the interface between ATM-based products (a router or an ATM switch) located in a private network and the ATM switches located within the public carrier networks. Also used to describe similar connections in Frame Relay networks. See also *NNI*, *Q.920/Q.921*, and *SNI*.

## unicast

Message sent to a single network destination. Compare with *broadcast* and *multicast*.

### unicast address

Address specifying a single network device. Compare with *broadcast address* and *multicast address*. See also *unicast*.

### Unicast RPF

Unicast Reverse Path Forwarding is an input function and is applied only on the input interface of a router at the upstream end of a connection.

### U-NII

Unlicensed National Information Infrastructure. Term coined by federal regulators to describe the access of information to citizens and business. Equivalent to the term "information superhighway," it does not describe system architecture or topology.

### uninsured traffic

Traffic within the excess rate (the difference between the insured rate and the maximum rate) for an ATM VCC. This traffic can be dropped by the network if congestion occurs. See also *CLP*, *insured rate*, and *maximum rate*.

### UNI-OSP

Feature that allows the authentication of outgoing Voice over IP (VoIP) telephone connections, using the Open Settlement Protocol (OSP).

### unipolar

Literally meaning one polarity, the fundamental electrical characteristic of internal signals in digital communications equipment. Contrast with *bipolar*.

### unity gain

In broadband networks, the balance between signal loss and signal gain through amplifiers.

### UNIX

Operating system developed in 1969 at Bell Laboratories. UNIX has gone through several iterations since its inception. These include UNIX 4.3 BSD (Berkeley Standard Distribution), developed at the University of California at Berkeley, and UNIX System V, Release 4.0, developed by AT&T.

### UNIX-to-UNIX Copy Program

See *UUCP*.

### unnumbered frames

HDLC frames used for various control and management purposes, including link startup and shutdown and mode specification.

**untrusted process**

System process that cannot affect the state of system security through incorrect or malicious operation, usually because its operation is confined by a security kernel.

**UPC**

usage parameter control. See *traffic policing*.

**upper-layer protocol**

See *U-law*.

**UPSR**

unidirectional path switched ring. Path switched SONET rings that employ redundant, fiber-optic transmission facilities in a pair configuration. One fiber transmits in one direction and the backup fiber transmits in the other. If the primary ring fails, the backup takes over.

**upstream**

Set of frequencies used to send data from a subscriber to the headend.

**UR**

User Registrar. One of the suite of software products included in the Cisco Subscriber Registration Center (CSRC) product. UR enables cable network subscribers to self-provision account registration, and to activate their cable modem and PC over the cable network using a Web user interface. User Registrar activates subscriber devices with account-appropriate privileges through updates to an LDAP directory.

**urban legend**

A story, which might start with a grain of truth, that has been retold and ends up on the Internet. Some legends that periodically make their rounds include "The Infamous Modem Tax," "Craig Shergold/Brain Tumor/Get Well Cards," and "The $250 Cookie Recipe." Urban legends are conceptually similar to space junk that stays in orbit for years.

**URI**

uniform resource identifier. Type of formatted identifier that encapsulates the name of an Internet object, and labels it with an identification of the name space, thus producing a member of the universal set of names in registered name spaces and of addresses referring to registered protocols or name spaces. [RFC 1630]

### URL

uniform resource locator. Type of formatted identifier that describes the access method and the location of an information resource object on the Internet. [RFC 1738] See also *browser*.

### usage parameter control

See *traffic policing*.

### USENET

Initiated in 1979, one of the oldest and largest cooperative networks, with more than 10,000 hosts and a quarter of a million users. Its primary service is a distributed conferencing service called news.

### user authentication

See *uauth*.

### user port

In the context of wavelength routing, a user port is a port that originates or terminates on a node; in other words, it is a port on the NE that points to a non–wavelength router NE.

### UTC

Coordinated Universal Time. Time zone at zero degrees longitude. Formerly called Greenwich Mean Time (GMT) and Zulu time.

### UTP

unshielded twisted-pair. Four-pair wire medium used in a variety of networks. UTP does not require the fixed spacing between connections that is necessary with coaxial-type connections. Five types of UTP cabling are commonly used: Category 1 cabling, Category 2 cabling, Category 3 cabling, Category 4 cabling, and Category 5 cabling. Compare with *STP*. See also *EIA/TIA-586* and *twisted pair*.

### UTS

Universal Terminal Support. A data link layer protocol (P1024C) that runs in full-duplex mode over synchronous serial (V.24) lines and uses the ASCII character set.

### UUCP

UNIX-to-UNIX Copy Program. Protocol stack used for point-to-point communication between UNIX systems.

### uudecode

UNIX-to-UNIX decode. Method of decoding ASCII files that were encoded using uuencode. See also *uuencode*.

### uuencode

UNIX-to-UNIX encoding. Method of converting binary files to ASCII so they can be sent over the Internet via e-mail. The name comes from its use by the UNIX operating system's uuencode command. See also *uudecode*.

### UVM

Universal Voice Module.

### UVM-C

Universal Voice Module-Channelized.

### UVM-U

Universal Voice Module-Unchannelized.

### V.24

ITU-T standard for a physical layer interface between DTE and DCE. V.24 is essentially the same as the EIA/TIA-232 standard. See also *EIA/TIA-232*.

### V.25bis

ITU-T specification describing procedures for call setup and tear down over the DTE-DCE interface in a PSDN.

### V.32

ITU-T standard serial line protocol for bidirectional data transmissions at speeds of 4.8 or 9.6 kbps. See also *V.32bis*.

### V.32bis

ITU-T standard that extends V.32 to speeds up to 14.4 kbps. See also *V.32*.

### V.34

ITU-T standard that specifies a serial line protocol. V.34 offers improvements to the V.32 standard, including higher transmission rates (28.8 kbps) and enhanced data compression. Compare with *V.32*.

### V.35

ITU-T standard describing a synchronous, physical layer protocol used for communications between a network access device and a packet network. V.35 is most commonly used in the United States and in Europe, and is recommended for speeds up to 48 kbps.

### V.42

ITU-T standard protocol for error correction using LAPM. See also *LAPM*.

### VAC

volts alternating current.

## VAD

voice activity detection. When enabled on a voice port or a dial peer, silence is not transmitted over the network, only audible speech. When VAD is enabled, the sound quality is slightly degraded but the connection monopolizes much less bandwidth.

### valid certificate

Digital certificate for which the binding of the data items can be trusted; one that can be validated successfully.

## VAN

value-added network. Computer network or subnetwork (which is usually a commercial enterprise) that transmits, receives, and stores EDI transactions on behalf of its customers.

### variable bit rate

See *VBR*.

## VBR

variable bit rate. QoS class defined by the ATM Forum for ATM networks. VBR is subdivided into a real time (RT) class and non-real time (NRT) class. VBR (RT) is used for connections in which there is a fixed timing relationship between samples. VBR (NRT) is used for connections in which there is no fixed timing relationship between samples but that still need a guaranteed QoS. Compare with *ABR, CBR*, and *UBR*.

## VCA

Virtual Communications Address. The standard and extended programming APIs for the Cisco VCO/4K product use a byte message scheme to facilitate communications between a controlling host application and the VCO/4K. Both source and destination VCA bytes are used to label and track communications between VCO/4K systems and host applications.

## VCC

virtual channel connection. Logical circuit, made up of VCLs, that carries data between two end points in an ATM network. Sometimes called a virtual circuit connection. See also *VCD, VCL*, and *VPI*.

## VCD

virtual circuit descriptor.

## VCI

virtual channel identifier. 16-bit field in the header of an ATM cell. The VCI, together with the VPI, is used to identify the next destination of a cell as it passes through a series of ATM switches on its way to its destination. ATM switches use the VPI/VCI fields to identify the next network VCL that a cell needs to transit on its way to its final destination. The function of the VCI is similar to that of the DLCI in Frame Relay. Compare with *DLCI*. See also *VCL* and *VPI*.

## VCL

virtual channel link. Connection between two ATM devices. A VCC is made up of one or more VCLs. See also *VCC*.

## VCN

virtual circuit number. 12-bit field in an X.25 PLP header that identifies an X.25 virtual circuit. Allows DCE to determine how to route a packet through the X.25 network. See also *LCI* and *LCN*.

## VCO

Virtual Central Office. VCO represents the Cisco VCO/4K product, an open, host-controlled, telephony switch capable of providing a wide range of enhanced services in the telecommunications market.

## VDC

volts direct current.

## VDSL

very-high-data-rate digital subscriber line. One of four DSL technologies. VDSL delivers 13 to 52 Mbps downstream and 1.5 to 2.3 Mbps upstream over a single twisted copper pair. The operating range of VDSL is limited to 1,000 to 4,500 feet (304.8 to 1,372 meters). Compare with *ADSL*, *HDSL*, and *SDSL*.

## vector

Data segment of an SNA message. A vector consists of a length field, a key that describes the vector type, and vector-specific data.

## Veronica

very easy rodent oriented netwide index to computer archives. Gopher utility that effectively searches Gopher servers based on a user's list of keywords.

## Versatile Interface Processor

See *VIP* in the "Cisco Systems Terms and Acronyms" section.

## VF

variance factor. One of three link attributes exchanged using PTSPs to determine the available resources of an ATM network. VF is a relative measure of CRM normalized by the variance of the aggregate cell rate on the link.

## VIC

Voice interface card. Connects the system to either the PSTN or to a PBX. Compare with *WIC*. See also *PBX* and *PSTN*.

## VID

VLAN ID. The identification of the VLAN, which is used by the standard 802.1Q. Being on 12 bits, it allows the identification of 4096 VLANs.

## VINES

Virtual Integrated Network Service. NOS developed and marketed by Banyan Systems.

## VIP

See *VIP* in the "Cisco Systems Terms and Acronyms" section.

### virtual access interface

Instance of a unique virtual interface that is created dynamically and exists temporarily. Virtual access interfaces can be created and configured differently by different applications, such as virtual profiles and virtual private dialup networks. Virtual access interfaces are cloned from virtual template interfaces.

### virtual address

See *network address*.

### virtual channel

See *virtual circuit*.

### virtual circuit

Logical circuit created to ensure reliable communication between two network devices. A virtual circuit is defined by a VPI/VCI pair, and can be either permanent (PVC) or switched (SVC). Virtual circuits are used in Frame Relay and X.25. In ATM, a virtual circuit is called a *virtual channel*. Sometimes abbreviated *VC*. See also *PVC*, *SVC*, *VCD*, *virtual route*, and *VPI*.

### virtual connection

In ATM, a connection between end users that has a defined route and endpoints. See also *PVC* and *SVC*.

**virtual IP**

See *VIP* in the "Cisco Systems Terms and Acronyms" section.

**Virtual Networking Services**

See *Virtual Networking Services* in the "Cisco Systems Terms and Acronyms" section.

**virtual path**

Logical grouping of virtual circuits that connect two sites. See also *virtual circuit*.

**virtual ring**

Entity in an SRB network that logically connects two or more physical rings together either locally or remotely. The concept of virtual rings can be expanded across router boundaries.

**virtual route**

In SNA, a logical connection between subarea nodes that is physically realized as a particular explicit route. SNA terminology for *virtual circuit*. See also *virtual circuit*.

**virtual subnet**

Logical grouping of devices that share a common Layer 3 subnet.

**virtual template interface**

A logical interface configured with generic configuration information for a specific purpose or configuration common to specific users, plus router-dependent information. The template takes the form of a list of Cisco IOS interface commands that are applied to virtual access interfaces, as needed.

**virtual trunk**

A portion of a physical interface that has the following characteristics: address space containing only one VPI and all VCIs underneath, bandwidth that is rate limited by hardware (VI), and ownership by a controller that uses it to interface to another peer controller.

**virtualization**

Process of implementing a network based on virtual network segments. Devices are connected to virtual segments independent of their physical location and their physical connection to the network.

## virus

Hidden, self-replicating section of computer software, usually malicious logic, that propagates by infecting—that is, inserting a copy of itself into and becoming part of—another program. A virus cannot run by itself; it requires that its host program be run to make the virus active.

## VLAN

virtual LAN. Group of devices on one or more LANs that are configured (using management software) so that they can communicate as if they were attached to the same wire, when in fact they are located on a number of different LAN segments. Because VLANs are based on logical instead of physical connections, they are extremely flexible.

## VLI

virtual LAN internetwork. Internetwork composed of VLANs. See also *VLAN*.

## VLR

visitor location register. A database that contains temporary information about subscribers who roam into an area controlled by another MSC. The VLR communicates with the HLR of the subscriber to request data about that subscriber.

## VLSM

variable-length subnet mask. Capability to specify a different subnet mask for the same network number on different subnets. VLSM can help optimize available address space.

## VMAC

Virtual Media Access Control.

## VNS

See *Virtual Networking Services* in the "Cisco Systems Terms and Acronyms" section.

## VoATM

Voice over ATM. Voice over ATM enables a router to carry voice traffic (for example, telephone calls and faxes) over an ATM network. When sending voice traffic over ATM, the voice traffic is encapsulated using a special AAL5 encapsulation for multiplexed voice.

## VoATM dial peer

Dial peer connected via an ATM network. VoATM peers point to specific VoATM devices.

## VoD

video on demand. System using video compression to supply video programs to viewers when requested via ISDN or cable.

## VoFR

Voice over Frame Relay. VoFR enables a router to carry voice traffic (for example, telephone calls and faxes) over a Frame Relay network. When sending voice traffic over Frame Relay, the voice traffic is segmented and encapsulated for transit across the Frame Relay network using FRF.12 encapsulation.

## VoFR dial peer

Dial peer connected via a Frame Relay network. VoFR peers point to specific VoFR devices.

## VoHDLC

Voice over HDLC. Voice over HDLC enables a router to carry live voice traffic (for example, telephone calls and faxes) back-to-back to a second router over a serial line.

## VoHDLC dial peer

Dial peer connected via an HDLC network. VoHDLC peers point to specific VoHDLC devices.

## Voice interface card

See *VIC*.

## Voice over Frame Relay

Voice over Frame Relay enables a router to carry voice traffic (for example, telephone calls and faxes) over a Frame Relay network. When sending voice traffic over Frame Relay, the voice traffic is segmented and encapsulated for transit across the Frame Relay network using FRF.12 encapsulation.

## Voice over IP

See *VoIP*.

## VoIP

Voice over IP. The capability to carry normal telephony-style voice over an IP-based internet with POTS-like functionality, reliability, and voice quality. VoIP enables a router to carry voice traffic (for example, telephone calls and faxes) over an IP network. In VoIP, the DSP segments the voice signal into frames, which then are coupled in groups of two and stored in voice packets. These voice packets are transported using IP in compliance with ITU-T specification H.323.

**VoIP dial peer**

Dial peer connected via a packet network; in the case of Voice over IP, this is an IP network. VoIP peers point to specific VoIP devices.

**VP**

virtual path. One of two types of ATM circuits identified by a VPI. A virtual path is a bundle of virtual channels, all of which are switched transparently across an ATM network based on a common VPI. See also *VPI*.

**VPC**

virtual path connection. Grouping of VCCs that share one or more contiguous VPL. See also *VCC* and *VPL*.

**VPDN**

virtual private dial-up network. Also known as virtual private dial network. A VPDN is a network that extends remote access to a private network using a shared infrastructure. VPDNs use Layer 2 tunnel technologies (L2F, L2TP, and PPTP) to extend the Layer 2 and higher parts of the network connection from a remote user across an ISP network to a private network. VPDNs are a cost effective method of establishing a long distance, point-to-point connection between remote dial users and a private network. See also *VPN*.

**VPI**

virtual path identifier. 8-bit field in the header of an ATM cell. The VPI, together with the VCI, identifies the next destination of a cell as it passes through a series of ATM switches on its way to its destination. ATM switches use the VPI/VCI fields to identify the next VCL that a cell needs to transit on its way to its final destination. The function of the VPI is similar to that of the DLCI in Frame Relay. Compare with *DLCI*. See also *VCD* and *VCL*.

**VPI/VCI**

See *VCI* and *VPI*.

**VPL**

virtual path link. Within a virtual path, a group of unidirectional VCLs with the same end points. Grouping VCLs into VPLs reduces the number of connections to be managed, thereby decreasing network control overhead and cost. A VPC is made up of one or more VPLs.

## VPN

Virtual Private Network. Enables IP traffic to travel securely over a public TCP/IP network by encrypting all traffic from one network to another. A VPN uses "tunneling" to encrypt all information at the IP level.

## VRF

A VPN routing/forwarding instance. A VRF consists of an IP routing table, a derived forwarding table, a set of interfaces that use the forwarding table, and a set of rules and routing protocols that determine what goes into the forwarding table. In general, a VRF includes the routing information that defines a customer VPN site that is attached to a PE router.

## VRML

Virtual Reality Modeling Language. Specification for displaying three-dimensional objects on the World Wide Web. Think of it as the 3-D equivalent of HTML.

## VS/VD

virtual source/virtual destination.

## VSA

vendor-specific attribute. An attribute that has been implemented by a particular vendor. It uses the attribute Vendor-Specific to encapsulate the resulting AV pair: essentially, Vendor-Specific = protocol:attribute = value.

## VSC

See *VSC* in the "Cisco Systems Terms and Acronyms" section.

## VSI

Virtual Switch Interface.

## VSI master

A VSI master process implementing the master side of the VSI protocol in a VSI controller. Sometimes the whole VSI controller might be referred to as a VSI Master but this is not strictly correct.

**1.** A device that controls a VSI switch, for example, a VSI label switch controller.

**2.** A process implementing the master side of the VSI protocol.

## VSPT

Voice Services Provisioning Tool. Provides end-to-end configuration for IP, trunk groups, trunks, routes, and dial plans for VSC3000 and VISM. Also known as Dart.

### VTAM

virtual telecommunications access method. Set of programs that control communication between LUs. VTAM controls data transmission between channel-attached devices and performs routing functions. See also *LU*.

### VT-n

Virtual Tributary level *n*. SONET format for mapping a lower-rate signal into a SONET payload. For example, VT-1.5 is used to transport a DS-1 signal. See also *DS-1* and *SONET*.

### VTP

Virtual Terminal Protocol. ISO application for establishing a virtual terminal connection across a network.

### vty

virtual type terminal. Commonly used as virtual terminal lines.

### VWP

virtual wavelength path. A VWP is a group of one or more channels between source and destination nodes. The term *virtual* indicates that the signal path can actually travel on different physical wavelengths throughout the network. All channels of the VWP transit the same path through the network.

### WAIS

Wide Area Information Server. Distributed database protocol developed to search for information over a network. WAIS supports full-text databases, which allow an entire document to be searched for a match (as opposed to other technologies that allow only an index of key words to be searched).

### WAN

wide-area network. Data communications network that serves users across a broad geographic area and often uses transmission devices provided by common carriers. Frame Relay, SMDS, and X.25 are examples of WANs. Compare with *LAN* and *MAN*.

### WAN interface card

See *WIC*.

### WAP

See *wireless application protocol*.

### watchdog packet

Used to ensure that a client is still connected to a NetWare server. If the server has not received a packet from a client for a certain period of time, it sends that client a series of watchdog packets. If the station fails to respond to a predefined number of watchdog packets, the server concludes that the station is no longer connected and clears the connection for that station.

### watchdog spoofing

Subset of spoofing that refers specifically to a router acting for a NetWare client by sending watchdog packets to a NetWare server to keep the session between client and server active. See also *spoofing*.

### watchdog timer

**1.** Hardware or software mechanism that is used to trigger an event or an escape from a process unless the timer is periodically reset.

**2.** In NetWare, a timer that indicates the maximum period of time that a server will wait for a client to respond to a watchdog packet. If the timer expires, the server sends another watchdog packet (up to a set maximum). See also *watchdog packet*.

### waveform coding

Electrical techniques used to convey binary signals.

### wavelength

The length of one complete wave of an alternating or vibrating phenomenon, generally measured from crest to crest or from trough to trough of successive waves.

### WCCP

Web Cache Communication Protocol. WCCP is a protocol for communication between routers and Web caches. Two versions exist: WCCP Version 1 (WCCPv1) and WCCP Version2 (WCCPv2). The two versions are incompatible. Cisco IOS images can support either of the two versions or both.

### W-DCS

Wideband Digital Crossconnect System. SONET DCS capable of crossconnecting DS-1 and VT1.5 signals. See also *DCS*, *DS-1*, *SONET*, and *VT-n*.

### WDM

wavelength division multiplexing. Multiple optical wavelengths can share the same transmission fiber. The spectrum occupied by each channel must be adequately separated from the others.

### Web

World Wide Web (also called WWW). A client/server system based on HTML and HTTP.

### Web browser

See *browser*.

### Web Console

A graphical user interface (GUI) application that communicates with the system by translating HTML pages into Cisco IOS commands.

### WEPD

Weighted Early Packet Discard. A variant of EPD used by some ATM switches for discarding a complete AAL5 frame when a threshold condition, such as imminent congestion, is met. EPD prevents congestion that would otherwise jeopardize the capability of the switch to properly support existing connections with a guaranteed service.

## WFQ

weighted fair queuing. Congestion management algorithm that identifies conversations (in the form of traffic streams), separates packets that belong to each conversation, and ensures that capacity is shared fairly between these individual conversations. WFQ is an automatic way of stabilizing network behavior during congestion and results in increased performance and reduced retransmission.

## WIC

WAN interface card. Connects the system to the WAN link service provider. See also *WAN*. Compare with *VIC*.

## wide-area network

See *WAN*.

## wideband

See *broadband*.

## wildcard

Wildcard is an unknown, unpredictable factor. The wildcard pre-shared key allows for a local router to authenticate remote peers using the pre-shared key, and not using the remote peer's IP address. The IP address of the remote peer is the unknown, unpredictable factor.

## wildcard mask

A 32-bit quantity used in conjunction with an IP address to determine which bits in an IP address should be ignored when comparing that address with another IP address. A wildcard mask is specified when setting up access lists.

## Wink Start

A method of E&M signaling. When the signaling leads indicate a change to an off-hook state, the other side must send a momentary *wink* (on-hook to off-hook to on-hook transition) on the correct signaling lead before the call signaling information can be sent by the sending side. After the call signaling information is received, the side that sent wink goes off-hook again and stays that way for the duration of the call.

## WinSock

Windows Socket Interface. Software interface that allows a wide variety of applications to use and share an Internet connection. WinSock is implemented as *dynamic link library (DLL)* with some supporting programs, such as a dialer program that initiates the connection.

**wireless access protocol**

A language used for writing Web pages that uses far less overhead, which makes it more preferable for wireless access to the internet. WAP's corresponding OS is that created by 3Com in its Palm Pilot. Nokia has recently adopted the Palm OS for its Web-capable cellular phone.

**wiring closet**

Specially designed room used for wiring a data or voice network. Wiring closets serve as a central junction point for the wiring and the wiring equipment that is used for interconnecting devices.

**WISCNET**

TCP/IP network in Wisconsin (United States) connecting University of Wisconsin campuses and a number of private colleges. Links are 56 kbps and T1.

**workgroup**

Collection of workstations and servers on a LAN that are designed to communicate and exchange data with one another.

**Workgroup Director**

See *VSC* in the "Cisco Systems Terms and Acronyms" section.

**workgroup switching**

Method of switching that provides high-speed (100-Mbps) transparent bridging between Ethernet networks, and high-speed translational bridging between Ethernet and CDDI or FDDI.

**World Wide Web**

See *WWW*.

**worm**

A computer program that can run independently, can propagate a complete working version of itself onto other hosts on a network, and can consume computer resources destructively.

**wrap**

Action taken by an FDDI or CDDI network to recover in the event of a failure. The stations on each side of the failure reconfigure themselves, creating a single logical ring out of the primary and secondary rings.

### WRED

weighted random early detection. Queueing method that ensures that high-precedence traffic has lower loss rates than other traffic during times of congestion.

### WRM

The Wavelength Router Manager™ is the trademarked EMS for the Cisco ONS 15900 Series Wavelength Router, both designed by Cisco Systems.

### WW TAC

See *Cisco WW TAC* in the "Cisco Systems Terms and Acronyms" section.

### WWW

World Wide Web. Large network of Internet servers providing hypertext and other services to terminals running client applications, such as a browser. See also *browser*.

### X Display Manager Control Protocol

See *XDMCP*.

### X Recommendations

CCITT documents that describe data communication network standards. Well known ones include X.25 Packet Switching standard, X.400 Message Handling System, and X.500 Directory Services.

### X terminal

Terminal that allows a user simultaneous access to several different applications and resources in a multivendor environment through implementation of X Windows. See also *X Window System*.

### X Window System

Distributed, network-transparent, device-independent, multitasking windowing and graphics system originally developed by MIT for communication between X terminals and UNIX workstations. See also *X terminal*.

### X.121

ITU-T standard describing an addressing scheme used in X.25 networks. X.121 addresses are sometimes called IDNs.

### X.21

ITU-T standard for serial communications over synchronous digital lines. The X.21 protocol is used primarily in Europe and Japan.

### X.21bis

ITU-T standard that defines the physical layer protocol for communication between DCE and DTE in an X.25 network. Virtually equivalent to *EIA/TIA-232*. See also *EIA/TIA-232* and *X.25*.

## X.25

ITU-T standard that defines how connections between DTE and DCE are maintained for remote terminal access and computer communications in PDNs. X.25 specifies LAPB, a data link layer protocol, and PLP, a network layer protocol. Frame Relay has to some degree superseded X.25. See also *Frame Relay*, *LAPB*, and *PLP*.

## X.25 Level 3

See *PLP*.

## X.25 Protocol

See *PLP*.

## X.28

ITU-T recommendation that defines the terminal-to-PAD interface in X.25 networks. See also *PAD* and *X.25*.

## X.29

ITU-T recommendation that defines the form for control information in the terminal-to-PAD interface used in X.25 networks. See also *PAD* and *X.25*.

## X.3

ITU-T recommendation that defines various PAD parameters used in X.25 networks. See also *PAD* and *X.25*.

## X.400

ITU-T recommendation specifying a standard for e-mail transfer.

## X.500

ITU-T recommendation specifying a standard for distributed maintenance of files and directories.

## X.75

ITU-T specification that defines the signaling system between two PDNs. X.75 is essentially an *NNI*. See also *NNI*.

## X3T9.5

Number assigned to the ANSI Task Group of Accredited Standards Committee for its internal, working document describing FDDI.

## XDMCP

X Display Manager Control Protocol. Protocol used to communicate between X terminals and workstations running the UNIX operating system.

## XDR

eXternal Data Representation. Standard for machine-independent data structures developed by Sun Microsystems. Similar to BER.

## xDSL

Group term used to refer to ADSL, HDSL, SDSL, and VDSL. All are emerging digital technologies using the existing copper infrastructure provided by the telephone companies. xDSL is a high-speed alternative to ISDN.

## XE

**1.** The VSC Execution Environment, a layer of software providing shared services for all application software on the VSC; and isolating higher-level software from operating system dependencies.

**2.** TransPath Execution Environment. Layer of software providing shared services for all application software on the TransPath and isolating higher-level software from operating system dependencies.

## Xerox Network Systems

See *XNS*.

## XGCP

Xternal Media Gateway Control Protocols. Includes SGCP and MGCP.

## Xid

See *termid*.

## XID

exchange identification. Request and response packets exchanged prior to a session between a router and a Token Ring host. If the parameters of the serial device contained in the XID packet do not match the configuration of the host, the session is dropped.

## XML

extensible markup language. A standard maintained by the World Wide Web Consortium (W3C). It defines a syntax that lets you create markup languages to specify information structures. Information structures define the type of information, for example, subscriber name or address, not how the information looks (bold, italic, and so on). External processes can manipulate these information structures and publish them in a variety of formats. Text markup language designed to enable the use of SGML on the World Wide Web. XML allows you to define your own customized markup language.

### XNS

Xerox Network Systems. Protocol suite originally designed by PARC. Many PC networking companies, such as 3Com, Banyan, Novell, and UB Networks used or currently use a variation of XNS as their primary transport protocol. See also *X Window System*.

### XOT

X.25 over TCP.

### XRemote

Protocol developed specifically to optimize support for the X Window System over a serial communications link.

### XStream

Major public PSN in the United States operated by MCI. Formerly called TYMNET.

### XTagATM

extended tag ATM.

**zero code suppression**

Line coding scheme used for transmission clocking. Zero line suppression substitutes a 1 in the 7th bit of a string of eight consecutive zeros. See also *ones density*.

**ZIP**

Zone Information Protocol. AppleTalk session layer protocol that maps network numbers to zone names. ZIP is used by NBP to determine which networks contain nodes that belong to a zone. See also *ZIP storm* and *zone*.

**ZIP storm**

Broadcast storm that occurs when a router running AppleTalk propagates a route for which it currently has no corresponding zone name. The route is then forwarded by downstream routers, and a ZIP storm ensues. See also *ZIP*.

**zone**

**1.** Collection of all terminals, gateways, and multipoint control units (MCUs) managed by a single gatekeeper. A zone includes at least one terminal, and can include gateways or MCUs. A zone has only one gatekeeper. A zone can be independent of LAN topology and can be comprised of multiple LAN segments connected using routers or other devices.

**2.** In AppleTalk, a logical group of network devices. See also *ZIP*.

**Zone Information Protocol**

See *ZIP*.

**zone multicast address**

Data-link–dependent multicast address at which a node receives the NBP broadcasts directed to its zone. See also *NBNS*.

**zone prefix**

A prefix that identifies the addresses to be serviced by a given gatekeeper. Zone prefixes are typically area codes and serve the same purpose as the domain names in the H.323-ID address space.

# Cisco Systems Terms and Acronyms

### AIP

ATM Interface Processor. ATM network interface for Cisco 7000 series routers designed to minimize performance bottlenecks at the UNI. The AIP supports AAL3/4 and AAL5. See also *AAL3/4* and *AAL5*.

### ALPS

airline product set. A tunneling mechanism that transports airline protocol data across a Cisco router-based TCP/IP network to an X.25-attached mainframe. This feature provides connectivity between agent set control units (ASCUs) and a mainframe host that runs the airline reservation system database.

### APaRT

automated packet recognition/translation. Technology that allows a server to be attached to CDDI or FDDI without requiring the reconfiguration of applications or network protocols. APaRT recognizes specific data link layer encapsulation packet types and, when these packet types are transferred from one medium to another, translates them into the native format of the destination device.

### ATG

address translation gateway. Cisco DECnet routing software function that allows a router to route multiple, independent DECnet networks and to establish a user-specified address translation for selected nodes between networks.

### ATM network

Traditional Cisco ATM network built around BPX switches.

### ATM network interface card

ESP card that is used as the OC-3 interface to the BPX's BXM.

### autonomous switching

Feature on Cisco routers that provides faster packet processing by allowing the ciscoBus to switch packets independently without interrupting the system processor.

## B

### BIGA

Bus Interface Gate Array. Technology that allows the Catalyst 5000 to receive and transmit frames from its packet-switching memory to its MAC local buffer memory without the intervention of the host processor.

### BOBI

break-out/break-in. VNS feature that allows interworking between Euro-ISDN (ETSI) and other VNS-supported signaling variants, such as DPNSS and QSIG.

### BPX Service Node

Closely integrated BPX switch, AXIS interface shelf, and extended services processor designed to support ATM and Frame Relay switched virtual circuits, as well as traditional PVCs.

## C

### CAM

Cisco Access Manager.

### CCIE

Cisco Certified Internetwork Expert.

### CCNA

Cisco Certified Network Associate.

### CCO

Cisco Connection Online. The name of Cisco Systems' external Web site.

### CCSRC

Cisco Subscriber Registration Center. An integrated solution for data-over-cable service providers to configure and manage broadband modems, and enable and administer subscriber self-registration and activation.

### CDP

Cisco Discovery Protocol. Media- and protocol-independent device-discovery protocol that runs on all Cisco-manufactured equipment, including routers, access servers, bridges, and switches. Using CDP, a device can advertise its existence to other devices and receive information about other devices on the same LAN or on the remote side of a WAN. Runs on all media that support SNAP, including LANs, Frame Relay, and ATM media.

### CEF

Cisco Express Forwarding.

### CET

Cisco Encryption Technology. 40- and 56-bit Data Encryption Standard (DES) network layer encryption available since Cisco IOS Software Release 11.2.

### CFRAD

See *Cisco FRAD*.

### Channel Interface Processor

See *CIP*.

### CIP

Channel Interface Processor. Channel attachment interface for Cisco 7000 series routers. The CIP is used to connect a host mainframe to a control unit, eliminating the need for an FEP for channel attachment.

### Cisco Discovery Protocol

See *CDP*.

### Cisco FRAD

Cisco Frame Relay access device. Cisco product that supports Cisco IOS Frame Relay SNA services and can be upgraded to be a full-function multiprotocol router. The Cisco FRAD connects SDLC devices to Frame Relay without requiring an existing LAN. However, the Cisco FRAD does support attached LANs and can perform conversion from SDLC to Ethernet and Token Ring. See also *FRAD*.

### Cisco Frame Relay access device

See *Cisco FRAD*.

### Cisco Internet Operating System

See *Cisco IOS*.

### Cisco IOS

Cisco system software that provides common functionality, scalability, and security for all products under the CiscoFusion architecture. Cisco IOS allows centralized, integrated, and automated installation and management of internetworks while ensuring support for a wide variety of protocols, media, services, and platforms.

### Cisco Link Services

See *CLS*.

### Cisco Link Services Interface

See *CLSI*.

### Cisco Network Registrar

A software product that provides IP addresses, configuration parameters, and DNS names to DOCSIS cable modems and PCs, based on network and service policies. CNR also provides enhanced TFTP server capabilities, including the generation of DOCSIS cable modem configuration files.

### Cisco ONP

The Cisco Optical Network Planner is the trademarked network planning tool designed by Cisco Systems, Inc. It is designed for use with Cisco ONS 15900 Series Wavelength Router network elements to optimize available optical network bandwidth.

### Cisco Optical Network Planner

See *Cisco ONP*.

### Cisco Wavelength Router Manager

See *Cisco WRM*.

### Cisco WRM

Cisco Wavelength Router Manager. Cisco's trademarked element management system designed for use with the Cisco ONS 15900 Series Wavelength Router.

### Cisco WW TAC

Cisco's World-Wide Technical Assistance Center. It is the focal point of all Cisco software and hardware maintenance and support services. Contact the Cisco WW TAC for help with installation and testing, performance, training, documentation, equipment repair Return Material Authorization (RMA) service, and equipment specifications. Refer to the About This Guide section of the user guides for additional information.

### ciscoBus controller

See *SP*.

### CiscoFusion

Cisco internetworking architecture that "fuses" together the scalability, stability, and security advantages of the latest routing technologies with the performance benefits of ATM and LAN switching, and the management benefits of VLANs. See also *Cisco IOS*.

### Cisco-trunk (private line) call

A Cisco-trunk (private line) call is established by the forced connection of a dynamic switched call. A Cisco-trunk call is established during configuration of the trunk and stays up for the duration of the configuration. It optionally provides a pass-through connection path to pass signaling information between the two telephony interfaces at either end of the connection.

### CiscoView

GUI-based device-management software application that provides dynamic status, statistics, and comprehensive configuration information for Cisco internetworking devices. In addition to displaying a physical view of Cisco device chassis, CiscoView also provides device monitoring functions and basic troubleshooting capabilities, and can be integrated with several leading SNMP-based network management platforms.

### C-ISUP

Proprietary Cisco protocol based on ISUP.

### CLS

Cisco link services. A front-end for a variety of data-link control services.

### CLSI

Cisco link services interface. Messages that are exchanged between CLS and data-link users, such as APPN, SNA service point, and DLSw+.

### CMNM

Cisco MGC Node Manager. The management system providing fault, performance, and security management for the VSC3000 (MGC) node. Also known as Rambler.

### CNS/AD

Cisco Networking Services for Active Directory, which consists of a port of Active Directory to Solaris and HP/UX, and an NT and UNIX client implementation of the LDAP API and GSS-API.

### coax cable

Type of cable used to connect Cisco equipment to antennas.

### configuration register

In Cisco routers, a 16-bit, user-configurable value that determines how the router functions during initialization. The configuration register can be stored in hardware or software. In hardware, the bit position is set using a jumper. In software, the bit position is set by specifying a hexadecimal value using configuration commands.

### CPP

Combinet Proprietary Protocol.

### CSM

Cisco Service Management system of Operations, Administration, Maintenance, and Provisioning (OAM&P) and management tools for service providers and large enterprise networks. CSRC is part of this system.

### CWAF

Cisco Web Application Framework. The underlying framework that manages the Web GUI for User Registrar and Modem Registrar.

### CxBus

Cisco Extended Bus. Data bus for interface processors on Cisco 7000 series routers. See also *SP*.

## D

### Data movement processor

See *DMP*.

### Diffusing update algorithm

See *DUAL*.

### DistributedDirector

Method of distributing Web traffic by taking into account Web server availability and relative client-to-server topological distances in order to determine the optimal Web server for a client. DistributedDirector uses the Director Response Protocol to query DRP server agents for BGP and IGP routing table metrics.

## DLSw+

data-link switching plus. Cisco implementation of the DLSw standard for SNA and NetBIOS traffic forwarding. DLSw+ goes beyond the standard to include the advanced features of the current Cisco RSRB implementation, and provides additional functionality to increase the overall scalability of data-link switching. See also *DLSw* in the main glossary.

## DMP

Data Movement Processor. Processor on the Catalyst 5000 that, along with the multiport packet buffer memory interface, performs the frame-switching function for the switch. The DMP also handles translational bridging between the Ethernet and FDDI interfaces, IP segmentation, and intelligent bridging with protocol-based filtering.

## DRP

Director Response Protocol. Protocol used by the DistributedDirector feature in IP routing.

## DSPU concentration

Cisco IOS feature that enables a router to function as a PU concentrator for SNA PU 2 nodes. PU concentration at the router simplifies the task of PU definition at the upstream host while providing additional flexibility and mobility for downstream PU devices.

## DUAL

Diffusing Update Algorithm. Convergence algorithm used in Enhanced IGRP that provides loop-free operation at every instant throughout a route computation. Allows routers involved in a topology change to synchronize at the same time, while not involving routers that are unaffected by the change. See also *EIGRP*.

# E

## EIGRP

Enhanced Interior Gateway Routing Protocol. Advanced version of IGRP developed by Cisco. Provides superior convergence properties and operating efficiency, and combines the advantages of link state protocols with those of distance vector protocols. Compare with *IGRP*. See also *IGP*, *OSPF*, and *RIP*.

## EIP

Ethernet Interface Processor. Interface processor card on the Cisco 7000 series routers. The EIP provides high-speed (10-Mbps) AUI ports that support Ethernet Version 1 and Ethernet Version 2 or IEEE 802.3 interfaces, and a high-speed data path to other interface processors.

### Enhanced Monitoring Services

Set of analysis tools on the Catalyst 5000 switch, consisting of an integrated RMON agent and the SPAN. These tools provide traffic monitoring and network segment analysis and management. See also *RMON* and *span*.

### ESP

Extended Services Processor. Rack-mounted adjunct processor that is co-located with a Cisco BPX/AXIS (all three units comprise a BPX service node) and has IP connectivity to a StrataView Plus Workstation.

### EXEC

Interactive command processor of Cisco IOS.

## F

### fast switching

Cisco feature whereby a route cache is used to expedite packet switching through a router. Contrast with *process switching*.

### FDDI Interface Processor

See *FIP*.

### FEIP

Fast Ethernet Interface Processor. Interface processor on the Cisco 7000 series routers. The FEIP supports up to two 100-Mbps 100BaseT ports.

### FIP

FDDI Interface Processor. Interface processor on the Cisco 7000 series routers. The FIP supports SASs, DASs, dual homing, and optical bypass, and contains a 16-mips processor for high-speed (100-Mbps) interface rates. The FIP complies with ANSI and ISO FDDI standards.

### FRAS

Frame Relay access support. Cisco IOS feature that allows SDLC, Token Ring, Ethernet, and Frame Relay-attached IBM devices to connect to other IBM devices across a Frame Relay network. See also *FRAD*.

### FSIP

Fast Serial Interface Processor. Default serial interface processor for Cisco 7000 series routers. The FSIP provides four or eight high-speed serial ports.

### FST

Fast Sequenced Transport. Connectionless, sequenced transport protocol that runs on top of the IP protocol. SRB traffic is encapsulated inside of IP datagrams and is passed over an FST connection between two network devices (such as routers). Speeds up data delivery, reduces overhead, and improves the response time of SRB traffic.

## G

### GDP

Gateway Discovery Protocol. Cisco protocol that allows hosts to dynamically detect the arrival of new routers as well as determine when a router goes down. Based on UDP. See also *UDP* in the main glossary.

### GRE

generic routing encapsulation. Tunneling protocol developed by Cisco that can encapsulate a wide variety of protocol packet types inside IP tunnels, creating a virtual point-to-point link to Cisco routers at remote points over an IP internetwork. By connecting multiprotocol subnetworks in a single-protocol backbone environment, IP tunneling using GRE allows network expansion across a single-protocol backbone environment.

## H

### helper address

Address configured on an interface to which broadcasts received on that interface will be sent.

### HIP

HSSI Interface Processor. Interface processor on the Cisco 7000 series routers. The HIP provides one HSSI port that supports connections to ATM, SMDS, Frame Relay, or private lines at speeds up to T3 or E3.

### HSCI

High-Speed Communications Interface. Single-port interface, developed by Cisco, providing full-duplex synchronous serial communications capability at speeds up to 52 Mbps.

### HSRP

Hot Standby Router Protocol. Provides high network availability and transparent network topology changes. HSRP creates a Hot Standby router group with a lead router that services all packets sent to the Hot Standby address. The lead router is monitored by other routers in the group, and if it fails, one of these standby routers inherits the lead position and the Hot Standby group address.

## I

### IGRP

Interior Gateway Routing Protocol. IGP developed by Cisco to address the issues associated with routing in large, heterogeneous networks. Compare with *EIGRP*. See also *IGP*, *OSPF*, and *RIP*.

### interface processor

Any of a number of processor modules used in the Cisco 7000 series routers. See *AIP*, *CIP*, *EIP*, *FEIP*, *FIP*, *FSIP*, *HIP*, *MIP*, *SIP*, and *TRIP*.

### IOS

See *Cisco IOS*.

### ISL

Inter-Switch Link. Cisco-proprietary protocol that maintains VLAN information as traffic flows between switches and routers.

## L

### LMT

Cisco's last mile technology.

### local adjacency

Two VNSs that control different VSN areas, but communicate with one another through a Frame Relay PVC, are considered to be locally adjacent.

## M

### MICA

Multiservice IOS Channel Aggregation. Technology that enables the simultaneous support of remote-access users through both analog modems and ISDN devices.

### MIP

MultiChannel Interface Processor. Interface processor on the Cisco 7000 series routers that provides up to two channelized T1 or E1 connections via serial cables to a CSU. The two controllers on the MIP can each provide up to 24 T1 or 30 E1 channel-groups, with each channel-group presented to the system as a serial interface that can be configured individually.

## NCIA

native client interface architecture. SNA applications-access architecture, developed by Cisco, that combines the full functionality of native SNA interfaces at both the host and the client with the flexibility of leveraging TCP/IP backbones. NCIA encapsulates SNA traffic on a client PC or workstation, thereby providing direct TCP/IP access while preserving the native SNA interface at the end-user level. In many networks, this capability obviates the need for a standalone gateway and can provide flexible TCP/IP access while preserving the native SNA interface to the host.

## NetFlow

Network flow is defined as a unidirectional sequence of packets between given source and destination endpoints. Network flows are highly granular: flow endpoints are identified both by IP address as well as by transport layer application port numbers. (NetFlow also uses IP Protocol, ToS,and the input interface port to uniquely identify flows.) Conventional network layer switching handles incoming packets independently, with separate serial tasks for switching, security, services, and traffic measurements applied to each packet. With NetFlow switching, this process is applied only to the first packet of a flow. Information from the first packet is used to build an entry in the NetFlow cache. Subsequent packets in the flow are handled via a single streamlined task that handles switching, services, and data collection concurrently.

## NETscout

Cisco network management application that provides an easy-to-use GUI for monitoring RMON statistics and protocol analysis information. NETscout also provides extensive tools that simplify data collection, analysis, and reporting. These tools allow system administrators to monitor traffic, set thresholds, and capture data on any set of network traffic for any segment.

## NMP

Network Management Processor. Processor module on the Catalyst 5000 switch used to control and monitor the switch.

## OPI

open peripheral interface. Cisco proprietary interface between Peripheral Gateways (PGs) and the ICM's Central Controller.

### OPT

Cisco's Open Packet Telephony architecture.

## P

### PIM

peripheral interface manager. The Cisco proprietary interface between a peripheral and the Peripheral Gateway (PG).

### PLIM

physical layer interface module. Interface that allows the AIP to a variety of physical layers, including TAXI and SONET multimode fiber-optic cable, SDH/SONET single-mode fiber cable, and E3 coaxial cable.

### process switching

Operation that provides full route evaluation and per-packet load balancing across parallel WAN links. Involves the transmission of entire frames to the router CPU, where they are repackaged for delivery to or from a WAN interface, with the router making a route selection for each packet. Process switching is the most resource-intensive switching operation that the CPU can perform. Contrast with *fast switching*.

### proxy polling

Technique that alleviates the load across an SDLC network by allowing routers to act as proxies for primary and secondary nodes, thus keeping polling traffic off of the shared links. Proxy polling has been replaced by SDLC Transport. See also *SDLC Transport*.

## Q

### QPM

QoS Policy Manager. Cisco policy server application for dynamically managing network traffic flows.

## R

### RP

Route Processor. Processor module in the Cisco 7000 series routers that contains the CPU, system software, and most of the memory components that are used in the router. Sometimes called a *supervisory processor*.

### RSP

Route/Switch Processor. Processor module in the Cisco 7500 series routers that integrates the functions of the RP and the SP. See also *RP* and *SP*.

### RSUP

Reliable SAP Update Protocol. Bandwidth-saving protocol developed by Cisco for propagating services information. RSUP allows routers to reliably send standard Novell SAP packets only when the routers detect a change in advertised services. RSUP can transport network information either in conjunction with or independently of the Enhanced IGRP routing function for IPX.

 **S**

### SDLC broadcast

Feature that allows a Cisco router that receives an all-stations broadcast on a virtual multidrop line to propagate the broadcast to each SDLC line that is a member of the virtual multidrop line.

### SDLC Transport

Cisco router feature with which disparate environments can be integrated into a single, high-speed, enterprise-wide network. Native SDLC traffic can be passed through point-to-point serial links with other protocol traffic multiplexed over the same links. Cisco routers can also encapsulate SDLC frames inside IP datagrams for transport over arbitrary (non-SDLC) networks. Replaces proxy polling. See also *proxy polling*.

### SDLLC

SDLC Logical Link Control. Cisco IOS feature that performs translation between SDLC and IEEE 802.2 type 2.

### silicon switching

Switching based on the SSE, which allows the processing of packets independent of the SSP (Silicon Switch Processor) system processor. Silicon switching provides high-speed, dedicated packet switching. See also *SSE* and *SSP*.

### SIP

**1.** SMDS Interface Protocol. Used in communications between CPE and SMDS network equipment. Allows the CPE to use SMDS service for high-speed WAN internetworking. Based on the IEEE 802.6 DQDB standard. See also *DQDB*.

**2.** serial interface processor.

### SP

Switch Processor. Cisco 7000-series processor module that acts as the administrator for all CxBus activities. Sometimes called CiscoBus controller. See also *CxBus*.

## SPA

Security Posture Assessment. Comprehensive security analysis of large-scale, distributed client networks conducted by Cisco Systems engineers.

## SPAN

Switched Port Analyzer. Feature of the Catalyst 5000 switch that extends the monitoring capabilities of existing network analyzers into a switched Ethernet environment. SPAN mirrors the traffic at one switched segment onto a predefined SPAN port. A network analyzer attached to the SPAN port can monitor traffic from any of the other Catalyst switched ports.

### SPNNI connection

Frame Relay connection between two VNSs in different areas or domains. The SPNNI connection gets its name from the proprietary Network-to-Network Interface protocol that operates over this connection.

## SSE

silicon switching engine. Routing and switching mechanism that compares the data link or network layer header of an incoming packet to a silicon-switching cache, determines the appropriate action (routing or bridging), and forwards the packet to the proper interface. The SSE is encoded directly in the hardware of the SSP (Silicon Switch Processor) of a Cisco 7000 series router. It therefore can perform switching independently of the system processor, making the execution of routing decisions much quicker than if they were encoded in software. See also *silicon switching* and *SSP*.

## SSP

Silicon Switch Processor. High-performance silicon switch for Cisco 7000 series routers that provides distributed processing and control for interface processors. The SSP leverages the high-speed switching and routing capabilities of the SSE to increase aggregate router performance dramatically, minimizing performance bottlenecks at the interface points between the router and a high-speed backbone. See also *silicon switching* and *SSE*.

## STUN

serial tunnel. Router feature allowing two SDLC- or HDLC-compliant devices to connect to one another through an arbitrary multiprotocol topology (using Cisco routers) rather than through a direct serial link.

## T

## TAC

A Cisco Technical Assistance Center. There are four TACs worldwide.

## TACACS+

Terminal Access Controller Access Control System Plus. Proprietary Cisco enhancement to Terminal Access Controller Access Control System (TACACS). Provides additional support for authentication, authorization, and accounting. See also *TACACS* in main glossary.

## THC over X.25

Feature providing TCP/IP header compression over X.25 links, for purposes of link efficiency.

## TRIP

Token Ring Interface Processor. High-speed interface processor on the Cisco 7000 series routers. The TRIP provides two or four Token Ring ports for interconnection with IEEE 802.5 and IBM Token Ring media with ports independently set to speeds of either 4 or 16 Mbps.

## TWS

two-way simultaneous. Mode that allows a router configured as a primary SDLC station to achieve better utilization of a full-duplex serial line. When TWS is enabled in a multidrop environment, the router can poll a secondary station and receive data from that station while it sends data to or receives data from a different secondary station on the same serial line.

## VIP

**1.** Versatile Interface Processor. Interface card used in Cisco 7000 and Cisco 7500 series routers. The VIP provides multilayer switching and runs Cisco IOS. The most recent version of the VIP is VIP2.

**2.** virtual IP. Function that enables the creation of logically separated switched IP workgroups across the switch ports of a Catalyst 5000 running Virtual Networking Services software. See also *Virtual Networking Services*.

## Virtual Networking Services

Software on some Catalyst 5000 switches that enables multiple workgroups to be defined across switches and offers traffic segmentation and access control.

## VSC

Cisco's virtual switch controller.

## W

### WorkGroup Director

Cisco SNMP-based network-management software tool. Workgroup Director runs on UNIX workstations either as a standalone application or integrated with another SNMP-based network management platform, providing a seamless, powerful management system for Cisco workgroup products. See also *SNMP*.